From Hearth to Horizons:

125 Years of the Social Science Club of Newton

Written and compiled by Marie Baroni Allen, Anne Larner, Vivi Leavy, Kathleen Rousseau, Mary Alice Stanton, Kate Stout and Duscha Weisskopf

Edited by Kate Stout

©2011 Social Science Club of Newton, Newton, MA
Layout and design — Riverview Press/Kate Stout

ISBN 978-0-557-93980-0

First Edition

*Cover photos: Mary Whiton Calkins, founding member; Adelaide Ball,
1953; Emily Hubbs Scott, current member*

TABLE OF CONTENTS

PREFACE

In 2007 the ambitious plan for this book, *From Hearth to Horizons*, was hatched. Its purpose was simple: to commemorate the Social Science Club of Newton's 125th anniversary in 2011. Undertaken by a dedicated group of member readers, the first part of the project was to digest the bulk of the Club's archived material in the Newton Free Library. The task was daunting. Digesting a century and a quarter of members' research papers and documents recording the Club's active interest in local, regional, national and international affairs took both dedication and good eyes.

For decades the Record Books (referred to in notes as RB) — accounts of business, annual and paper-sharing meetings — were handwritten. In the early years of the Club the papers themselves were not preserved. Instead the recording secretary reported the events of every meeting and wrote a lengthy summation of the paper in a hand both elegant and often well faded on the page. The recording secretary's synopsis more often than not caught the spirit of the topic at hand but was spottier when it came to providing insights into both the discussions that followed and the members' reactions.

All that reading and deciphering resulted, in 2009, in the Annotated Bibliography now archived alongside other Club records and materials at the Newton Library. Special thanks is therefore due to the members who sometimes were immersed in, and sometimes simply slogged through, mountains of Club records. In addition to my own compilation of the Bibliography, these readers were: Marygrace Barber, Vivi Leavy, Mary Alice Stanton, Duscha Weisskopf, Carol Robinson, Carole Simon, Nancy O'Brien, Liza Martin, Kathleen Rousseau, Barbara Hawkins and Jean Kennedy.

The next phase of our project was to draw on the Annotated Bibliography to help direct our work. Occasionally outside sources were tapped to lend illumination to the accomplishments and evolution of this Club. We conceived of the book in four sections — Club history, the Club and Newton, the Club in the broader wider world and, finally, the Club and women's issues — and recruited committees to write and compile them. Inevitably the project grew, eventually into the six chapters to come. Footnotes became endnotes, which can be found at the end of each individual chapter, in an effort to make the reading as smooth as possible.

Each writer, editor and abridger is given due credit in these pages in the form of a byline. The writing of *From Hearth to Horizons* was a monumental effort, requiring near-monthly powwows for two-plus years in which we negotiated issues both large and small, including problems of style and even our identity, then and now. As you read these pages and encounter those bylines, you cannot fail to note, and I trust silently thank, the women of the book committee for their devotion and competence.

Throughout *From Hearth to Horizons* we have tried to give a flavor of the Club's principle endeavor, the writing of lengthy research papers, through as many excerpts as possible. Inclusion of entire papers was impractical, owing to their average length (some ran close to 50 pages!). All quotes not otherwise identified are from members' papers or from Club records. It must be remembered, too, when reading these excerpts that they were written for oral presentation. This can affect the tone as well as the style of the selection. The writers did not know, after all, that their papers might one day be published.

For many of us 21st century participants in the *From Hearth to Horizons* project there were also some points of distress — first, that so many papers and all that intellectual energy are gone. Prior to the early 1950s virtually no papers survive. Only two papers were saved during the decade 1952–1961; only 12 papers exist from 1961–1971. It was not until the mid-1980s that papers were routinely collected and filed in the archives. The lack of those earlier papers and the voices behind them is an immeasurable loss.

Another question that pervaded both the reading and the writing portions of this project was this: Who were these women? Until well into the second half of the 20th century Club members were uniformly addressed in the minutes by their husbands' names — Mrs. Wolcott Calkins, Mrs. Francis Hornbrooke, etc. Only if they were unmarried did they have first names. This formal style of address was so thoroughly adhered to that some of the early members might have been robbed of their given names altogether had it not been for diligent research. It was important for us to give our members a personal identity, at least in these pages.

Furthermore, who these women were in their own lives and times is largely lost to us. It was not until 2002 that then Club president Mary Robinson instituted the practice of expanded introductions of the authors before each paper was given, allowing in theory for these mini-biographies to enter the record. Unfortunately even these have not been rigorously preserved. What we know of most of our early members' lives and accomplishments, including what motivated their interest in becoming — and staying — members of the Social Science Club, has vanished.

The question of Who Were These Women eventually morphed into the issue of Who Are We Today? The fact that for most of its 125 years Club members were ladies was indicative not just of comportment but also of social status. In today's 21st century Club, however, many of us have lived through, fought for and been shaped by the women's movement in America. While our mothers may have wished 'ladyhood' on us as children we have lived our lives carrying the banner of personhood before us. To this end, throughout *From Hearth to Horizons*, we authors refer to Club members as women but we allow earlier members through their excerpted papers to be true to themselves and their own times — that is, both ladies and their husbands' wives.

This does not mean that 21st century Club members balk at donning hats and gloves at our annual meeting. On the contrary we cherish the ladies of yesteryear and have tried diligently to honor them here in these pages. Given their love of intellectual challenge and ever-ready social activism in their own eras, we believe that those ladies would take very real pride in the women we've become and in the Club itself as it marches on in its second century of research, writing and contributions to society.

— Kate Stout, editor
March, 2011

Andy Marshall and Lavinia Tomb decked themselves out in turn-of-the-century garb at the 1979 annual luncheon to honor Club founders.
(Photo by Emily Hubbs Scott)

CHAPTER ONE

FROM AMIABLE IGNORANCE TO ENLIGHTENED EQUALITY: THE SOCIAL SCIENCE CLUB OF NEWTON, 1886–2011

by Mary Alice Stanton

Lucy Newhall Sawyer, then president of the Social Science Club of Newton, wrote the following for the World's Columbian Exposition in Chicago, 1893. A leather bound copy was included in the collection of the Women's Club materials displayed in the Women's Building at the Exposition.

The Social Science Club of Newton did not spring into life Minerva-like. It grew out of the needs of a few women in their daily life. But, like the growth of nations, its development has been slow, unfolding from its past into an ever-advancing present. It has sought to become strong by slow degrees. Its purpose is to broaden the life of women by turning their thoughts persistently upon interests that touch men and women as gathered into society.

Women have for ages recognized the part that they ought to perform in the family as companion of the husband, as educator of the children. In the changed life of today, they find that wider interests are necessary for the just performance of domestic duties.

Patriotism is by slow degrees beginning to burn with a purer and more intense flame in the hearts of the American people than ever before. Public opinion needs education and women should cease to be stumbling blocks through amiable ignorance. Educated to think wisely on social questions, they become a medium for the transmission of advanced thought to men engrossed with business, who, it should always be remembered, are the members of society by whose effort thought is made effective.

Such clubs as ours are very active means by which the attention of women is turned to subjects that receive the unremitting and earnest attention of all members of society. It is largely in this way that the present indifference to public needs can be overcome, and a better and safer society be built up.

* * *

"On the cold winter morning of January 22, 1886, two Newton Corner ladies put on their cloaks and bonnets and walked a few steps to the house of a neighbor, Mrs. Henry Wellington, on Fairmont Avenue. Mrs. Wolcott Calkins, the wife of the minister at Eliot Church, came from nearby Bellevue Street, Mrs. Francis Hornbrooke, also a clergyman's wife, came from Lombard Street. Mrs. Lincoln Stone, a doctor's wife, and Mrs. J. Herbert Sawyer of Chestnut Hill came."[1] Though Mary Calkins had to send her "regrets," she is still listed among the founders. Indeed, as she was a single woman, she is the only founder defined by her own accomplishments. Mary Calkins became the first professor of physiological psychology at Wellesley College.

The creativity, energy and leadership of the others emerged in time: Lucy Sawyer launched the first Vacation Industrial School in the country; Orinda Hornbrooke worked in tandem with the newly founded Audubon Society and the Massachusetts legislature to safeguard birds from sacrificing their feathers to the millinery industry; Lydia Wellington was an outstanding organizer and leader; and Charlotte Calkins was effective in her outreach to other clubs and gave the Social Science Club its motto.

This handful of women began the Social Science Club of Newton with the goal "to learn more and do something about the social problems of their time."[2] They started the Club to study and present papers on different issues of the day. They undertook to investigate and shape their rapidly growing country, to move on from the tragedy of a civil war and, along with a great wave of immigrants, to help build its education system and governance.

Mary Whiton Calkins at about 25 years old.
(Courtesy of Wellesley College Archive)

The first paper, titled "Prison Reform," was given by Charlotte Calkins who had visited local prisons to observe and report on conditions. This was typical of the kind of subject treated in subsequent presentations. They ranged widely over national and local matters: "The Political Status of the Negro," "The Indian Question," "The Poor of Newton: How Can We Help Them," "The Labor Question," "Divorce," "Free Trade and Protection," "Is Modern Society a Success?" Other papers were titled "The Speakeasies in Nonantum," "Needed Reform in the Observance of the 4th of July" (which led to the banning of firecrackers in Newton), "Fisheries," "Industrial Education" and "Mormonism" (by a member who traveled to Utah and interviewed an Elder, his five wives and 26 children). They studied "The Chinese Question," "Child Instruction in the Mystery of Life," "Social Progress as the Result of Fixed Universal Principles" and "The Physical Value of Sunday."

Early meetings were quite formal with the ladies wearing hats and gloves. Meetings were not allowed to end before noon so that every member had an opportunity to discuss the topic after the paper was read or to give a presentation of her own in response. Papers were occasionally reread if many members had missed the first presentation.

Such was the nature of the members that it soon became clear that the

Club would not content itself to just study issues. A year into its existence, the minutes of January 26, 1887, describe the Club's aim thus: "It was not [created to be] a literary club nor a social event. It aims at beneficent work in arousing an interest among its members in the social needs of the community and country." Some of the women went out to give lectures to other clubs and local societies. Others lobbied their legislators for laws to improve conditions for prisoners, the unemployed, the poor and immigrants. They also fostered legislation regarding the environment, including native birds, trees and water pollution.

In November 1886 members voted to collect an annual fee of 25 cents, and to change the meeting day to Wednesday. By February 1887 they were working on the Club's first constitution and bylaws. These were adopted after a year of discussion and rewriting. Meeting chairs owned by the Social Science Club were stored in a member's stable and were driven by horse and wagon to the home of the hostess every week.

The "season" went from November through May and comprised about 24 meetings. A typical year in the early decades included between five and eight guest speakers, usually clergymen, educators and local government officials. The first meeting of each month was strictly for business. Paper writing was a mixture of volunteering and assigning — resulting in some impromptu performances and some cancelled meetings. By 1893 the idea of a year-long topic had evolved and clear assignments were set.

By 1898 the membership was so large that the Club stopped meeting in private homes and rented space in the newly built Hunnewell Club. Located at the corner of Church and Eldredge Streets, the Hunnewell Club has changed its name and function over the years. Long known as the Pomroy House, the white structure now houses condominiums.

Education was always foremost on the

When the Club outgrew members' homes for meetings, it rented space in the Hunnewell Club on Church St. The building now houses condominiums.

agenda. In April 1887, a paper on vocational and industrial schools led many members independently to visit and research industrial schools such as the South Boston Cooking School and the North Bennet Street Industrial School. The minutes from April 27, 1887 state: "The idea was suggested . . . there should be an industrial school . . . in our own city . . . and ladies of the Club should be the prime movers in this good work . . . thus showing that the Social Science Club could act as well as talk."

And act they did! In 1887, thanks to the vision and leadership of Lucy Sawyer, the first Vacation Industrial School in the nation was launched. The school ran for ten weeks, five days a week during the summer. The students, averaging about 12 years of age, were taught cooking, sewing, dressmaking, millinery, basketry and woodworking. The school and its teaching staff were managed by Mabel Hall, a Club member and educator. Members of the Club served as assistants. After the first year the school moved to the Nonantum area where Lydia Wellington and her husband Henry gave the use of an entire building, the Athenaeum Building, to the school.

Vacation Industrial School enrollment grew from a dozen girls in the Thompsonville sewing school in 1888 to 555 boys and girls in Nonantum by 1908 when the City of Newton assumed full responsibility. In the 20

Children pose with their handiwork in an Industrial School basketry class.

9

years of the school's existence the Club raised more than $10,000 to support it. The transfer to the city, which was a goal of the Club almost from the start, was a very slow process during which the Club learned how to build political support for their work. Patience and ingenuity led to some years of sharing expenses with the city and finally to the city's entire takeover of the Nonantum school.

In 1909 the Club's Industrial School Committee became the Philanthropic Committee, now the Scholarship Committee, and in 1925 it began awarding a college scholarship to a Newton High School girl.

Students in a class circle at the Industrial School.

In the early 1900s the Club had as many as 14 committees charged with fulfilling its mission in originating, shaping and overseeing its local and far reaching concerns. The Home Economics Committee, for example, monitored the local milk, meat and butter inspection laws. The efforts of this committee led to the current silver fund. Pennies were collected to pay for milk for the school children at Underwood School. Years later the silver fund money became the source of summer camperships for Newton children. Once in a while a penny will show up among the dollar bills in the silver basket as a reminder of the original purpose and an acknowledgment of the good work done by those early members of the Club.

Another manifestation of the Club's interest in education was its close relationship to the Newton school system. In the early decades Club members worked closely with the school administration in evaluating its programs and setting priorities. At the same time they responded to requests for help in building libraries in Georgia, Tennessee, North Dakota and even Alaska, long before it was a state. With the cost of a book at five cents, five dollars went a long way.

In its 12th year the Club reached 100 members. The following year, at the suggestion of Charlotte Calkins, they adopted as a motto "Privilege is Obligation" and chose green and white as Club colors. These actions were influenced in part by the many other women's clubs active in Newton and in other towns in Massachusetts (*see* pg. 16). The SSC kept informed of their activities through membership in the General Federation of Women's Clubs, the national group, and the Massachusetts Federation of Women's Clubs, the state organization. In the spring of 1895 members of the SSC were instrumental in forming a Newton Federation of Women's Clubs. Through it they lobbied for their reform efforts throughout the city.

Charlotte Althea Dudley Calkins at about 25 years of age.

Courtesy of Evan Calkin.

The women's response to World War I is reflected in their individual projects of knitting, and quilting for soldiers, and in their philanthropic efforts for France, Belgium, Armenia and Syria. Patriotic songs became a part of every meeting. There was also a heightened awareness of environmental concerns. This was expressed locally in their willingness to contribute to the salary of a Nature Study teacher at the High School and globally in the 1919 report of the Conservation Committee: "The war has shown sooner than could have been brought about in any other way (that) the most fundamental question of the day is the conservation of natural resources — minerals, oil, natural gas, soil, water, forests and all useful plant and animal life — not only each nation for itself but each nation in co-operation with every other. It is the most fundamental question because upon these resources alone depend the life of the world." Today's challenges have been evident for quite a while!

In 1936 Lenice Ingram Bacon wrote a play called "Letitia's Triumph" to mark the 50th year of the Club. The play traced the history of the organization and was performed by the members a second time to mark the Club's 75th anniversary.

Through the 1950s Club membership remained high and steady, between 80 and 100. In the 1960s, however, the introduction of the school lunch program signified a cultural shift. It was no longer necessary for a woman with school age children to be home at midday. A woman could go shopping in town, or possibly hold a job. Wednesday morning, Club meeting time, was not so sacred. Philanthropic work continued, a science committee was added, and mayors and school committee members still addressed the Club regularly, but membership declined sharply. The women made vain measures to bolster their numbers. In the early 1970s there was a call for each member to solicit three others. The Club began to reach beyond Newton Corner for members. But by 1978 when active membership dipped under 40, the Club restructured and moved their meeting site to the Farlow Hill home of member Emily Scott. From then on the Club met 12 times a year including an opening tea and a holiday musicale. The musicale was frequently held at the home of Inge Saraceno who delighted her fellow Clubwomen with her handmade European pastries.

Further changes took place in the 1990s as membership stabilized and evolved. In 1993 Virginia Munkelwitz noted that, "as a working woman it would be much easier for me to take a long lunch than a morning off." From this suggestion and a group survey, the Brown Bag Lunch developed. For years meetings had not been held in January or February, partly due to weather and partly to Florida migration. But in 1995 the Club decided to try this less formal 'bring your own lunch to a member's home' model. Lunch programs often focus on Club history, but have also included book swaps and guest speakers from the community. By 1998 the Club was able to return to Grace Church for its regular meetings.

Now, as the Club enters the second decade of the 21st century, membership remains around 40 and the Club continues to attract an active group of women with a rich variety of interests and talents. The group continues to contribute to the community. They fostered the building of the new Newton library and provided one of the study carrels. As global and local needs shift, the Club responds — in the 1980s the Club facilitated the sale of Hmong women's needle work and helped the adult special needs community in Newton. More recent philanthropic interests have included women in Afghanistan and orphans in Tanzania. The Newton high school scholarship endures and summer camperships continue.

Underlying all its activities and forming the very backbone of the Club from the start is the quality of friendship that the members have found in one another. Even Aristotle recognized that the richest friendships arise from work done in unison for a goal outside oneself. May the women of the Club carry on into the 21st century a work so well begun in the 19th.

Milk Cures and Bed Rest: Trying to Keep the Thinking Woman Down

by Kate Stout

In March 1994 Club member Sylvia Skinner delivered a paper on Nobel Prize winner Jane Addams (1860–1935). The theme that year was "Nobel Peace Prize Winners." Within Skinner's eloquently written paper on Addams, who was the founder of Hull House in Chicago and so a driving force behind the settlement movement in America, was a mini-essay on the Victorian presumption that intellectual activity in women was quite literally bad for their health. It is excerpted here because it sheds riveting light on a little-known reason why many intelligent women found refuge in women's clubs of all natures, not least among them the Social Science Club of Newton.

Jane Addams, Skinner writes, had very real physical problems that bedeviled her health in many ways. As a child Jane had frequent illnesses, including tuberculosis of the spine, which left her with a slight curvature of her back and an awkward gait. Allen Davis in his biography of Jane Addams writes: "Despite her complex family and her frequent sicknesses,

Jane had a happy rural childhood not significantly different from others of her generation, except that she early developed a sense of purpose and commitment. She was sickly, but she never became a hypochondriac."

With this understanding of her subject directly addressed, Skinner goes on to a broader canvas — how women of intellectual strength were dealt with by a nay-saying society and how that society gave muscle to its mores by couching them in the 'objectivity' of a medical diagnosis. Addams, Skinner says, was among the first wave of college-educated women, which meant she was a tacit threat to the very fabric and order of American life in the late 1880s.

Skinner writes:

> This first group of college-educated women had considerable difficulty after they graduated finding a role for themselves that could incorporate their hard-won knowledge and new view of themselves. After the excitement of learning new ideas and discussing them intensely with one another, they re-entered a world in which women's roles did not include this kind of intellectual activity.
>
> Jane Addams suffered a great deal with this dilemma after she left Rockford Seminary. She wanted very much to attend Smith to continue her education, and also enrolled at Women's Medical College in Philadelphia, but her health became a serious problem, with her back causing her difficulties again. The doctors prescribed that she should spend months in bed, and when this did not help, she had surgery on her back, followed by more months in bed.
>
> The college-educated woman of this period was very susceptible to illness. It was almost expected of her, since intellectual activity was seen as leading to physical and mental breakdown. William Dean Howells said in 1872 that "American society seemed little better than

a hospital for invalid women." Tom Lutz has written a very interesting book on neurasthenia called *American Nervousness 1903: An Anecdotal History,* in which he describes an epidemic of this disease at the turn of the century, afflicting a large number of well-known people including Theodore Roosevelt, Edith Wharton, William and Henry James, William Dean Howells and Jane Addams. It was a nervousness, which was "a mark of distinction, of class, of status, of refinement. Neurasthenia struck brain-workers but no other kind of laborer."

But although men and women received the same diagnosis, the prescription for cure was gender specific. In the most widely known treatment for women [that of physician Weir Mitchell], the patient was prescribed bed rest for a month or longer, was not allowed visitors or permitted to read or write, and was spoon-fed a diet of milk by a nurse. . . . In contrast to this infantilization and enforced debilitation, Theodore Roosevelt, Thomas Eakins, Frederic Remington and Owen Wister were all sent to the Dakotas for rough-riding exercise cures (the latter two by Mitchell). Henry James was sent to hike in the Alps. . . . Other men congregated at resort spas to play sports and to ride for exercise.

Neurasthenia was considered a form of nervous exhaustion, and while women needed rest and quiet so that they might passively build up their reserves of nerve force, men needed actively and vigorously to build up theirs. Women became exhausted through too much exposure to the world, and so the rest cure, during which women were to center their thinking on their families, functioned to refit them for their basic social role. Neurasthenia in men made them unfit for a successful life in the world, and the survivalist, competitive, aggressive exercise cures can be seen as a way of refitting them in the basics of their available roles. Both cures were represented in terms of a return to traditional values of passive femininity and masculine activity.

In her paper on Jane Addams, Sylvia Skinner is moved to speculate what, in light of medicine as oppression, becomes painfully obvious: "I wonder if the Social Science Club in Newton was in part an expression of the yearning at this time for validation of the role of the thinking woman."

The Roots of Social Science

Virginia Munkelwitz presented this paper on March 6, 1991. The topic for the year was Critical Issues for Women Today. *Edited and abridged by Kate Stout.*

The Social Science Club of Newton sprang from a massive women's club movement that began after the Civil War and lasted until suffrage was obtained in 1920. Clubs such as the SSC performed significant civic functions in virtually every community in the United States. At the height of the women's club movement women of all social and ethnic groups worked through clubs to effect change. This does not mean the clubs were inclusive, because they were not. There was a good deal of snobbery and, unfortunately, on-going racism. But different clubs existed for different groups and they worked through a national network to achieve significant results.

Clubs provided a tool that women used to influence public policy. Clubs created a new public space between the formal public structure of government and the private arena of the home. Women learned to use this public space to redefine their own identities and to challenge the larger structures of business and politics. As both domesticity and religion became marginalized, women joined with ministers to reassert moral values, to make domesticity more meaningful and to change the public sphere.

The emergence of women from the private, isolating and confining realm of the home into the forbidden public sphere has been termed "Domestic Feminism." During the second half of the 19th century, women formed widespread literary societies. These societies were formed not at the expense of the home but to enhance it; not as a departure from the role of 'ladydom' but as a way to strengthen and nurture the family. The literary clubwoman retained her ladylike behavior but at the same time she carried on radical political activities. The forerunners of the literary societies were Sorosis in New York and the New England Women's Club in Boston.

Jane Cunningham Croly founded Sorosis in 1868. [The club's name comes from the Latin for sister, hence a society of sisters.] Croly was a feminist and journalist and, for many, the single most important person in the women's club movement. She encouraged women to participate in the public arena but also to improve their lives at home, to move beyond the social conventions that had been set for them but to fully respect their roles as mothers and homemakers. She chose not to join the suffragists, who advocated power outside the home and whose radical political means offended the vast majority of men and women.

Jane Croly gathered several of her friends to form Sorosis with the purpose of bringing women together to increase their self-knowledge and self-respect.

> The object of this association is to promote agreeable and useful relations among women of literary and artistic tastes .... It recognizes women of thought, culture, and humanity everywhere, particularly when these qualities have found expression in outward life and work.... It aims to establish a kind of freemasonry among women of similar pursuits, to render them helpful to each other, and bridge over the barrier that custom and social etiquette place in the way of friendly intercourse. ... It affords an opportunity for the discussion among women of new facts and principles, the results of which promise to exert an important influence on the future of women and the welfare of society.[3]

Sorosis met twice a month to discuss business and social matters.

Lunch was followed by papers, entertainment or speeches. Most members were career women. Original members were writers and journalists but as the club grew, artists, historians, teachers, philanthropists, architects, photographers and physicians joined. Despite the variety of occupations, these women shared a sense of adventure; they were women who explored avenues unknown to most women of their time. They were women who were not in the mainstream of American culture, and Sorosis offered them the opportunity to associate with other women like themselves. As a group, they could discuss the difficulties of reconciling their femininity and their careers.

It is important to realize that Jane Croly's objectives were radical, even though her methods were moderate. She did not join the suffragettes because she realized how unpopular they were and, consequently, how long it would take them to obtain the vote. She said, "There is no need of waiting until men give us a vote, we take it without asking, and we apply ourselves at once to an examination of the causes of the evil we deplore, and of the remedy to be applied."[4]

She urged women to accept responsibility for their own issues and advocated a Women's Parliament that would concern itself with women's issues. "[I]t will be understood that the Parliament has nothing to do with the demand for 'Women's Rights,' so-called; it simply recognizes women's duties, and proposes a way to perform them."[5] The Parliament was a failure. Croly's small, elite, activist group was not representative of most women of the time, and the idea of a national women's group did not resurface until 1873.

That year Sorosis created the Association for the Advancement of Women (AAW). Unlike the Women's Parliament, the AAW was an elite national organization that espoused the ideas of Sorosis and those of the New England Women's Club (NEWC), which had been founded by Caroline Severance and her friends, also in 1868. The women in Severance's club were less career-oriented and contributed social reform to the club movement. They worked in education, politics, women's careers and clothing design to reform American life. They actively

18

supported suffrage, established a horticultural school for women, ran a store which sold sensible clothing and formed a lobby to elect women to the Boston school board. The NEWC brought to the AAW its strong sense of social reform, adding that imperative to Croly's own Domestic Feminist ideals. For instance, the seventh AAW annual meeting encouraged women to join state boards of education, and to manage insane asylums and reformatories. Later assignments included investigating the conditions of children in state institutions. However, the greatest contribution of the New England club was suffrage. Members of the NEWC were able to reconcile the Domestic Feminist and Suffrage movements, and thus pave the way for moving suffrage into the mainstream. They subordinated suffrage to Domestic Feminism and claimed it would result in "better schools, better order, better protection of women, juster legal verdicts, less crime, fewer divorces."[6]

The AAW met annually for 25 years. It did not try to induct women into the club movement but tried to unify women who were already club members. Ironically, it succeeded in creating more women's clubs. It also created a feeling of sisterhood among the women who attended as well as one of social reform action in its members.

* * *

Literary clubs were formed across America from 1870–1900 and succeeded in reaching the vast majority of women. The Social Science Club of Newton, founded in 1886, began during this phase of the women's club movement, and in many ways fit the pattern of the literary club although founding members objected to that description.

Club membership was usually based on some common factor: school, community, religion, profession or economic status. The majority of these clubwomen were over 40 and past childbearing age. They were not career women, but women whose duties of tending children and keeping house were lessening, and who now had time for other activities. Many of them were college graduates who had put aside their dreams in order to raise a family. Housework during this period was intense and tedious even for those who were lucky enough to have domestic help. When the last child had grown a woman had time to think about her own needs again. As one woman said, "'We were no longer in our first youth, our babies were out of our arms and their bringing up was past the nursery stage with its insistent claims, while their future opened wide vistas, where we needed all the wisdom we could get.' In a society that valued a woman for her maternal duties, the woman finished with child rearing had a void to fill. She was ready for a role that gave her self-esteem and importance in life. Rather than push her children into paths she may have regretted not taking, she could forge her own."[7]

A small percentage of members were single. A single woman in the 19th century usually lived with her relatives and was considered an outsider in a culture that revered motherhood. If she worked, she suffered job as well as social discrimination, so the club provided social support as well as activity.

Literary clubs studied culture. This was a departure from the earlier moral reform societies that existed to improve society; they more closely followed Sorosis' aim to study for enjoyment and to meet for camaraderie. Unlike Sorosis, literary clubwomen did not produce scholars or career women, but their strivings for self-improvement should not be underrated. This was an era that defined women as selfless agents but through literary clubs women were taking an important step toward improving their status.

The format for most clubs was to give papers on an annually elected topic. Controversial topics were avoided. Literature, mythology, classics, the Bible, art, music and history were popular topics. The Social Science Club was on the left side of the spectrum with early topics such as "The American Indian Problem," "The Political Status of the Negro" and "The Perils of Divorce." In most clubs, though not in Newton, paper presentations were followed by refreshments, which served an important purpose as expressed by a Chicago clubwoman: "Many of us mute, inglorious Miltons who had not the courage to speak our minds before several hundred in formidable array, expressed our humble opinions freely over the teacups."[8]

Women benefited in many ways from literary clubs — they obtained public-speaking experience; they developed a strong sense of sisterhood; they found self-esteem while researching and writing papers; they learned to organize committees, lead meetings and use Parliamentary procedures; and they entered a new realm through their study of culture. As author Karen Blair says in her book *The Clubwoman as Feminist*, "Clubs developed in women a sisterhood which extended beyond the membership to all women, a respect for women's sphere, and a critique of male values in addition to expanding their intellectual aspirations. In the face of ridicule and censure, women learned that silence was no longer the virtue it once had been. Instead of feeling intimidated by large groups or impolite for asking questions, women found it smarter to probe, first about problems in the arts, and then about the problems of women in society. Gradually, they were moved to act on their own behalf, in the form of establishing scholarships and clubhouses and later through grander programs. Club life succeeded at reaching and assisting a large body of American womanhood to grow, by altering their expectations of both their social functions and their ability to carry out change."[9]

In 1877, a new organization was formed in Boston — the Women's Educational and Industrial Union (WEIU). It enlarged the club movement by introducing cross-class sisterhood and 'municipal housekeeping,' ideas that would grow to be incorporated into literary clubs. The use of the word 'union' in its name is a clue to increased identification with working-class women and their problems. The WEIU incorporated the earlier social reform ideals of the New England Women's Club in its efforts to deal with working-class poverty. However, the WEIU identified with working-class women in a deeper sense: they believed that like working-class women, housewives were dependent on their husbands and could only gain independence through paid work.

Harriet Clisby, a London-born physician, established the WEIU to discuss women's potential moral power. The response was immense. After one year there were 400 members; after ten years there were 1200. But it was Abby Morton Diaz who guided the organization from the discussion of moral power to an application of moral power. The WEIU created job opportunities for women who wanted to work. They opened a store where housewives could sell their homemade goods, calling it "The Mother of Exchanges"; they opened several lunchrooms which provided jobs as well as inexpensive and nutritious food; they established dressmaking and millinery courses, a School of Salesmanship, and a School of Housekeeping; and in the process, they elevated many women's domestic responsibilities to professions.

The WEIU's other significant contribution was the new Municipal Housekeeping movement that served to move women from social reform to civic reform. "Woman has a special function in developing the welfare of humanity, which man cannot perform. This function consists in her power to make, of any place in which she may happen to live, a home for all those who come there. Women must now learn to make of their cities great community homes for all the people."[10]

The Municipal Housekeeping movement addressed civic industrial issues. Volunteers established a Protective Committee to provide legal assistance to women with employment-related grievances; they investigated pollution caused by industrial smoke; they interested themselves in street cleaning; and they improved working conditions for women and children. By taking action on community problems, they pushed women farther into the public sphere and set a precedent for public action that would be expanded upon by the General Federation of Women's Clubs. Municipal Housekeeping reached its zenith with the establishment of this federation of clubs of all types in 1890 by Sorosis founder Jane Cunningham Croly. The Federation resulted in cooperative collective action.

Clubs began their reform work with those institutions most closely associated with culture. Due to the efforts of these clubwomen, libraries were established. They began by forming traveling libraries and moved on to obtaining rooms, books and, eventually, buildings. The American Library Association credited women's clubs with establishing 75% of all public libraries in existence in 1933. The Federation guided these groups not only in their objectives but by presenting papers such as "How to Start Small Libraries," "How to Stimulate Interest in Local Libraries" and "Should Public Library Boards Include Women?"[11]

Clubwomen moved quickly from establishing school libraries to school reform. The Social Science Club was a pioneer in this area. In 1887 — three years before Jane Croly began her federation — the SSC established and ran the Vacation Industrial School. Education, however, was only the starting place of club work. Clubwomen were responsible for civil service examinations; planting trees and protecting the environment; amending child labor laws; establishing public parks and gardens; making public transportation safer; building public restrooms; providing sewage and garbage collection. They set up tuberculosis camps, sanatoriums, clinics and hospitals; hired district nurses and state bacteriologists; and established pure food laws. Women accomplished these tasks with the firm belief that they were morally superior to men and therefore responsible for applying virtue to their homes, their communities and their country.

A growing level of feminism accompanied these vast accomplishments. As women became more involved in the male public sphere, they did not draw such tight lines around the male and female arenas. They saw the value of both spheres and sought to merge them. The result was increased education for women in areas that had traditionally been considered male, and an emerging conviction that men should share in household duties. They wanted a man "who, beside earning his share of the living, will expect to do as much as the mother does toward making the home a lovely place in which to live; who will take an intelligent interest in the education of the children and, by example and works, foster spiritual life in the child."[12]

Running parallel to a new brand of feminism was the emergence of popular support for suffrage. At a 1908 Federation meeting in Boston the issue was openly discussed and two years later a majority voted in its favor. Clubwomen already believed that home values belonged in the world, and the vote would further that belief. In 1914 thousands of delegates endorsed suffrage. They represented 1,700,000 clubwomen.

The Senate approved the Nineteenth Amendment on August 26, 1920. But for the women's club movement suffrage was a double-edged sword. Women now had a direct relationship with the state, and this undermined their need for collective action. Women's political activism had succeeded in creating government agencies that handled social problems. Social workers replaced club workers in settlement houses and while this provided jobs for women, clubwomen no longer played an active role. They did not mobilize for new causes. Never again did they assume the kind of involvement that had existed at the height of the Federation. Ironically, the success of the club movement was instrumental in undermining the club movement itself.

Profile of a Founding Member: Orinda Dudley Hornbrooke
by Vivi Leavy

Orinda Hornbrooke, a founding member of the Social Science Club of Newton, was in many respects a typical clubwoman of the end of the 19th century. She was comfortably off, the wife of a successful clergyman. Her husband, Dr. Francis Bickford Hornbrooke, came to Newton in 1879 to lead Channing Unitarian Church and retired with many laurels 21 years later.

Born in St. Albans, Maine on November 8, 1846, Orinda Althea Dudley was the second daughter and fourth child of Harrison and Elizabeth Prentice Dudley. Her parents were both of hardy Puritan stock, her father tracing his lineage back to Thomas Dudley, second governor of Massachusetts Bay Colony. The family lived in several communities in Maine and Massachusetts while the children were growing up including Fall River and finally Cambridge. Orinda was probably educated in the local free (public) schools as was at least one of her brothers.

Orinda met her husband-to-be Francis Bickford Hornbrooke in Cambridge shortly after he arrived there in the fall of 1871 to attend Harvard Divinity School. He was 22 and grew up in Wheeling, West Virginia. Orinda was three years older. They were engaged the following

24

year but, as was the custom, did not marry until September of 1874 when Bickford had graduated from Union Theological Seminary and received a call to minister to a small parish in East Hampton, Connecticut, and thus could support a wife. The wedding took place at the home of the bride's parents at 53 Dunster Street, Cambridge.

By 1886 Orinda was 39, the mother of two sons, ten-year-old Dudley and six-year-old Bickford. As a busy minister's wife, she was probably also deeply involved in Channing Church work, women's circles and philanthropic activities. They must not have been enough to absorb her passion, energy and ambition for, on January 22, she was one of the five women who met at Lydia Wellington's house on Fairmont Avenue to start the Social Science Club. Charlotte Calkins, the wife of the pastor of Eliot Church and also among those first five, met her there for the first time. "I have a memory of a rather youthful face with fair hair and a winning smile. A touch of pink in her hat suited her delicate coloring," Calkins recalled in her tribute to Hornbooke 34 years later.[13]

Orinda Hornbrooke was not a force among the founding women. Calkins described Lucy Sawyer and Lydia Wellington, as "the two originators of the Club. . . . Both were thoughtful women of strong character . . . eager to serve wherever the need was discovered."[14] Hornbrooke, who was known for her eloquence and her sense of humor,[15] didn't even hold office for a few years. Eventually she took her place as one of six vice presidents, then as acting president in 1901 while Calkins was abroad, and finally as president (1902–04). Calkins judged her "a most efficient presiding officer. I think no woman in the Club has given us so many papers, all of vital interest, as she."[16]

Orinda Hornbrooke, true to her old New England roots, had a conservative cast of mind. While suffrage was an important issue of the 1890s, she had many reservations. On April 22, 1891, she attended a 'guest meeting' where the clergyman Russell Ballou, husband of Club member Augusta, addressed the members and their guests on the controversial matter of "Women and Natural Law," an issue which played an important role in the question of women's suffrage. The Club's recording secretary reported that Mr. Ballou argued that "from the standpoint of natural law we must agree that women's best work is done in the domestic sphere." There was a great deal of discussion, some of it in dissent, picking up on the suffrage issue. "Mrs. Walton gave some examples from her experience in temperance work. In her opinion the votes of women are most needed. Mrs. Wilson spoke of the duty of women to study political science with a view to relieving the burden of ignorance. . . . At the close of the discussion, Mrs. Hornbrooke spoke a word for the anti-suffrage side of the question, pointing out the local and transitional nature of this privilege, even for men, and speaking of the power already possessed by women without this right."

Hornbrooke's views on suffrage were reported again at a Club meeting on January 24, 1894. At issue was the Municipal Suffrage petition to be presented at the State House. Members had been asked to prepare themselves to vote on it at the previous meeting. "Mrs. Hornbrooke . . . thought that women lack the business training to satisfactorily perform the duties pertaining to the government of a city, and that in its broader sense, suffrage would prove an inconvenience and not a benefit. Mary Lathrop Tucker voiced the opinion of many present in declaring a belief in suffrage for women, but not in universal suffrage for either men or women." Hornbrooke's anti-suffrage stance was not only philosophical but practical and represented the views of enough of her fellows that support for the petition was stymied.

That wasn't always the case. Club member Helen Howes Gleason reported that "Mrs. Hornbrooke . . . once told me that at the State Federation meeting in Swampscott suffrage was endorsed over her bitter protest. 'I did all I could,' she said, 'but in vain, so I went out and sat on the stairs and wept.'"[17] At the Club's 25th anniversary celebration, she told the crowd "in her usual humorous way [that] she thought she had been voted down more often than any other member of the Club."[18]

A few years later, on April 22, 1896, Hornbrooke became interested in another controversial topic, immigration. She presented her paper, "A Study of Our Foreign Populations," to a largely sympathetic audience of

Club members. The recording secretary synopsized her talk: "From the nature of American institutions and the character of the first settlers, Mrs. Hornbrooke differed from Mr. Garrison's 'pretty theories' concerning immigration by classifying all those who came to these shores before the Revolution as Native Americans and all those who came later as immigrants." William Lloyd Garrison, a strong supporter of the right to free immigration was on the wrong track according to Hornbrooke. She feared "the mental and moral effects of such an influx of immigrants," considering them to lead to the "decline of native stock" and the growth of slums, and called for a tariff to limit immigration.

The discussion that followed was very fully covered; immigration was a hot topic in the 1890s in the halls of government and in the newspapers of the day as well as at the Social Science Club. "Mrs. Merrill viewed both sides of the problem and thought that as a Christian people we have a duty to perform. . . . Mrs. Sondericker expressed sympathy for the quiet, unobstructive element which makes good citizens." But Mary Billings agreed with Hornbrooke that "it was wise to eliminate this [undesirable] element," and Harriet Bowman feared "the danger of being foreignized ourselves." Even Lucy Sawyer believed that "charity should be subservient to order."

The following winter, Hornbrooke found a topic, the preservation of birds, that not only was close to her heart but evoked enthusiastic support from fellow Club members. She and her husband were well placed in Newton society through his profession and her ancestry; they also had many contacts in Boston and Cambridge through his clubs and her family. It is likely that she was invited to one of the series of teas that Boston social leader Harriet Hemenway of Boston and her cousin Minna Hall gave in the autumn of 1886 to publicize an issue which had recently come to their attention, the killing of birds to adorn ladies' hats. "In the 1880s trendy bonnets were piled high with feathers, birds, fruit, flowers, furs, even mice and small reptiles. Birds were by far the most popular accessory; women sported egret plumes, owl heads, sparrow wings and whole hummingbirds," ecologist Jennifer Price explains.[19] Hornbrooke

27

did her research, wrote her paper and presented it to the Club on December 16, 1896, but there was a snowstorm and only 23 ladies made it to the meeting. The stalwart attendees knew a great paper when they heard it. Not only did they schedule Hornbrooke to give her paper again, but they decided to place a synopsis in the *Boston Evening Transcript*, overriding their normal aversion to newspapers and publicity.

Thus, on January 20, 1897, Hornbrooke faced a full house. Ethie Howe, who took notes that day, remarked that "the meeting was unusually large, called together from interest in the subject of the morning, 'Ornamentation at the Expense of Animal Life,' and the knowledge that it was treated in a masterly manner by Mrs. Hornbrooke." She called her paper "A Plea for the Birds."

Ethie Howe's notes, written out by the official recording secretary Elizabeth Whittier, undoubtedly don't do justice to Hornbrooke's eloquence. "Man is the inheritor of the earth. Formerly all life was preserved; now man wages warfare on the beasts of the field and the fowls of the air," she argued. "Birds are among the highest forms of animal life as shown in their care of their young and faithfulness to one mate, practical monogamists . . . . Authorities agree that there are fewer birds than formerly. Birds are powerful friends and allies of man, exterminating many insects injurious to harvests. Who are these that kill the birds? Who are these who thus disturb the balance of nature? The ones who would be expected to be their protector — the women!"

She tugged on her audience's heartstrings and their religious training: "Herons in Florida, so beautiful and graceful are doomed to extinction to fill the demand for their aigrettes from millinery houses. They are readily taken when their nests are full of little birds, as the mother will not leave her young. They live in colonies so many are killed at once and the little birds are left to die of starvation. And yet Christian women read, 'not a sparrow falls to the ground without the Father.' Christ said, 'As you have done it unto the least of these you have done it unto me.' Cruel vanity ignores all but its own desires."

She rallied her fellow Clubwomen: "This is an abominable blot on our escutcheon in this, the woman's century. The receiver [of stolen goods] is as bad as the thief. If women would not buy or wear these decorations, the birds would not be killed. She is responsible! . . . We could accomplish much if we would join the crusade!"

Her listeners' reaction must have been gratifying. "The reading of the paper was listened to with the greatest interest and attention and was followed by an animated discussion by members of the club and some guests. The main point was what can we do to aid the cause? The following resolution was passed: 'Let our club draw up a paper that can be presented to others.' Adelaide Blodgett made a motion that such a petition to the legislature be drawn up by Hornbrooke and signed by members of this club and others desirous of so doing. The resolution was adopted by unanimous vote of the club."

There was strong follow-up to Hornbrooke's talk. On March 17, 1897, Mary Stetson (the chairman of the Club's Board of Directors, the officer in charge of seeing activities were carried through, not just discussed) read a circular from the newly formed Audubon Society hoping Newton women would unite in work with them on the issue. Lifetime membership was 25 cents and Harriet Barrows had brought membership forms. She also read a long list of the names of members (among them the conservationist, Mary Lathrop Tucker [Mrs. Fred H.] who had so opposed Hornbrooke's stands on suffrage and immigration) wanting "to work for a meeting to interest young people in the cause of birds." Hornbrooke seems to have been suffering a letdown from her normal sure self that day. It was reported that "she spoke of the misunderstanding of the Audubon Society in regard to the purpose of the Newton women. She reported utter discouragement in sending petitions to the legislature, for this year at least, as other societies had utterly failed in this purpose." Trying to be positive, the president [Susan Baker] "noted that this year Jordan Marsh [Department Store] had stopped importing bird feathers."

Two weeks later (March 31, 1897) it was announced that Hornbrooke was taking her "Plea for the Birds" to the Newton Federation and a young people's group. By January 1905 she noted that her paper had been given

61 times to various men's and women's groups. Although the Audubon Society was not her cup of tea, Hornbrooke did become an associate member of the older and more scientific American Ornithologists Union in 1897.

During Orinda Hornbrooke's presidency of the Club in 1902, she was one of the Clubwomen involved in what must have been a shocking development to members. Newtonites opening their *Boston Globe* on Tuesday, August 19, 1902, found large black headlines, "Clubwomen Sued," and in slightly smaller type, "Buckley Claims They Lost His Albany House License." How many Club members could remember the quick vote they took back on April 23 that Hornbrooke, as president, should represent the Club in the matter of "formulating a concerted appeal [with many local women's clubs] for the suppression of the nuisance maintained at the Albany House, Brighton"? The 'nuisance' at the Albany House hotel, members didn't need to be told, was its saloon. As for the targeted proprietor, Timothy F. Buckley, his name was surely never mentioned. The *Boston Journal* reported that Hornbrooke herself "seemed very much surprised that a suit for damages had been brought." [20]

Here is her story to the *Journal*:

> I had no information that such a thing would happen either
> when the petition for the suppression of the house was
> presented to the governor or later. Such a thought never
> entered my mind. We were asked by the members of the
> Brighthelmstone Club of Brighton to help in absolving a
> nuisance there known as the Albany House. Fifteen of us
> . . . early in June waited upon Governor Crane. There was
> no written petition drawn up or anything of the kind. Mrs.
> Bates of Brighton simply told the governor the situation
> in a few words and we all seconded it. Three days later
> we saw by the papers that the Albany House was closed,
> and from that time until this I have thought nothing of
> the matter. In fact I had completely forgotten the incident.

Then she got up on her high horse. "This is really too ludicrous to talk about," Mrs. Hornbrooke, said smiling. She continued:

> Why the man won't dare to take the case to the courts.
> If he does, he will be cutting his own throat. We have all
> the facts on our side. This wasn't started in a hurry-flurry
> sentimental sort of way, you understand. We went at the
> wiping out of this place in a systematic business manner.
> It was simply a hearing before the governor of the state, a
> private hearing in which a few women desired to tell the
> officials of the Commonwealth just what was going on in
> Brighton. The governor listened to us with the result that
> the Albany is at present not running. I think Mr. Buckley
> or whoever the man is, had better sue Governor Crane
> — that's the man he wants to deal with. Oh he's only
> trying to scare us women, you know, but I think I will
> sleep just as soundly tonight . . . as ever before.

Mr. Buckley saw it differently of course. According to the *Globe*, he had purchased the property from the Boston and Albany Railroad about 18 months before, made improvements on it to the tune of $20,000, and operated both the hotel and the bar for a year under a hotel license. The license came up for renewal in April and the Boston Police Board voted favorably on it. A week later, on the same day the new license was to take effect the women met with the governor and presented their petition. The Police Board then reneged and the license was not forthcoming. Without the license Mr. Buckley claimed his property was worthless and brought suit for $50,000. The *Globe* noted that "the [petition] is one of the consequences of the anti-saloon agitation in Allston at the time the licenses were last issued." What the Anti-Saloon League gentlemen could not accomplish, the women did.

All the fuss quite quickly withered away to nothing. As another clubwoman petitioner pointed out to the *Journal*, "there isn't $50,000 in all the clubs put together . . . .These clubs have no corporate existence." And the sentiment of the times was not on Buckley's side. As Hornbrooke said, possibly exaggerating a bit, "Think of it! 5,000 women were represented and of the same opinion!"[21]

Perhaps that triumphant statement to the *Globe* reporter marked the apogee of Hornbrooke's political efforts and interests. The sudden death of her beloved husband at the age of 54 in December 1903 did not end her Club activities, but it seemed to change them. Her energies in the immediate future went largely into preserving and enhancing her husband's memory. She wrote the lively and revealing "Sketch of His Life," published two years after his death and prepared for publication a book he left nearly finished among his papers. Meanwhile for the Club she put politics aside and wrote more literary papers: "Benjamin Thompson, Count Rumford" (March 28, 1906); "The Poets Laureate of England" (March 13, 1907); "Margaret Fuller" (February 23, 1910); and many others. She wrote her last paper in 1916 before a debilitating illness curtailed her activities and forced her to become bedridden prior to her death in November 1920.

Orinda Hornbrooke may or may not have been 'typical' but she was emblematic of an early Social Science Club member in the issues that engaged her, her time of life, her social standing in the community, her enthusiasm for learning and for helping others, and also that she was first and foremost a wife.

Social Science or
How Long Does It Take for a Century to Turn?

Written and presented by Alison Umbsen on January 8, 1986, as part of the Club's centennial observance. The topic for the year was, "Study the Past and Shape the Future." Edited and abridged by Vivi Leavy.

Many years ago when the 19th century was turning into the 20th my two older sisters were beginning to entertain. When they had a dinner party, little sister Alison would be sent to the country to her grandmother Buswell's in Newton. So at an early age I began to hear and learn about the Social Science Club. I would much rather have stayed at home watching and listening but apparently I was using my talent as a snoop in Newton. I am amazed at how much I recall.

The Buswells moved to Newton in 1889. Soon after, Grandmother [Susan Buswell] joined the Club. It was always called the Club, [but] when Grandfather [Charles H. Buswell] said 'the Club' he meant the Hunnewell Club. My mother Alice Buswell Towle graduated from Smith College in 1889 and joined the Club the next fall. This was most unusual; 30 years of age was considered the criterion. By that time one's background and intellect would be merged into the perfect candidate. In my mother's case, Miss Mary Calkins had persuaded the powers-that-be that by having such a recent college graduate as a member, especially one who had graduated with honors in the classics, the whole Club would benefit.

Alison Umbsen
(Photo by Emily Hubbs Scott)

Mother was engaged but living at home. My father was busy becoming a doctor (Harvard 1888, Boston University Medical School, internship at Boston City Hospital and then Massachusetts General). They were engaged ten years. You didn't get married until you were earning! So Mother became busy in all sorts of projects, as did most of the members of the Club. One of Mother's pet projects was The Working Girl's Club. Very often she read to them to uplift their minds. She told me that when she read *Pride & Prejudice* one of the girls came to her afterwards and said, "That is the kind of lady I would like to be." The end of Mother's active Social Science membership came when she married my father and went to live in Boston.

The third member of my family to belong to the Club was my aunt, Carrie Buswell Hollings. She belonged to the Club as soon as she was eligible but it was an off and on relationship. In 1910 (the year I was born) she married a school classmate, William Hollings. They lived in Denver, Washington and Charleston, West Virginia. It wasn't until after World War I that they returned to Newton. Then she became a steady member. Her dramatic flair made her papers outstanding. Her paper on Martin Luther was used by her young relatives at Winsor, Harvard, Dartmouth and Bennington Junior College. I never dared ask about plagiarism!

* * *

There was a network of Social Science Club members in the neighborhood of my grandmother's house on Franklin Street: Mrs. Ralph Angier, the quiet one; Miss Grace Weston, affectionately called 'the Town Crier'; Mrs. Samuel Braman, the parliamentarian; Miss Miriam Dewey who could talk faster than anyone known to man and still be able to answer questions without pausing for breath. Aunty Hollings was known as 'the trotter.' Up the hill there was Mrs. Everett Kemp, the boss; Mrs. George Angier, the practical one; and Mrs. Bemis Gleason who kept track of things that needed to be done and did them. After all, Mayor Neddy Child's sister was a member.

It was the custom of these ladies to have 'at-home' days where tea would be served. Grandmother Buswell had tea served every day. Her house was a gathering place, not only because of the tea but also because it was the halfway point up the hill when walking. Quite often these tea parties became unofficial board meetings, especially if it was the first Monday [sic] of the month when there had been the monthly board meeting that morning. There was always a residue from these meetings that would ordinarily have to wait until the next month. If a decision was reached at Grandmother's the network would be contacted and very often at the next board meeting a recommendation would be presented for consideration.

As was the custom of the day I was often asked to recite a poem. I had been well coached by my governess. For me this was a form of torture left over from the Victorian era. One day, my sister Caroline came to my rescue. Out of my sweet, innocent little mouth came this ditty: "Can the chatter, kid! Or I'll give you a slug in the mug that will knock your blinkers all over your hash trap." I couldn't understand why some of the ladies asked to be excused. Later I was told that Grandmother turned pink and went right on serving tea. I was never asked to recite again either in Newton or Boston.

Sometimes my grandfather would arrive home from Boston in time for tea. After greeting the ladies he would ask, "And what is the burning question today?" He would then be given a rundown. But the ladies never gave us [children] any of the sacrosanct information.

Membership was very hush-hush. It would be a month after the candidate's name had been presented to the Board before the name could be brought to the Club for a vote. This gave the Board plenty of time to look into the background of the candidate. It also provided time for the future member to be brought to a scheduled guest meeting. [Eight such meetings were scheduled per year, with members who brought a guest paying a 25 cent guest fee]. After finally being voted in, the lucky person would be visited by the Chairman and a member of the Membership Committee. They would ask if she would be interested in joining the Club. Never did the candidate find out who had proposed her. . . . Do you remember Patty Calkins telling of the time she ate her 'nay' ballot because she didn't know what to do with it and still have the unanimous vote the Club wanted? I also know of someone who was black-balled because she asked if she could join.

The annual Christmas donation brought forth a debate as to whether to give just food, or should a monetary donation be included. It would be so nice for "Johnny to have a new pair of shoes and Daddy could have a new shirt to wear while hunting for a job. Five dollars would suffice."

There wasn't time for business on paper days. Papers were supposed to last until 12:00 noon. If they didn't, the time was filled in with a report on a recently read book, or perhaps a description of a recent trip.

* * *

Magazines were one way members kept up with the times. There was a regular clientele and magazines were passed along. Quite often I was the errand girl for this activity. I remember *The Atlantic Monthly, Harpers,*

Punch, London Illustrated, Scribners and *National Geographic*. No one ever found out that this city girl was terrified of the quiet Newton streets. The route went from Grandmother's on Franklin, through Waterston Road to Ruthven, to Park and to Sargent, ending at Mrs. Day, Senior's. Nearly always I was sent back with more magazines and a bunch of flowers — Mrs. Day was very gracious with her flowers.

Improving the mind was definitely one of the goals of the Social Science Club. Look how we have super paper after super paper! And how often are they uncannily timely? Do you remember Mrs. Schofield who gave a brilliant paper pulling scraps of paper from the four pockets of her suit coat? It came out in perfect form and well organized.

What are some of the highlights you remember? What will some of the highlights be in the next 100 years? Will some of our present concerns still be with us in the future? How is Prison Reform doing?

Note: In 1986 Anne Purple noted some biographical information on Alison Umbsen's foremothers:

> I found the name of A. M. Buswell signed as Recording Secretary and asked Alison Umbsen if this was her grandmother. It was her mother! There were many references to her serving on committees and taking part in discussions as well as reading very fine papers, but the following quotations are what interested me most. From the minutes of December 7, 1898: 'Mrs. Emerson recommended omitting or postponing the next meeting of the club in honor of Miss Buswell's wedding but after discussion the motion was lost.' Later in the meeting it was voted to send flowers from the Club to Miss Buswell on December 14th [her wedding day]. The next entry is dated December 28: 'By decision of some of the officers, the meeting of the 14th was omitted.' Then on May 3, 1899: 'The resignation from membership of Mrs. Alice Buswell Towle was announced. After unanimous

expression of regret and expression of appreciation of the benefit of her logical mind and sweet temper, so helpful to this club, it was voted to accept her resignation with a suitable testimonial of the club sentiment.'

Club Giving Ain't What It Used to Be

Anne Purple presented her paper "Social Science Club Finances 1886-1986" on December 4, 1985. The theme for papers that year was Study the Past and Shape the Future. Looking at the past and considering the future must have been much on the minds of Social Science Club members in that centennial year. The following, compiled and edited by Vivi Leavy, is based on that paper.

Philanthropy has been a major aim of the Social Science Club, although it plays a smaller role today than when the Club was founded. In the early days work as well as money was expected of members, especially in support of the Vacation Industrial School. The School was within the Newton community which made it especially worthy, although many 'outside' projects gained the interest and support of the Clubwomen, particularly after the School was taken over by the City of Newton in 1908 and the burden of underwriting it was lifted. The scholarship for a Hampton Institute student, which started in 1892, was continued until 1984. A local college scholarship was established in 1925. According to Jan Cadwell (1975), "The Scholarship Fund at the Newton Classical High School was established in 1925 and the recipient was Miss Elizabeth Marcy, a second year student at Wellesley." She goes on to relate that 'Dr. Marcy' went on to a long teaching career at Hunter College. That scholarship continues to this day (2011). Contributions were made to many other health and education-related efforts over the years, especially within the City of Newton.

In her centennial paper, "Finances" (1985), Anne Purple makes an illuminating comparison of the philanthropy budgets of the Club in 1910 and 1970; 2010 is included here to bring it up to date.

One Hundred Years of Club Giving

1910	$	1970	$	2010	$
Nonantum Day Nursery	225	College Scholarship	800	College Scholarship	2500
Hampton Scholarship	70	Hampton Scholarship	100		
Tuberculosis Work	50	Newton YMCA Dirctor's Fund	50	Newton Y Campership	225
Newton Hospital	100	All-Newton Music School	50		
School Gardens	25	Museum of Science	100		
		WGBH	50		
		American Field Service	15		
		Underwood Library	25		
		Newton Boy's Club	50		
TOTAL	470		1240		2725
Total (in 2008 $)	10,987		6870		2725
Per Capita (in 2008 $)	110		113		75

Summarized and 2010 figures supplied by Vivi Leavy.

Don't forget that a dollar in 1910 was worth more than $23 in 2008 dollars, the latest year for which data exists. So the 1910 club spending on philanthropy $470 is equivalent to about $10,987 today. The 1970 budget of $1240 (when a dollar was worth $5.54 in current dollars) is worth about

$6870 in 2008 dollars. Thus philanthropic spending declined a bit less than 40% in the 60 years between 1910 and 1970, and by another 60% in the last 40 years.

Over the last 100 years, membership too has declined from 100 with a waiting list in 1910, to an active membership of 36 in 2009–10. Per capita philanthropic spending in 2008 dollars was $109.87 in 1910 and in the neighborhood of $75 today. Since inactive members also contribute in varying amounts to today's income, the actual per capita amount for philanthropy is closer to $70 in 2010. However, the percentage of philanthropy dedicated to the Newton community has increased over the years, from about 75% in 1910 to more than 85% in 1970 to 100% today.

Why Our Motto Matters

by Duscha S. Weisskopf, April, 1997

The meaning of the Social Science Club's motto, Privilege is Obligation, has been questioned by some of our members. The following is an attempt to speak to the motto's significance by this member, who thinks it has not lost its relevance.

Social Science is the study of the institutions and functioning of human society. If we look at contemporary society as a whole we must be struck by the incontestable privilege attached to being a resident of the United States, to say nothing of the City of Newton with its outstanding public resources. Old-fashioned as the use of the word 'privilege' may be, it seems to me to apply to the status of the Club's members. It is a word aptly applied to a group which exists to "arouse interest in the social needs of community and country," and which does this by presenting papers written by members who have the leisure to reflect on issues, read books and gather their conclusions in literate, persuasive form.

This privilege led the founders of the Club to conclude that they owed society a special effort: to improve conditions impeding the very equality which those who object to our motto are seeking. Obligation is the condition, in our case, of being morally bound to take thought and

39

action. When prospective members contemplate joining they will find [in our Club's history] a record of issues that concerned our predecessors. They will read, in plain English, that this is "not a literary club or social event" but an attempt by intellectual and moral effort to raise our and the community's consciousness, the very object of much ongoing agitation for reform today.

The continued use of the 1890s phrase will preserve unbroken a sense of community with those who came before us, while leaving us free to choose themes relevant to our own times. A sense of obligation to the past will increase our awareness of the effort, and sometimes courage, that was involved in bringing about improvements in social conditions of the past. It will make us more sensitive to the intractability and complexity of some problems, and perhaps spur us on to more forceful, more whole-hearted participation in the endeavor envisioned by our founders.

Poetry in the Social Science Club
by Vivi Leavy and Kathleen Rousseau

Poetry has always been an integral part of the Social Science Club. In 2010 every meeting still begins with a reading of poetry or philosophy and year-end reports at the annual meeting are given in rhyme, blank verse or even haiku. Club celebrations include poetry. The printed menu card from the 10th anniversary gala luncheon at Mary Billings' house started:

> The Gang sits down to feast and chat,
> To revels gay, but dignified,
> Such as befit these learned dames
> Who "vital" problems oft decide.

Mary Lathrop Tucker, chairman of the Program Committee, was such a gifted poet that her year-end report, "Our Club Topics," at that luncheon was carefully kept, copied and read at future occasions. The excerpt below was quoted by Charlotte Calkins, a founding member of the Club, as part of the entertainment after the annual luncheon in April 1924.

But perhaps the favorite topic
Of this tireless S.S.C.
Was Woman, past and present
And what she was to be.

Once woman, lovely woman,
In castle sat and spun,
Or lounged away the empty day
Till setting of the sun;

While her knight upon his charger,
With helmet, shield and sword,
Went forth to conquer all the world
At his fair lady's word.

We've changed all that: 'tis woman
Now girds the armor on;
With spear and sword and charger bold
She battles with the wrong.

Will she succeed where man has failed?
Methinks she cannot do it;
For both must join to win the fight,
Or both will always rue it.

So this Club they talked of woman,
Past, present and to come,
In all possible relations,
Or by herself alone.

While on many other subjects
Too numerous to relate,

Did they study and ponder,
And eagerly debate.

* * *

And in the dim, dim future
When this Club has ceased to be,
Some brilliant Thirtieth Century Club
Their work perchance will see, —

And will put among its topics
I dare to prophecy
"The Newton Social Science Club:
What it Did for Moral Progress,
Wherein it Failed and Why."

Poetry and poets have also been the subject of many papers over the years from Orinda Hornbrooke's March 1907 discussion of "The Poets Laureate of England," through Gertrude Dennison's work on "Poets of the Post War" in February 1934, an undated paper on the 18th century Black poet Phyllis Wheatley and Jean Kennedy's biography of "Anne Dudley Bradstreet, America's First Poet" in April 2006.

Poets have read their work to Club members: Grace LeBaron Upham in April 1893, Pearl Strahan in November 1945 and Erica Funkhouser in March 2008 among them.

The appropriateness of studying poetry has been a subject of debate among Club members. Influential founding member Lucy Sawyer reminded members at the opening meeting of the 1893 season that "We are not a literary club . . . so topics should be treated so as to draw the lesson that will point toward the life of today." But by April 1921 the discussion of whether time spent on literature and art was in accordance with the purpose of the Club ended with the statement that "in these uncertain and troubled times the . . . uplift of such subjects is what we most need."

In addition to writing verses for Club reports, a few gifted members wrote poetry and plays that were given as 'entertainments' for various occasions. Irene Young's poem "Die-Hards" was performed in an antiphonal dramatic reading for the annual meeting in April 1936, the 50th anniversary year. The poem's rollicking rhythm almost obscures the serious theme of division over the mission and format of the Club.

Die-hards
by Irene H. Young

Die-hards
We are the women of Newton
Scientific, but not very social.
Long have we clung to tradition
Meeting each Wednesday for study.
Now by revolt we are shaken;
Now we are threatened with faction.
Now has tradition been challenged.
Sacred our customs and by-laws;
Sacred our minutes and roll-call;
Sacred, most sacred, our motto:
Privilege is obligation.
What do we do in the summer
But wait for our tea in November.
What do we do in the springtime
But think of our annual luncheon.
What do we do in the winter
But plan for another year's program.
These are the signs of the season.
Nothing must happen to blight them.
Sacred are all our traditions.
Brightest of all days are Wednesdays.

Agitators

We are the women of Newton
Social but not scientific.
Weary we sit Wednesday mornings
Listening or seeming to listen.
Thinking of home and our duties.
What if the telephone rings —
Rings — who shall hurry to answer?
Who shall say, "No," to the cleanser,
"No" to the Eagle and Tiptop?
What if the Fuller man comes,
Brings a small brush for a present,
A present and none to receive it?
Furtively watching the clock,
Listening or seeming to listen,
We wait for dismissal at midday.
Now is the moment for questions,
Now shall the speaker make answer.
School will be over and children
Out in the world unattended,
Playing in pond and in puddle.
Often have babies and children
Suffered and swooned from starvation
Wednesdays while mothers were watching,
Furtively watching the clock,
Listening or seeming to listen,
Hardest of all days are Wednesdays.

Think of what Boston can offer
Wednesdays from ten until midday.
Mornings of wit and diversion,
Musicales, pictures, Avery,
Snow-White and the Copley.
Windows new-dressed for the shopper,

Latest creations for Easter,
Costumes for skiing and sunning,
Bargains upstairs — in the Basement.
None will remain by tomorrow.
Hostess gowns gone by tomorrow.
Cocktail coats! taken by others.
Linens — first showing in Boston;
Stockings of silk from the Orient.
Never could wear them on Wednesdays.
Perhaps Mrs. Lennox might see them.
Furtively watching the clock,
Listening or seeming to listen,
Waiting for end of the questions.

While we are holding our meetings
Outside the Great World is waiting,
Waiting for us until midday.
Crippled the work of the churches,
While we take time out for study.
Helpless the poor and the aged,
No one is there to protect them.
Charity ceases to function.
Only the vicious are busy.
Sinners are rampant on Wednesdays,
Rampant from ten until midday.
Why should we get here so early?
Let's not begin till eleven.
Why should we loiter till midday
Just to be learning and listening.
Let's have a club without speakers.
Let's have a club without papers.
Let's have a club without meetings.
Let's have a week without Wednesdays.

We're tired of Greeks and Egyptians.
Who are they but dead men and mummies?
We're tired of Crete and of Persia.
Who cares where the Hebrews once wandered?
We long for the new and the timely;
For Hitler and Franco, and Eden.
For Roosevelt, and Jackson, and Ickes,
For unions with Green fighting Lewis,
For everything up to the minute.
We women love things controversial,
Love things controversial on Wednesdays.

Die-hards

We're wise, we've learned history's lesson.
The new things are only the old ones.
Remember the Code Hammurabi,
Remember the corn laws in Egypt.
The wise man must always look backward.
The future is frightfully shoddy.
We women hate things controversial,
Hate things controversial on Wednesdays.
Were we not founded for study?
To make ourselves fit for our husbands?
To talk to them over the beefsteak
On subjects of weight and importance?
Now we have ceased to be pupils,
Ceased, and instead become teachers.
Who would enlighten our men folk
Did we not meet every Wednesday?
Tell them to write to the Senate,
Take them by force to the hearings,
Train them to vote for the righteous?

46

Men are all hostile to culture.
We must bring light to their darkness;
Privilege is obligation.

Agitators

Now you have brought us to reason.
Men are all hostile to culture.
We must bring light to their darkness.

Die-hards

Now is the menace averted.

Agitators

Now we are caught in the meshes.

Die-hards

Now we shall meet every Wednesday.

Agitators

Now we must promise to listen.

Die-hards

Now we shall live for our motto.

Agitators

Who can remember the motto?

Die-hards

Privilege is obligation.

Agitators

Privilege is obligation!

Irene Young was unique and celebrated by her fellow members. A selection of her poetry and a play she wrote based on T.S. Eliot's *Murder in the Cathedral* were read and performed at her Tribute in April 1971. A poet of her stature has not been revealed among the Club membership since.

Endnotes

1   Margaret Sudbey, "History," Social Science Club Annual Program, 1994.

2   Ibid.

3   Blair, Karen, *The Clubwoman as Feminist, True Womanhood Redefined, 1868–1914.* Holmes & Meier Publishers, NY, NY, 1980, p. 23.

4   Ibid., p 39–40.

5   Ibid., p. 40.

6   Ibid., p.53

7   Ibid., pg. 60.

8   Ibid., pg. 67.

9   Ibid., pg. 71.

10 Ibid., pg. 74.

11 Ibid., pg. 98.

12 Ibid., pp. 107–08.

13 Social Science Club, Record Book following December 1, 1920.

14 SSC, RB, April 30, 1924. "Reminiscences of the Early Days of the Social Science Club," by Mrs. Wolcott Calkins, p. 1.

15 Ibid., p. 4.

16 Ibid., p. 7.

17 SSC, RB, November 2, 1955. "The Social Science Woman Emerges," by Helen Howes Gleason, p. 13.

18 SSC, RB, "Reminiscences," p. 4.

19 www.audubonmagazine.org/features0412/hats.

20 *Boston Journal*, August 19, 1902.

21 *Boston Globe*, August 19,1902.

CHAPTER TWO

THE CLUB AND THE CITY OF NEWTON

by Vivi Leavy

Since the Club's founding the City of Newton has provided a primary stage for members to express many of their civic, philanthropic and historical interests. Through the Club, members have supported, investigated, critiqued and tried to influence — often successfully — the school system, the city government, immigrant services, health and morals, conservation and much more.

Drawing on information in the Club's Record Books, the first section of this chapter traces the Club's interactions with the schools and with services for needy women and children. It describes how the members kept informed of issues within the city and, finally, how changes in the relationship of women to the work force in the 1960s affected the Club and its connections to the city. The rest of the chapter includes excerpts from some of the papers concerned with Newton that Clubwomen have presented over the years. Historian Thelma Fleishman investigated the East Parish Burying Ground to shed light on the founding of Newton in the 1600s. In 2010 archaeologists are continuing her original work. Club members have been very active as volunteers and supporters of the Newton-Wellesley Hospital. Beverley Lovell's paper describes its founding and the medical climate of the time. Brooke Lipsitt's work on Norumbega emphasizes how the development of transportation affected the growth and decline of the city's renowned amusement park. Margaret Gerrity's informal tale of the beginnings of the Stanley Steamer reflect the entrepreneurial spirit of two Newton citizens and contrasts with Margaret Snider's research on ornithologist Charles Maynard who was promoting habitat conservation for birds from his workshop in West Newton at just the same time. Finally, Jean Husher's carefully researched biography of the reclusive Newton philanthropist Mabel Louise Riley depicts the life of a woman whose story is otherwise lost to the louder voices of history.

Shaping the Schools

From its very beginning members of the Social Science Club have had a strong interest in education, which often focused on the nearest target, the local public schools. That interest evolved quickly from study to action. In March of 1887, with the ink barely dry from Mary F. Linder's first draft of the Club constitution, members discussing the social and economic value of Boston's new North Bennet Street Industrial School decided to help create a similar school in their own city. From that germ of an idea came the Thompsonville Girl's Sewing School in the summer of 1888. The next summer the school moved to Nonantum, where the majority of the immigrant families who were intended to be its main beneficiaries lived, and became the Vacation Industrial School. There it grew and flourished under Club management, staffed by Club volunteers and paid for by Club members' work and ingenuity for 18 years until the city was finally persuaded to assume responsibility for what had become a serious burden to the Club. That is a well known story. What is less familiar is the multitude of other means Club members used through the years to influence and shape the Newton Schools for the better education of their own children.

Women's suffrage and using the power of the ballot to elect women to the Newton School Committee was one avenue to shaping the schools. As early as the 1870s women were elected to membership on school boards in Lynn, Beverly and Boston, and by 1879 the state legislature voted to allow women to vote for the school committee as well as serve on it. This was not uncontroversial and it took time and work to promote the idea. The Club received an appeal from the School Suffrage Association in February 1892 urging the women of Massachusetts to use their right to vote to improve the schools. "Mrs. Wellington made some very eloquent remarks in support," Club minutes recorded. About half the members present voted that they were ready to join a movement for "awakening interest in Newton women." But the following year the women were still discussing the pros and cons of the school suffrage law and the difficulties in registering in order to vote. It was not until December 1894 that the Club was fully engaged, voting to pay nine dollars for a campaign circular for a Mrs. Martin who was re-elected to the school board. Two years later they were faced with the situation of the nomination of a woman candidate they opposed despite her gender. The Education Committee decided that "it was inexpedient to take any action" in opposition to her.

Relations between the Club and the school board flourished at the turn of the century. In the spring of 1897, according to Club minutes, members voted to pay for the distribution of supplies stored in the cellars of some schools and needed by other schools. That fall Club members decided to "devote definite time to the study of Public Schools" by surveying the kindergarten system, the science and English curriculums and the role of the public library in relation to the schools. A series of papers was presented on every aspect of this research and a dialogue with the superintendent of schools was cultivated. Later the Club petitioned the school committee to replace the Bigelow School building which had been condemned. And finally in late winter the Club asked the school committee to establish cooking classes by September 1898. When the city did agree to build a new Bigelow School, the Club took issue with its location.

The following year, 1899, the minutes report that the Club carried out another check on the kindergarten and a review of the curriculum in the high school and was invited by the school board to consider the instruction in grades four through eight. Three and sometimes more members visited the schools and reported to the board. Among their notes: "74% of time is for fundamental studies, no overcrowding, elocution needs work." Singing, drawing, nature study and physical education were also evaluated. By the following winter a study committee was appointed "to consider the advisability of keeping Mr. Aldrich as superintendent of schools." While there is no notation of their findings, the new superintendent, Dr. Frank Spaulding, addressed the Club in January 1905. He was an advocate of the most modern educational theories of the day, those that Club members had presented in their papers over the previous decade, and spoke of "the current transition from where education is given, to where children are really educated in mind, body and emotions."

This intense study and critique of the school system was all taking place at the same time the Club was working hard to convince the city to take over the Industrial School. Educator James Monroe, who addressed the Club in December 1906 on "Manual and Industrial Training," must have had a very favorably disposed audience when he made the case for manual training starting in kindergarten to promote the development of both mind and body. On the political front, the Club agreed to share the campaign expenses of Club member Dr. Deborah Fawcett, a local doctor and 1903 graduate of Boston University's School of Homeopathy, when she decided to run for the school committee in 1905. When the city finally agreed to take over the management and cost of the Vacation Industrial School in the late fall of 1907, the minutes note that "there was great applause" from Club members. They had certainly worked creatively over many years to bring about that decision.

The Club's role in the schools immediately became less political and less involved with curricular matters. One reason must have been that Dr. Spaulding, who served as superintendent from 1904 until 1914, was a vigorous, creative and respected educator and administrator. He had their confidence. Club interest in the schools began to be directed more toward the health and character formation of the students.

In their characteristic way, in early 1908, Club members invited a guest speaker to address them on "Stamp Savings in the Public School"[1] and allocated ten dollars to start a "stamp savings system" at the Bigelow

School. They liked to be informed before they acted, and promoting the moral welfare of young children through teaching them thrift was a worthy goal. Within three months there were 228 depositors at Bigelow and the program was operating at Underwood and Lincoln elementary schools.

The same spring the Reverend Alfred Brown spoke to the women on "The Movement to Place Nurses in our Public Schools." He told how nurses had been introduced into the Boston schools a few years earlier with great success. The Club may not have succeeded immediately in bringing school nurses to Newton since it was a full two and a half years later that the Club invited Miss Gertrude Melnick to describe how "School Nurses for Newton" would work. She emphasized the need for cleanliness and explained that the toothbrush program would not only instruct but also hand out brushes. Meanwhile, the Newton Federation of Women's Clubs had put drinking fountains in the high school and supported providing dental work for poor school children.

Members of the Club Education Committee resumed some of their activist ways in March 1912, reporting to members the results of their inspection of the lunchroom at the high school and explaining the need for an "Emergency Room" for girls. Conditions for girls at the high school continued to be a concern. In 1914 the Club invited a speaker who made a plea for the appointment of a Dean for High School Girls. She explained that "character building is the aim of education, and that the dean would act 'as a supervisor or big sister.'" The outcome must have been favorable, for the high school girls dropped from focus. The next request was for the Club to give financial support for restrooms at Underwood. The usual response to such a request was to send a subscription sheet around at a meeting giving each member a chance to sign up to donate if she could.

In early 1917 Club members agreed to a substantial financial commitment when they voted to contribute to the salary of "an excellent teacher of Nature Study at the high school" in order to retain him. Apparently the school board felt they could not afford his salary, and the Club, no doubt encouraged by influential advocates for nature and conservation among the membership like Orinda Hornbrooke and Mary Tucker, wife of the school committeeman Fred Tucker, jumped into the breech. As a 'thank-you,' the teacher, Mr. MacDonald, gave a talk to the ladies that March. Once they were involved in matters of teachers' pay, Club members persevered. In March 1919 when they were told that Newton teachers had "hesitated to make public the real conditions of living which they were compelled to face through inadequate salaries," they decided to cooperate in an attempt to raise teacher salaries. In response, at the end of the year the Board of Aldermen agreed to pay an additional $200 to every teacher.

In the early 1920s the Club was still likely to swing into action or make a contribution in response to education concerns that were brought to their attention. When Miss Mabel Grigg, the assistant superintendent, explained how the schools were "succeeding in making health habits fashionable and popular," members made a donation to the school nurses for glasses for poor children. They also voted to pay for a school attendant in Thompsonville, inspired by an account of the "splendid Americanization work being done at the school." They voted to send a recommendation to the school board and the Board of Aldermen that Bigelow School be made "into a fully equipped building [suitable for] real junior high school needs."

While the Club's Education Committee was less involved in day-to-day school operations, as the decade went on it still kept members informed about the schools through reports at business meetings and by sponsoring a speaker once a year. Records show that leaders from the Newton school department were frequent guests of the Club until the late 1970s when the Club eliminated most outside speakers. In the winter of 1924, Club members came up with a project to encourage higher education for women that turned into a lasting interest. They decided to give a college scholarship to

The 2009 scholarship recipient Jasmine Pullen-Smith receives a Club pin from education committee chair Anne Larner.

a Newton girl and within a few weeks raised $200 to support it. From then on, selecting the appropriate scholarship recipient became an important project. The scholarship was continued even through the Club's lean years, and in 2011 is a mainstay of its philanthropy and a symbol of its continuing commitment to educating women.

Settlement Work: From Day Nursery to Pomroy House

Sometimes the Club's broad interests in social improvement combined to good effect. As early as 1901 the Club asked the aldermen to provide playgrounds for Wards 1 and 7, the Newton Corner area where most members lived, and playgrounds were forthcoming as long as the Club came up with the final $500 to make it possible. Eight years later they sponsored a speaker who assured them that supervised playgrounds were vital for sound development in cities to help fend off gangs and delinquent behavior; good examples could be found in Boston and even in Waltham next door. So by 1911 the ground was laid for the Club to support the hiring of a playground supervisor at the Nonantum Day Nursery and respond to a request for materials and games for the children.

The Day Nursery was an outgrowth of the Industrial School, which had remained under the wing of the Club after the school was taken on by the city. Its original mission was to care for young children of working mothers, as the name implied, but with the addition of the playground located near the Stearns School came a variety of new activities. A Club report of April 26, 1911, noted that the nursery "is developing into a Social Settlement and doing remarkable work." It had an "average attendance of nine children plus 19 clubs and classes for boys and girls, a mothers' club and classes . . . a milk station where 33,106 bottles of milk were distributed last summer and a successful playground." By the early fall of that year the "playground was a great success with up to 400 children per day." At Christmas 175 gifts were given out and 105 children showed up for a sewing class designed for 60.

The Stearns School Center continued to thrive even as the original

55

Nonantum Day Nursery closed down by February 1914 "because not enough babies needed it," as the matron, Miss Taylor, reported to Club members. She explained that "a greater work" was being directed from an office at the Stearns School, "classes in sewing, cooking, crocheting and English for about 5000 people in all, mostly foreign born." The Stearns Center had only one paid professional. Volunteers, many of whom must have belonged to the Club, carried on most of the work with children and families. The Club also gave it substantial financial support from 1913 forward, as it had supported the Day Nursery before it. When it was merged with the Rebecca Pomroy House in 1939, Club support was maintained. By the 1960s the Club's interest in Pomroy House was still so strong that one of the Club's two representatives to the Newton Community Council was dedicated to its interests. Funding for Pomroy House Summer Camperships continued through the decade until it was merged with the Newton Community Service Center in 1968, an example of the growing trend of the public sector to absorb previously privately funded community organizations.

The Committee System

Committees helped members of the Club keep their fingers on a lot of pulses within the City of Newton as well as outside it. Proposed in April 1913 by a member who felt that, since the Vacation Industrial School had been given up, "no real work had been accepted by the club as a whole," by 1917 there were 16 committees, of which only six dealt with the nuts and bolts of running the Club. The other ten represented interests and activities. If there was a project, there was a committee to report on it and keep it on track. Some, like Birds, Conservation or Legislation, had a wider realm of interest but also focused closely on Newton — sponsoring Orinda Hornbrooke's 'save the birds' speeches to schools and clubs; investigating conditions in Newton police stations and advocating separate quarters for women and minors being held; or reporting on ravages by gypsy and brown-tailed moths in city trees.

Other committees were set up specifically for Newton projects. The Information Committee ran an "Information Bureau" for 21 years starting in 1898 which provided a clearinghouse for domestic help of all sorts. The Stamp Savings Committee initiated and monitored a savings program within Newton elementary schools. The Moving Picture Committee kept an eye on offerings at the Newton Opera House and let members know when they had misgivings; in January 1914 a member reported that a recent performance "was somewhat unsatisfactory owing to the objectionable vaudeville." Two years later the Club wrote the mayor protesting "the erection of a Moving Picture House in Newton." The project-based committees expired when the projects came to an end, but the broader committees, although they were merged and renamed as interests shifted, remained until the end of the committee system in 1976. After that date Club members had to rely on local papers to track city events since there was no longer a regular schedule of speakers from the school department or the city government. Members' interests were more engaged in broader national and international issues and the world of work.

Membership Decline and the End of Newton Proper

Ironically the publication of Betty Friedan's *The Feminine Mystique* correlated with the first concerns of the Social Science Club executive board about membership in 1963. Speaking for the Education Committee, its chairman Anne Purple "expressed the embarrassment of the committee and program chair due to the low attendance when excellent and busy speakers are engaged for our group." The board decided to postpone the roll call until after the speaker so he wouldn't have to hear all the regrets and they noted that the exact same discussion had occurred a year earlier. Membership was 84 at the beginning of the decade of the 1960s, apparently still healthy, but something was happening to the interests of members. When long-time and very active member Esther Gleason resigned in February 1964 because of full-time work, the board seemed shocked. Mary Kent, a member for 55 years, resigned at the same time, a harbinger of the retirements of members who had joined long ago and been mainstays of the Club through the decades. There was low attendance at the 1964 Musicale and only 52 members at the Welcome Tea in November 1965. The board considered the issue and in March 1967 the membership chairman read a statement to the Club that the board had decided that while Club by-laws required that members reside in Newton and Newton had been "traditionally construed to mean Newton Proper" (the area now referred to as Newton Corner) it was to be regarded as the whole city from then on. Expanding the geographic range of membership was little help, however. Over the next decade membership fell from 61 in 1970 to 45 in 1975. Reform efforts, which had begun in 1970 with the appointment of a Committee of the Concerned to poll members and make recommendations, came to naught because members could not agree on the nature of the problem or the solution. The president, Lavina Tomb, remarked that while the poll indicated members did not want change, "this does not solve the problems we face." By 1973 they did agree on a few changes to the by-laws to decrease the size of the executive board; but it was not until 1976 that really substantial changes simplifying the structure of the club were enacted, enabling the Club to go forward with a smaller but committed membership.

By 2011 membership had expanded to include women from several different communities in the western suburbs of Boston, although many still had a Newton connection having previously lived there. The typical member joins the Club after retirement from paid work, in contrast to the early days when Club activities were an important part of a member's work. Membership numbers have stabilized at slightly under 50 including some ten 'inactive' members.

The East Parish Burying Ground: Where Newton Began

Thelma Fleishman, a historian, long-time volunteer at the Newton History Museum and author of nine books, presented the paper from which this excerpt was taken in October 1991. The study topic for the year was unspecified, Personal Choice. She later wrote a much fuller illustrated handbook published in 2004 by the Newton Historical Society, Where Newton Began: A Guide to the East Parish Burying Ground. *Edited and abridged by Vivi Leavy.*

Thelma Fleishman
(Photo by Emily Hubbs Scott)

The oldest burying ground in Newton by more than a century is the East Parish Burying Ground, commonly known as the Centre Street Cemetery, at the corner of Centre and Cotton streets. It is where Newton as a community did in fact begin and today is to me the most valuable of the city's historic assets, but also the most fragile. It is, incidentally, one of the few cemeteries in the country included in the National Register of Historic Places as an individual site.

Although Newton celebrated 300 years of settlement in 1930 and there are markers [noting that] in various parts of the city, not least at the entrance to the burying ground, no one actually lived [in the area] until the end of the [1630s] when about half a dozen families were granted land in Newtown, later renamed Cambridge. Being part of Cambridge was a geographical absurdity and highly inconvenient . . . and by 1654 many of the families living on the south side of the river started holding separate religious meetings probably in the home of Edward Jackson (who later built the first house on the site of the Jackson Homestead for his son Sebas). At the same time the families petitioned the General Court to excuse them from paying for the upkeep of the ministry in Cambridge and, although this was refused, they decided to build their own meetinghouse anyway. Probably in 1660 John Jackson, one of the first settlers...who by this time owned many acres of land, gave one as a site for the meetinghouse and to be used as a burying place. . . . At about the same time the name 'Cambridge Village' came into use.

In 1662 the General Court acted in favor of the Village residents and permitted them to withdraw from the congregation in Cambridge, and the First Church in Newton was officially gathered. The first minister, John Eliot Jr., son of the Apostle to the Indians, was ordained in 1664. He died four years later and was buried near his meetinghouse. The tomb [now there] is not the original, but was rebuilt along with those of other early ministers at the expense of the town. Eliot's first wife Susan, who died in 1665, was probably the first person buried there, although there is neither record nor trace of her grave. The site of the meetinghouse is marked by a marble obelisk, the Settlers Monument, erected by the descendants of the early settlers in 1852.

Acquiring their own burying ground, meeting house and minister, although major steps in the process of breaking away from Cambridge, were only a beginning. Villagers still had to go to Cambridge for town meeting and training days for the militia; and if the children went to school, they had to make their way there too. The Charles River could be crossed by canoe or over one of two bridges: the Great Bridge (now Lars Andersen) which connected Cambridge and Brighton and which the villagers still supported with their taxes, a bone of contention for many years to come, and the bridge in Watertown.

After a series of further petitions, in 1672, the four-mile line between Cambridge and the Village was at last confirmed, and the villagers were authorized to elect three selectmen and a constable. For some reason this right was not exercised until 1679, when on August 27 the first town meeting was held in the meetinghouse. This is also the date on which the town meeting records begin and the one appearing on an early version of the town seal, although 1688 is regarded as the official date of incorporation. In December of that year five selectmen and other town officials were elected and the Village was released from paying a share of Cambridge taxes for the upkeep of its schools. It was also allowed to elect its own deputy to the General Court. The name Newton, unless we misread the photocopy, was granted in 1691.

The original meetinghouse building served until 1697 when a new one was built, traditionally on the opposite side of Centre Street on land given by John Spring. However, I have reason to believe the second building too may very well have been within the confines of the burying ground, which in 1701 was enlarged by a gift from Abraham Jackson, son of the original donor. This further acre was also to accommodate the training field for the militia and the school. In the same year Jonathan Hyde gave an acre for a school in Oak Hill for the benefit of the children in the southern part of town. One schoolmaster was appointed to run both. The first to occupy the post was John Staples, whose house, much altered, still overlooks Waban Square . . . Abraham Jackson's grave is unmarked but an exquisite bit of carving marks that of his three children.

Thus by the beginning of the 18th century, Newton's first center was well established. We know the stocks were there too, kept in the schoolhouse when not in use and the pound[2] was almost certainly very close by. This was to change with the death of Nehemiah Hobart, the second minister, in 1712. He had been much loved and respected by his parishioners who had dutifully journeyed from the outlying areas in the south and west to attend meetings. After his death they were no longer prepared to do so. After much petitioning, negotiating and arbitrating, a new meeting house was built in the geographical center of the town at the corner of Homer and Centre streets in 1721. The schoolhouse and the pound followed soon after and, as a new and larger training field had been in use since about 1710, all that remained and still remains, of the original town center is the burying ground.

The Newton Cottage Hospital

Beverley S. Lovell presented this paper November 12, 1975. It was part of the bicentennial year topic, New Town to Newton, with authors researching some aspect of the history of the city and its reflections in the current day. Edited and abridged by Vivi Leavy.

Beverley S. Lovell
(Photo by Emily Hubbs Scott)

It was nearly midnight on a chilly October night. A messenger hurried through the dark streets and banged on the door of the Grace Episcopal Church rectory. "The doctor wants you to come," Rector George Shinn was told. "A woman is dying. She is not of your flock but she's old, she's friendless and she needs your presence." Quickly the clergyman dressed and hastened along the rutted roads of the village of Newton Corner to stand vigil at the bedside of the dying woman. Unexpectedly, she rallied. Still very sick, she needed to be tended through the night. The doctor and the minister went out in search of someone to sit with 'the stranger within our gates' until morning. Many people were roused and asked, but could not or would not come. Finally a warm-hearted Irish woman left her own brood of children to come and do what she could for the poor old soul. The doctor and the clergyman, tired and troubled, turned to each other. "We must have a hospital," said the clergyman. "Indeed we must," replied the other. "The time has come." It was 1880, less than 100 years ago.

Away off in Boston, Dr. John Collins Warren had founded the first general hospital in the area, the Massachusetts General Hospital, in 1821, almost 60 years before the knock on Reverend Shinn's door. Hospitals were then thought to be for the indigent poor who had no one to take care of them. A hospital was a place where a person went to die. Newtonians were cared for in their own homes. They gave birth, got sick and well, or died, properly in their own beds. Disease was a manifestation of the wrath of God; recovery and good health were evidence of God's favor. The night breezes, the damp sea air, these were dangerous.

But in Germany in 1880, Robert Koch, working on the principles laid down by Louis Pasteur some 15 years earlier, established the guidelines by which bacteriology became a science. He proved that microbes cause diseases like diphtheria, typhoid and other scourges. While there was skepticism about the germ theory in some parts of this country at the end of the 19th century, in most places and certainly in Newton, doctors began to wash before treating patients, and to dress in clean white gowns. They sterilized instruments and introduced rubber gloves. Patients began to survive operations.

In enlightened Newton change and hope were in the air. Reverend Shinn called on the mayor, the Honorable Royal M. Pulsifer, to convince him of the "desirability of establishing an institution for the care of the sick, and for kindred objects." In response, the mayor called a meeting of prominent citizens from all parts of the city and "it was unanimously voted that it was expedient to establish a Cottage Hospital," the records say. The names of some of these Newton citizens would have been familiar to early members of the Social Science Club. Besides Pulsifer, there were Ellison, Burr, Pierce, Claflin, Calkins, Lord, Converse, Morse, Lawrence and others. In December 1880, 43 gentlemen and ladies were named members of the new hospital association. Twenty-four trustees were chosen, "equally," the record says, "between the sexes."

By 1884 enough money was raised (12 subscriptions of $500 each) to buy nine acres of land from the Granville Fuller estate on Washington Street in Lower Falls "near the gasometer," and an architect was hired. By June of 1886 the Newton Cottage Hospital was dedicated and open for patients.

It must have been very attractive. Certainly the townspeople of Newton were very proud of it and descriptions abound in old records. The *Boston Herald* (June 9, 1889) included a lengthy description of the new hospital: "It has a pleasant location, the buildings standing on a gentle elevation and surrounded by well-kept grounds. In the rear are extensive gardens where much of the vegetable supply is raised. The hospital has its own chickens

and also its own cows, guaranteeing the purity and freshness of the milk
. . . . The floor is bare but for a rug here and there; the walls are unpapered
and untinted . . . over each window is a transom to aid in ventilation. The
object of these arrangements is to prevent the accumulation of dust or the
lodgment of disease germs."

The hospital was laid out with a central administration building with
corridors radiating from it containing separate wards for men, women and
children. They were bright and very, very clean. The *Herald* informed its
readers that, "Visitors will be welcome at the hospital on Wednesdays and
Saturdays between 2:00 and 4:00 pm. Anyone will feel well repaid for the
trouble he experiences in reaching the building. It is but a short distance
from the Woodland Station of the Newton Circuit Road [railway] and the
trains run at frequent intervals."

The executive head of the hospital was a young woman, a rather unusual
situation which was described as "an experiment" in *A Brief History of
the Newton Wellesley Hospital*. The position was a demanding one. The
History explains that the head had to be "an educated and skillful nurse
capable of taking charge of the hospital under the direction of a Medical
Board, and of instructing pupils in nursing. In addition, she must keep
a book recording the name, age, birthplace, residence and disease of
each patient admitted, the date and on what terms, and finally the date
of discharge and in what condition, or the date of death and to whom the
body was delivered. Besides rendering a quarterly accounting of receipts
and expenditures, she must keep a perpetual inventory of hospital property
and a tally of money or other property belonging to patients."

Lest you think that this capable young woman was handling all the sick
people in the town of Newton, you must understand that many diseases
were unacceptable to the admitting nurse that first year. You could not get
in if you suffered from measles, chicken pox, diphtheria, mumps, scarlet
fever, whooping cough, pneumonia, or any other infectious or contagious
disease. If you were incurably ill, you could not come to the hospital.
A grand total of 26 patients were cared for during the first year, with an
average stay of four weeks. However, very soon two 'contagious wards'

were constructed to care for victims of scarlet fever and diphtheria, the leading killers of the day. Another ward was presently constructed for smallpox patients. These were built at some distance from the main hospital and had their own administration building. Not until 1930, as vaccination became widespread, did these diseases abate and the 'pest houses' were torn down. Thus, the community acquired a hospital, and by the standards of the day it was a good hospital, one of about 500 in the nation at the time.

The extraordinary thing about the Newton Cottage Hospital was its medical staff, equally divided between homeopaths and allopaths. Medical practice at the time could be confusing. A dismayed observer characterized the practice of medicine as "a bedlam of allopaths of every class of allopathy, homeopaths of high and low dilution, hydropaths mild and heroic, chromo therapists, Thomsonians, mesmerists, herbalists, Indian doctors, clairvoyants, spiritualists with healing gifts, and I know not what besides."[3]

The practice of homeopathic medicine had burgeoned in the villages of Newton since German native, Dr. Joseph Barnstill, settled in Newton Corner in 1849 and introduced the practice. This school of medicine was brought to the U.S. in 1825 by Dr. Samuel Hahnemann who established the first homeopathic medical college in Philadelphia in 1850. His theory was that "disease can be cured by medicines which cause in a healthy person symptoms similar to those caused by the disease itself." Bear in mind that this was all prior to the discovery of germs and their relation to disease!

The traditional treatments for 'universal fevers' were bloodletting (in most cases 10-14 ounces, but in apoplexy 40-50 ounces), physicking, sweating, diuretics, induced vomiting and blisters.[4] It's no wonder that people stayed away from doctors if at all possible. The lotions and potions, often herbal, of the homeopathic doctors were gentler than the usual practices and enjoyed great success. In addition to Hahnemann Medical College, Boston University and Harvard also graduated doctors with degrees in homeopathic medicine.

The two factions of medicine dwelt together, according to historic record, "in most perfect harmony." Neither one infringed upon the other. If patients were admitted without a preference for one school or the other, they were assigned alternately. The schools existed until 1930 when homeopathy was relegated to a separate department and gradually faded away.

Finally, let us not forget the longevity and devotion of the Hospital Aid. The enthusiastic ladies of the village of Newton Corner founded this group when the hospital was hardly more than an architect's dream. The first president was Mrs. Alvah Hovey the grandmother of Social Science Club member Leni Hovey's husband. The ladies met in the parlor of the Eliot Church to plan Hospital Sunday, their first big project. "On the Sabbath before Thanksgiving in the churches of the City" the offering collected that day was to go for the support of the hospital. This practice was carried on for 38 years and a total of almost $550,000 was donated through the churches.

The Aid group expanded to take in all seven wards of the city and drew up by-laws spelling out its mission, "to furnish the hospital and assist in its maintenance in such ways as shall be deemed suitable." The suitable ways have included donating and mending linens, canning and donating garden produce, rolling bandages, making hospital johnnies, and similar direct, useful activities.

Today, in 1975, the Newton-Wellesley Hospital Aid is still a vital contributor to the hospital. While we no longer give 'Birthday Pennies' (a penny for each year given on your birthday), contributions in money and time are the envy of many other hospitals. This year's fund raising event furnished a new mental health unit; last year the money paid for a kidney dialysis machine. Old time rummage and bake sales have evolved into a most attractive gift shop and coffee shop staffed by volunteers.

The Newton Cottage Hospital of old, the pride of the community, has developed into a full-service teaching hospital affiliated with Tufts University. The nursing school, originally taught by the matron of the hospital, and consisting of half a dozen girls "not older than 35 or younger than 23, of good health and unimpeachable character, and with the rudiments of a good common school education" has become one of the nation's finest with an enrollment of 170 women and men from all over New England.

You can still get to the hospital from Woodland Station. It's just a short walk and visiting hours are daily now. Many members of the Social Science Club are among the volunteers who devote time to the hospital. Others of us have been patients there. All of us can take pride in our excellent non-profit community hospital just as our ancestors did.

Norumbega Park: Where Newton Celebrated

Former president of the Newton Board of Aldermen Brooke K. Lipsitt presented this paper December 4, 2002. The study topic for the year was How the World Celebrates. Edited and abridged by Vivi Leavy.

Norumbega Park was where I celebrated in June 1959, at my Newton High School Senior Prom, held in the Totem Pole Ballroom. Though I had certainly visited the park with its rides and playgrounds, to my eyes Norumbega was first and

Brooke Lipsitt
(Photo by Emily Hubbs Scott)

foremost a place for Newton to celebrate grand occasions. It was that, of course. It was also a great deal more.

Norumbega Park was a product of its time, 1897. Newton was a very different community 105 years ago, particularly in the area of transportation. Until late in the 19th century most land transportation in the United States was animal powered. A horse provided a seat or pulled a carriage, or man traveled on 'shank's mare,' by foot. The first horse-drawn bus service, in the 1820s, was followed by steam-powered railroads and subways by mid-century. Two transportation developments were particularly significant for Newton. The Boston & Worcester Railroad introduced passenger service to Newton in 1834. And the invention of electric traction, in 1888, provided another major boost to urban transit systems. Electric-powered subways were in use in New York and Boston by the early 1890s. In a parallel development, an interurban system of electric surface trolleys was developed, serving neighboring cities and suburban areas.

William Jackson had taken advantage of the railroad's arrival in Newton Corner in 1834 to lay out and sell, at a handsome profit, the early suburban subdivisions of Walnut Park and Waban Park. It probably was no coincidence that he sat on the Board of Directors of the Boston & Worcester Railroad. And when the railroad was extended to the area that came to be known as Auburndale three years later, he was determined to duplicate the feat. Though located on the Charles River, Auburndale did not have the natural falls to provide the water power that had allowed Upper and Lower Falls to develop as industrial villages with relatively substantial populations. Thus in 1847, when William Jackson and his partners formed the North Auburn Dale Land Company to develop the area adjacent to the railroad tracks, the village had just a few dozen families. Now, for a round-trip fare of 75 cents, the well-to-do who had had their summer homes in Brookline and other out-of-town locations could live outside the city of Boston year round. Other developers followed and the village was firmly established by the 1860s.

The first horse-drawn street railroad came to Newton in 1868. The Waltham & Newton Horse Railroad Company began operations on the River Street line with two cars and eight horses plus a plow and a sleigh for winter travel. The company electrified the line in 1889 and extended it east. Other independent companies were also granted charters along major roads linking village centers. The companies were usually backed by real estate operators and landowners who wished to enhance the value of their properties by making them accessible by mass transit. In this environment, in 1895 the Commonwealth Avenue Street Railway opened an electric trolley route from Lake Street in Brighton to Newton Centre. During the next two years Commonwealth Avenue and the trolley tracks in its central green were extended to the Newton/Weston line at the Charles River. To put this endeavor in context it is useful to consider that there were only two dozen houses built on Commonwealth Avenue for the entire distance the trolley traversed when it inaugurated its service.

Now, let's consider the challenge to Adams D. Claflin, Newton resident and president of the Commonwealth Avenue Street Railway. The company had invested in the infrastructure of a transit system and needed riders to support it. So he did the obvious: he opened an amusement park at the end of the line. Voila! Norumbega. The theory was that the company could afford to lose money on the park but that the enhanced revenue from the trolley would offset the losses. So, on opening day in 1897, 15 cents bought a roundtrip ride from Lake Street, including admission to Norumbega Park. Without the ride, the admission was 10 cents, and it remained 10 cents, with children under 12 admitted free, well into the 1930s.

The success of Norumbega Park was immediate. On opening day, June 17, 1897, more than 12,000 people came. Ladies in long dresses and hats, men in suits, ties and straw toppers, filled trolleys with the words "Norumbega Park" emblazoned in a gold arc on the front of each car. For comparison, the population of the entire city of Newton in 1897 was about 20,000. Almost everyone, except for the fortunate few neighbors, came by trolley, and given that trolleys could take at most two or three hundred passengers per trip, there were nights, at the height of Norumbega's popularity, when trolleys had to run until 5 a.m. to get everyone back to Lake Street.

When it opened on a 21-acre site between Commonwealth Avenue and the river, Norumbega had something for everyone in the family. It had a penny arcade, a merry-go-round, a deer park of more than an acre, the largest zoo in

Norumbega Park — the Casino and Main Entrance, Auburndale.

New England, extensive picnic grounds, and bicycles and canoes for rent. It also featured racks for storing more than 1000 bicycles. Remember, these were the days before widespread ownership of automobiles. Refreshments were available at booths around the park and on a small island in the river connected by a footbridge. The proprietors were careful to provide adequate security for unescorted women and children and even provided a Woman's Cottage where they could rest. The colored lights that played over the fountain in the huge pool were powered by the same electrical system that ran the trolleys, at a time when many homes were still lighted by gas lamps.

Additional facilities included the Pavilion Restaurant, the largest building in the Park, which seated 250 people in a second floor dining room located to take advantage of the breeze over the water. It was managed by Joseph Lee, a former slave, who owned the Woodland Park Hotel at the corner of Woodland Road and Washington Street, one of those comfortable locations for those who could afford to flee downtown Boston's summer discomforts in the days before air-conditioning.

Of course there was entertainment. A vaudeville theatre with seats for 1200 put on two performances a day. Free band concerts on the edge of the Charles each Friday and Saturday evening and Sunday afternoon drew crowds of up to 1000 canoes. The young couples came equipped with pillows, mosquito netting, food and drink, and if the evening was particularly hot, you might find some of the canoes still occupied in the morning. To prevent any untoward goings on, the Metropolitan Police established a station in Auburndale in 1904. In addition to their living and working space and several cells, the police maintained a drying room and wringers for the clothes of boaters who capsized as well as an upstairs telescope with which to check on distant canoeists. There was even a photography lab in which to develop prints for evidence in case the police needed to file complaints against "disorderly proceedings along the Charles River."

The time was perfect for development of a facility like Norumbega. The Victorian interest in the out-of-doors brought wide participation in active and passive recreation by people of all ages. It was the period that saw the founding of the Appalachian Mountain Club and the State Parks Commission. Private boat clubs abounded.

While some of its sister parks struggled over the years, Norumbega succeeded in large part because its proprietors continually reviewed their product and updated it. In 1904 the directors built a roof over the outdoor Rustic Theatre to protect patrons from the weather and increased its size to accommodate 3000 customers. As cars became popular the Park bought ten acres across Commonwealth Avenue and created a parking lot and, later, a gasoline and repair station. New amusements were added each season. John T. Benson, a noted animal expert, was hired to manage the zoo, also increasing its size. In 1916 he took over as manager of the entire park. Benson later founded Franklin Park Zoo and Benson's Wild Animal Farm in Hudson, New Hampshire. He may have been more of a showman than a serious naturalist. Some claim to remember that the rabbit cage at the Wild Animal Farm was labeled "snake food."

Norumbega always had its ups and downs. There was a period during and just after World War I when attendance was down significantly and there was thought of closing the Park. In fact, Norumbega's sister park in Lexington was closed at this period. Here, though, the Park's directors decided to invest and stay in business. They noted the success of Nutting's-on-the-Charles, a large dance hall over a boathouse in Waltham. Nutting's had opened in 1914 and quickly had become a popular spot for dancing and listening to jazz. In response Norumbega's directors increased the size of their restaurant and added a dance floor so that, by 1919, diners could listen and dance to the music of the Norumbega Dance Orchestra.

By the time the Totem Pole Ballroom opened in 1930, there were more than 100 ballrooms in and around Boston as well as gigantic multi-band dances at the Boston Garden almost every weekend and moonlight cruises with dinner and dancing in the harbor. The competition was fierce. Yet the Totem Pole became one of the best-known ballrooms in the country with its 12-foot high totem poles, custom-made in Seattle, at either side of the bandstand. Famous band leaders and their swing bands played there —

Jimmy and Tommy Dorsey, Benny Goodman, Gene Krupa, Harry James and Artie Shaw all brought their bands to Auburndale-on-the-Charles. Though there were plush accommodations for 500 couples, loveseats reserved for 50 cents and larger couches at $1, there were many occasions when it was standing room only with over 1000 couples in attendance. The ballroom was as fine as any in the country and it was next to an amusement park. What more could one ask?

The Depression ended the heyday of Norumbega. The park provided inexpensive entertainment, but all was not cloud-free. The dolls and pennants offered as prizes along the midway were replaced with flour and sugar. A number of the boathouses along the river were destroyed by flood in the mid-1930s and few were replaced. As the Depression continued attendance dropped and the Park and ballroom came close to closing.

An entrepreneur named Roy Gill was determined to save Norumbega. After two seasons as the concessionaire for the merry-go-round and a couple of the popular rides, he took over as manager of the entire facility in 1938. To improve the tone of the park he prohibited drinking at the ballroom and instituted a 'no stags' policy to prevent crowding of the dance floor with non-dancers who only came to listen to the music. He also insisted on a dress code — no slacks or bobby-sox for women, jackets and ties for the men. Gill clearly saw the future of the park in the Totem Pole.

He saw another opportunity when he visited the World's Fair in Flushing Meadow in 1939 and 1940. Soon he was the proud owner of the Fair's collection of 65 paddleboats, purchased for $1.00 each plus shipping. They were an immediate hit on the Charles and Gill soon had dozens more built at Norumbega and at another local boatyard.

With the conclusion of the War there was another surge of popularity for the Totem Pole. For the first time a whites-only policy was dropped and black musicians and patrons arrived. And then there was another transportation innovation. In 1951 Route 128, a six-lane highway, was opened. It was right there, just down Commonwealth Avenue from Norumbega. It could bring more traffic but, more significantly, it made it easier for urban and suburban dwellers to travel farther afield. Attendance dropped as other options became more easily accessible.

This is the period that I remember, though I certainly did not know that the Norumbega Park of my youth, with the Dodge-em Cars, the carnival games in the booths under the trees, the merry-go-round and the fabulous ice cream was long past its prime. I never realized that my senior prom — dancing to Bob Bachelder and his orchestra at the Totem Pole, sitting in the velvet banquettes with the little lamps on the tables between — represented the reflection of an era bygone. To me, Norumbega was magic.

The reality was a little different. In 1956 after 18 years of ownership Roy Gill sold the park. The new owner installed more modern sound equipment at the Totem Pole and once again brought in big bands such as the Glenn Miller Orchestra and Guy Lombardo. He hired Bob Bachelder as his regular bandleader. But times had changed. More young people took their dates out in cars than in canoes and the drive-in was less expensive than the Totem Pole. Others stayed home and watched television. The ballroom remained busy only on Saturday evenings.

After just a few years the park was sold to Peter Kanavos, a developer who had ambitious plans for the site at the 128 interchange. And that was the end of Norumbega. The Park closed on Labor Day 1963, the Totem Pole, the next February. The days of the trolley parks and the big ballrooms were over. Modern transportation produced Norumbega Park and modern transportation sounded its death knell.

The Birth and Early Days of Newton's Stanley Steamer

This paper by Margaret Gerrity was presented October 8, 1975, under the theme Newtown to Newton. Both Augusta and Flora Stanley were early members of the Social Science Club. Gerrity implies that she acquired the letters she quotes and the stories she tells directly or indirectly from them. Edited and abridged by Vivi Leavy.

The Gay 90s marked the golden era of fast horses and bicycles. Strangely enough they both played an important role in the construction of the first

Stanley Steamer, completed in September 1897. The Stanley twins, Francis Edgar and Freelan Oscar, had been Newton residents for seven years at that time. They looked so much alike that most people couldn't tell which one was Frank and which one was Freel. One was called "F.E." and the other "F.O." They had moved to Newton along with their photographic dry-plate business from Lewiston, Maine, where the business had developed to a point requiring the establishment of a larger plant nearer the market, where there were better railroad facilities. So the Stanley Dry-Plate Company moved to Newton in the spring of 1890. The business flourished and its product became known throughout the world.

F.E. lived in a house of his own design at the corner of Centre Street and

Augusta May Stanley was the wife of F.E. Stanley and a Social Science Club member.

(Courtesy of the Stanley Museum, Kingfield, Maine)

Hyde Avenue. F.O. lived on Hunnewell Avenue until he built his large brick house on Waverley Avenue which he occupied for the rest of his life. F.E. was more athletically inclined than his brother. He enjoyed bicycling immensely and wanted his wife to be able to ride with him. Augusta Stanley was a large woman and did not look with favor on taking up cycling. Her husband tried to teach her to ride, though without much success. One day, out on Centre Street, she actually rode her bicycle about 30 feet but then fell off and was both bruised and scared. "Never again!" she said to her husband. "Never you mind, Gustie," he replied helping her up, "I will build something so that we can ride in safety and comfort, side by side."

Horses, too, convinced F.E. that some means of getting places other than by his old Taffy would be fine. Horses had minds of their own and sometimes went places their owners didn't like. F.O. had a roan colt in 1897 and had been trying to break him to harness all the previous winter and spring without much success. In June he ran away, throwing his trainer out of the carriage near Newton Corner. The horse bolted up Park Street and then through much of residential eastern Newton before ending up back home in his own stable. The driver was not injured and the carriage none the worse for the trip, but F.O. gave the colt away the next day to a man who promised to keep him out of Newton.

In April 1897 Mrs. F.E. Stanley sailed for Europe. F.E. sold his last horse soon after and made up his mind to get rid of his carriages before his wife returned. In June of that year he wrote his wife, "I am all out of horses and shall not own a horse again until I have seen the outcome of the motor carriage business movement." In July he told her, "I wrote you some time ago about motor carriages. Well, I'm building one. I am making all the plans and it will weigh only 350 pounds and will be four inches wider and five inches longer than our best buggy was. It will cost me about $500 and will be finished the first of September or soon after you get home. It will not be afraid of a steamroller and will have no bad habits. It will stand without hitching, and perhaps that is all it will do." Finally in August he wrote, "I am surprised to know that motor carriages are not more numerous in Paris. . . . You could not be in Boston as long as you have been in Paris without seeing more than two!"

The first Stanley Steamer was indeed completed in September 1897. Here is what one of the Stanley twins wrote recalling the first ride in that strange, frail-looking vehicle: "I shall never forget our first ride. We went out our alleyway onto Maple Street, and turned toward Galen Street. A horse hitched to a produce wagon was standing at the side of the road. He heard the car coming, turned his head and took a look, gave a snort and jumped so quickly that he broke the whippletree but did not move the wagon. He ran out to Galen Street, turned around, took one more look, and then raced up Galen Street, through Newton Square and did not stop running until he reached Newtonville Square. This occurred in the forenoon. That afternoon the owner called at our office and told us we owed him $25. We claimed we owed him nothing. But we said if he would take his harness and wagon up to Murray's and have them repaired we would pay the bill. The bill amounted to two dollars. That first trip we went as far as Newtonville and back without further trouble."

At first F.O. Stanley was not too interested in the steam carriage which brother F.E. had made. Both brothers were up to their necks in the photographic dry plate business and F.O. was devoting his time mainly to that. Nevertheless, F.E. had been bitten by the horseless carriage bug and he took steps to prove that the car he had built opened up new horizons that few had even dreamed of.

One reason for F.O.'s lack of enthusiasm was the failure of the little car to make the run from Newton to Poland Springs in Maine in one day. On July 8, 1898, F.E. left his Centre Street home at 4:00 o'clock in the morning and got as far as Mystic Park where he punctured a tire. He had taken the precaution to take along a new tire and in about 20 minutes he had put it on. All went well until he reached Hamilton where he punctured another tire. He called F.O. who sent a boy on a 'wheel' [bicycle] with a new tire. He then returned to the shop in Newton by 12:30 p.m. having covered 76 miles.

In a letter to Flora Stanley who was summering at Lake Placid, New York, her husband Freel wrote a short account of F.E.'s second attempt at driving to Poland Springs: "Before starting, Frank was told to give his carriage a more thorough test as he had put on a new body, a new engine and two new tires of a different make. The next morning he started again to do the trick. When he got to Kennebunkport his steering bar broke when he was going at high speed and the carriage ran plumb into a ledge, breaking both front wheels and damaging the body badly. Frank jumped, landing in a brush pile, and was not injured. Had he met with no accident he could easily have reached Portland by noon and Poland Springs by 5:00 p.m. His handlebar had broken once before and was entirely unsafe. By the time you get home my carriage will be ready and we will have some fun."

The newspapers in Boston and Lewiston, Maine, covered F.E. Stanley's trip to Maine. Although he did not reach his goal, people were amazed that a motor carriage could travel as far as it did. Everybody wanted to see the car and its maker. That same year, 1898, the first exhibition of motor vehicles in the United States opened in October in Mechanics Hall in Boston with four exhibitors. Following this showing of early motor carriages there was a meet for automobiles on Charles River Park track. The *Boston Herald* (November 10, 1898) reported that, "This meet has brought Boston up to date with London and Paris. It was high time that the horseless carriage should make its speedy entrée to public consideration here.... The meet has done much to familiarize people with automobiles, and this contest must give tremendous impetus to interest in this invention.

The Stanley twins, Francis Edgar and Freelan Oscar, F.E. and F.O. respectively, ride the streets of Newton in the world's first 'motor carriage.'

... It is doubted if any of the spectators at the meet said they did not care to have such a vehicle."

In its report of the meet, *The Horseless Age* reported that the Stanley Steamer won the hill climb in a walkover. The event featured an 80-foot-long wooden structure with a 35% grade. The Stanley Steamer made but one trial run and with a rush ma.de the 80 feet in 4.6 seconds. The article further stated that F.E. Stanley evoked great applause when he appeared on the track in his light and trim steam carriage, which he took for an exhibition spin, doing the mile in two minutes 11 seconds and two miles in five minutes 19 seconds. Both Stanley brothers were aboard the little car with F.E. at the helm. Following this spin around the track people flocked around the car and besieged the Stanleys with questions. Many wanted to know when they could get one and how much it would cost. Sensing the tremendous interest shown at the meet, F.O. capitulated, and from that day joined his brother in the company, aiming to produce Stanley Steamers by the hundreds.

F.O. lost no time in furthering publicity for the car. On August 31, 1899, he and Mrs. Stanley made the ascent to the top of Mt. Washington via the carriage road in about an hour and a half running time. They were the first to reach the summit in an automobile, a feat which was front-page news not only in Boston but also around the world. By then, Stanley cars were in production with parts on hand for building 200 and a factory equipped to assemble them. Orders were coming in faster than the Stanleys could fill them. However, earlier that summer the brothers had accepted a bid to buy their motorcar design. The buyers included Amzi L. Barber, the owner of an asphalt paving company. Mr. Barber set up the Locomobile Company of America and started turning out 'Stanley Carriages' by July, taking advantage of the publicity.

Although the Stanley twins had agreed not to sell automobiles for one year from the date of sale, that did not mean they were out of the car business. They lost no time making plans for a much better steam car than the model they had sold. They introduced it in 1901 to great praise. George Eastman, founder of the Eastman Kodak Company, which later purchased the Stanley Dry Plate Company, bought a Stanley motor carriage in 1902. He wrote enthusiastically, "For real dead game sports the Stanley machine is the only one. I have just gotten a new one from the Stanleys. If the electric [car] is a peach, the Stanley is a peacherina."

Not every owner was as enthusiastic. While the running quality of the Stanley Steamer was unequalled, it did have one major drawback. A steam car will not run without steam and the fire to make it. The burner had a pilot light just like a gas stove today, and as long as the pilot light was lit it would maintain steam pressure. If the pilot light was allowed to go out, it could take from 15 minutes to half an hour to get up enough steam to run the car. As long as gas car users had to crank their engines by hand, many people preferred the steam car despite its defects, but the invention of the self-starter sounded the death knell of the steamer.

While this story of how the Stanley Steamer first came to be built has been printed in books and magazines many times, as is usually the case with the tellings of beginnings by people who were not there, the true facts of its birth and infancy as related here rarely appear.

Charles Johnson Maynard 1845–1929

Margaret J. Snider presented the paper from which these short excerpts were taken on February 4, 1976. Snider was the reference librarian for the Newton Free Library and a paper writer in the bicentennial year when the topic 'From Newtown to Newton' explored facets of the city of a century earlier. She was an amateur birder and became interested in finding out more about Charles Maynard when, prowling about in the Library's basement on another task, she came across a set of his 12 small volumes which listed birds seen on walks in Newton, Plum Island, Maine, and some further fields in the early decades of the century. Not only had he written up accounts of the birds sighted, but he had published the small books himself in West Newton where he lived and worked, yet Mrs. Snider had never heard his name. Even now his entry in Wikipedia is a very short paragraph.

In her paper Snider noted that the library owned many of Maynard's books on birds, butterflies, shells and even gravestones. While his name may have faded from history, in his day he was a significant figure in the world of natural history and birding. He was vice president and editor of the Bulletin of the Nuttall Ornithological Club of Cambridge founded in 1873, the first of its kind in this country, and he was a founder and president of the Newton Natural History Society and published many of its bulletins and member talks. He taught in the summer school of the Massachusetts Agricultural College, now the University of Massachusetts

Amherst (1910–1919) and ran a store called The Naturalist's Bureau on Crafts Street near his home, which carried all kinds of natural history materials and where he gave classes in taxidermy. He taught bird classes beginning in 1868 and for many years led popular bird walks scheduled for weekends especially so teachers could attend.

A West Newton farmer's son, his early experience as a taxidermist reflected and increased his interest in the natural world and made up in part for his lack of formal scientific education. From his writings, especially his 1907 article "Birds of Newton" in Mirror of Newton Past and Present, *Snider considered him one of the early conservationists. He decried the loss of habitat, "the little brook, once the home of the rail and bittern, the old apple trees in the orchard that had attracted the warblers"; and spoke out strongly against spraying pesticides. He called for the restoration of native shrubs and plants and recommended that "public parks should have whole sections left perfectly wild for birds, without trimming or without underbrush or fallen leaves being removed." His message is the same one birder David Sibley voices today.*

In addition to reading his books Snider interviewed Howard Rich who as a child went on Maynard's bird walks. She wrote:

A friend of the family, knowing of his interest in birds, put him in contact with Mr. Maynard who was well known to the Rich family since they attended the same church. Thus began the nature trips, always on Saturday, for Sunday was for church going. On these trips Mr. Rich felt sure he had walked 14 miles instead of the four listed.

Each member was given a small brown folder containing the date and place of the next meeting and a report of the trip of the week before. Usually two meetings were listed, Saturday and Sunday; Mr. Rich always went on Saturday. An advertisement for one of Mr. Maynard's books or the *Records* was printed on the covers inside. Each brown folder listed the volume and subscription rates: $2.00 for the set of 40 (in a bound volume); $1.00 for 20; 50 cents for ten; 25 cents for five; six cents each, payable in advance. Nine volumes bound formed an attractive set of the *Records* and sold for $12.80. [The advertisement claimed that] "this publication contains weekly news of value to nature students throughout the world. Notes on various subjects, but especially birds, gathered by experienced observers appear on its pages. The attention of all nature lovers, and especially of librarians, is called to these important volumes. They will be sent to anyone for examination." The fees for the walks were listed as follows: single walk, 50 cents; ten-walk ticket, $4.00. Often a review of one of Mr. Maynard's books was included. . . . Mr. Maynard knew the value of including the names of those spotting a bird and calling attention to it for the group. Credit was given in the report of the walk appearing the following week in the *Records*. It was smart business practice, for it is hard to find the person who does not like to see his or her name in print; besides, it added prestige and helped to sell more copies of the *Records*.

Birding is now far easier than in those days when a trip to Plum Island meant taking the street car at Newton Corner to Park Street then to North Station and the train to Ipswich, then walking to the boat landing where you boarded a boat for the island. Once there you did your birding, looking for Taras, Sharp-tailed Sparrows and other native birds, and returned to Newton in reverse order. No wonder such a trip bore the notice, 'bring your lunch.'. . . Now all you do is hop in your car and drive to Plum Island.

Mr. Rich remembers his afternoon excursions to Mr. Maynard's home which was in the Albemarle area near the Fessenden School. He went on his bicycle and would find Mr. Maynard busy amid the clutter of type, his printing press, drawers of specimens, skins, and materials for his woodcuts and lithographs. He did his own woodcuts and lithographs, and either did himself or supervised the hand-coloring of the plates, setting the type, and

"Young of Common Tern"— A woodcut by Charles Johnson Maynard.

81

printing many of the books and articles he wrote. If he was lucky Mr. Rich would return home with a prize, a bird skin which was about to be discarded as being the worse for wear. Once home Mr. Rich would 'prop it up' and draw and paint it.

In concluding, Snider wrote:

According to the account in the *Dictionary of American Biography* Mr. Maynard was a keen observer who had no hesitation in publishing his observations. While his observations were often original and voluminous, covering a wide field, "his lack of early scientific training was frequently evident in his publications and he fell short of the accomplishments which might have been his had he had a thorough foundation in science." However, one of his biographers in noting this lack commented, "It is possible this would have spoiled his independence and originality and made a narrow specialist of him." In any case, he did serve as an inspiration and mentor to those many young people and adults with whom he came in contact.

Note: Charles Johnson Maynard's books are now in the public domain. The Warblers of New England *is available online on Google Books and is a fine example of his work, right down to hand-colored plates.*

Who was Mabel Louise Riley?
This paper by civic leader Jean M. Husher was written and presented on March 8, 1978. The year's theme was Contemporary Women of Influence. Edited and abridged by Vivi Leavy.

The Mabel Louise Riley Charitable Trust is a very large foundation which in 1976 alone gave out more than $800,000 in support of a wide variety of good causes. The foundation is mainly interested in pilot programs in education, health, social welfare and community development, particularly proposals coming from Newton and Cotuit, Massachusetts, the communities where Miss Riley lived almost all her life. The Charles

River Watershed Association; Freeport, Inc.; Newton Historic Preservation Association; Newton Community Development Foundation; Newton Community Services Centers, Inc.; Newton Youth Foundation; and Grace Episcopal Church were all recipients of grants from the foundation in fiscal year 1976.

Who was Mabel Louise Riley? It seems reasonable that information about this gracious lady should be available, yet surprisingly little is. Not even a photograph of her has been found. The booklet distributed by trustees of her foundation include but two brief paragraphs identifying her. No obituary, other than a brief death notice, was published in the newspapers when she died in 1971. A month later when the terms of her will and the size of her estate were made known, almost no information about her was revealed. The church she attended did not know when or where she was born or where she received her education. Since she was 88 years old upon her death, the likelihood of discovering a close friend of her own generation still living is remote. Her personal papers, diaries, journals, letters, photos and so on, seem to have been destroyed in settling her estate.

Who was Mabel Louise Riley? Clearly research in uncovering this fast-disappearing person, whose large estate has solved some of the financial needs of so many worthy organizations, would have to be done by personal interview, and most certainly it should be done very soon before all the people who knew her are gone.

Mabel Louise Riley began her life on February 26, 1883, in Boston, the only child of Agnes Winslow Riley and Charles Edward Riley. Her father was born in Burnly, Lancashire, England in 1852 and educated at St. James School and Mechanics Institute. His education terminated at an early age and he was hard at work in a cotton mill while still quite young. His first job was changing empty bobbins for full ones and then carefully attaching the threads so the weaving machines could continue their work. England's fluid society, at least in the industrial realm, allowed Charles Riley, a bright and ambitious boy, to work his way up out of the factory into management. In 1879 when he was 27 years old, he was appointed representative of a cotton textile machinery manufacturer and sent to the United States. It was not long before he met and courted the lovely Agnes Winslow of Philadelphia. The Winslows were rather new to Philadelphia society, having originally come from an old Massachusetts family. But clearly they recognized the potential of this good-looking, ambitious young Englishman in spite of his humble beginnings. The couple married sometime in 1881.

Time out for courtship did not slow down Charles Riley's business pursuits at all. Perhaps, indeed, it served as an impetus, for somehow he raised $100,000 to purchase the American rights to manufacture his employer's machinery under the name H & B Machine Company in Pawtucket, Rhode Island. Soon after marriage, the young couple moved to Boston where Charles established his office under the name C. E. Riley Company. Boston was a textile center but also a cultural center with more appeal than Pawtucket. It was there that Mabel Louise was born.

When Mabel Louise was still a young child of five her parents bought the stylish Queen Anne house at 93 Bellevue Street in Newton that was to be her home for so many years. The Charles Rileys had owned the house for about ten years when they decided that the Queen Anne style was quite outdated and something must be done. The tower peaks, the carved panels, the side porches, and the small portico were all stripped off and the house was almost doubled in size with generous additions to the rear and each side. A handsome *porte-cochere* and classic balusters were added to the roof so that the house took on the characteristics of the Federal Revival style so popular at the time. The continuing success of Charles Riley's textile interests allowed him to purchase the vacant lot next door on which he built a magnificent carriage house and, like other Newton families of the era, laid out handsome gardens and a greenhouse filled with exotic plants. It must have seemed to Charles Riley that he had achieved his dreamed-of position as a member of the landed gentry in the best English tradition, for he remained truly English through and through.

Mabel Louise spent her childhood years as a much-loved daughter in this spacious home on the top of Mt. Ida overlooking the plains of Newton

Corner and Watertown to the hills beyond. Little is known of her during those years. Newton School Department records show she was not in any school at seven years old, so perhaps she had a governess and was taught at home. In 1891 it is recorded that she was attending private school, as she was six years later when she was 14, although there is no record which one. It can be inferred from the comments of those acquainted with her later in life that her upbringing fostered the qualities of self-discipline, modesty, courtesy to all, and of quiet generosity, for these attributes were much a part of her personality all her life. One person described her as 'to the manner born.' Whether born to the manner or not, she clearly was trained to it from early childhood.

One contributor said that Mabel Louise was presented to society upon completion of her education. Her parents had been listed for some time in the annual Newton Blue Book which recorded the names of families considered important in Newton society. When Miss Riley was 21, she was listed separately and was 'at home on first Mondays.' However another contributor noted that her family was received into Newton society with some reserve, at least by those whose families dated back to the colonial period, for her father had come up through the factory. It was not unusual in the 'Gilded Age' of the 1880s and 1890s for ambitious, creative, imaginative young men to push ahead in the business world and then demand entrance into the ranks of society, but the reserve of older families in receiving them was not unusual either.

Mabel Louise must have been an attractive young lady for it has been reliably reported that she was tall and well formed with lovely, curling reddish-blonde hair. Those who knew her well said she had a dry sense of humor and a noticeable twinkle in her eye. The proprieties becoming a young lady forbade her boisterous laughter, but she was known to make quiet and humorous observations on the follies of mankind. As a young adult she was much interested in horseback riding and driving sporting carriages. One contributor recalls as a child sitting on a wall edging the street and waving as Mabel Louise drove by in her open carriage. She graciously acknowledged the child by dipping her long whip in a most dignified manner. Dozens of ribbons and awards for competition in riding, driving and showing horses, along with photographs of her prize horses, were found in the carriage house after her death.

Whatever may have been the social world for Mabel Louise and her mother, it is clear that Charles Riley was very well received in the strictly male worlds, be it business, social, philanthropic or political. The list of his memberships to social and business clubs was lengthy. His business prospered and he was widely recognized in Boston business circles. He must have appeared somewhat overwhelming to his daughter, raised at a time when restrictions on the ambitions and interests of most females severely inhibited all but the few given to 'kicking over the traces.' No contributor has revealed that Mabel Louise was among these, but rather that her strong self-discipline would never have allowed her to do so. By all reports, she was very close to her parents, particularly admiring her father who instructed her in the management of the estate and directed that generous philanthropy be a part of this.

By the time that Mabel Louise was ready to take up her role in the social world, her father had earned a large fortune. In addition to her personal reserve toward people, this may have given her some problems. Although ever most gracious, she was, by all reports, not given to fluent small talk or the flirtation so common to sociable young ladies. One can imagine that her wealthy parents might be concerned that she not be courted by those primarily interested in her money. Such concern might well stretch itself to unwonted suspicion of all young men coming to call. One tale, true or not, has it that whenever a young man came to call on Mabel Louise, he was invited into her father's library. Charles Riley would light up a large and expensive cigar and demand of the young man what his intentions were towards his daughter. If this were indeed fact, it would be enough to scare off the most hearty of possible suitors.

Around 1910 Mabel Louise was asked to join the Board of Directors of the Rebecca Pomroy Home for Orphan Girls, beginning her many, many years of active social service and generous giving in the tradition of her father. The resident director, Miss Clara M. Hayes, was regarded as a martinet but neither Mabel Louise not the treasurer, Oliver Fisher, were taken in. It is reliably reported that these three had a fine time together exchanging witticisms. Miss Riley served actively on this board for several decades and privately provided many niceties for the home: milk from the family cows; fresh vegetables from the large farm garden across Bellevue Street; flowers in season; and a generous sum donated each year toward the summer camp.

In the years prior to and following World War I, Mabel Louise Riley liked to entertain with musicales that were generally regarded as delightful. Although she did not play an instrument herself she was very appreciative of classical music and attended Boston Symphony concerts until well into her eighties. She also appreciated good theater all her life and was a member of the Theatre Guild. Although several people have suggested that she made the usual trip to Europe, she was not in any way an adventurous person, so it is unlikely that she enjoyed travel.

In June of 1929 when Mabel Louise was 46, the family purchased a home and extensive acreage at Cotuit on Cape Cod. It was there that her great love of plants came into its own as she developed, with her gardeners, some six acres of gardens, formal and informal, woodlands, ponds and marshes. She was especially fond of her primrose collection and made a special trip down to Cotuit each spring to see them in bloom. Equally gorgeous were her tea roses, some 450 bushes. The pond area included a rustic bridge and a garden house perfect for bird watching which Miss Riley enjoyed. Indeed no expense was spared in the design and maintenance of these gardens or the ones at Bellevue Street, for they gave Miss Riley perhaps her greatest pleasure. She shared her flowers with friends and sent bouquets to organizations in which she had an interest as long as she lived, and she supported regular plantings of spring bulbs on the grounds of her two favorite social service organizations, the Pomroy House and the Stone Institute.[5]

The same newspaper which announced the purchase of the Cotuit property by the Riley family also noted the arrival of the new minister of Cotuit's Federated Church, Walter Craft, and his wife Ruth. Miss Riley treasured the friendship of this family and in her quiet way assisted in the education of their son. She also enjoyed the social life of Cotuit. She belonged to the Wianno Club, the Beach Club in Centerville and the Oyster Harbor Club, and took part in their activities. She purchased a cabin cruiser large enough to accommodate half a dozen people in its lounge and hired a captain to run it.

By the 1930s Charles and Agnes Riley were becoming quite elderly. While Agnes had been in poor health for years, her vigorous husband died first after a short illness in 1937. Agnes passed away in 1941. Charles Riley had been most interested in the Stone Institute, serving as president of the Board of Directors for some 25 years. Upon his death his daughter was invited to join the board and she maintained an active interest in this organization for many years.

Miss Riley was a life-long member of Grace Episcopal Church in Newton, attending services fairly regularly but only rarely its various functions. She could be counted on to give $50 a year to the Church Periodical Club, but the chairman had to make a point of writing a formal letter requesting a donation. In addition, and again in her most quiet way she observed which church members appeared to need help in providing for themselves and would take them shopping for some new clothes at R. H. Stearns Department Store from time to time.

She was sought by many organizations to join their boards of directors and occasionally she would, but only as an honorary member and she would not attend meetings. Among those were the Newton Boys Club and the Family Service Bureau. She apparently felt that her active service for the Pomroy House and the Stone Institute was putting her time and energy where her heart was. She was, however, most generous in support of many local organizations. She was a member of the Newton Community Club and several other social organizations and, though she rarely attended meetings, she could be counted on to purchase tickets to all their events. She felt quite miffed one time when a representative of a Newton organization came to visit seeking her continued financial support. Unfortunately he dropped a file card with her name on it and the notation, "This person can give more." She never gave them anything again.

Her wealth was sometimes a source of unhappy thoughts, justified or otherwise. Once when asked to pour at a tea at church she let slip that, "No one has ever asked me to pour before. People just ask me for my money." She was a person of considerable reserve and it was generally difficult for people to feel that they might make friends with her. She was tall and dignified and seemed sometimes, probably without ever intending to as is the way with shy people, somewhat imperious and unapproachable. She did not indulge in small talk and innocent gossip. Thus a wall was built which seems to have isolated her in Newton, at least from all but a few intimate friends. Even her lawyer of many years always called her 'Miss Riley.'

To her closest friends, however, she was highly intelligent with a fine character and a good appreciation of the ridiculous. She was well organized, running her complicated households on strict schedules. Those serving her knew what was expected and were well paid. Miss Riley was thoughtful of their needs and appreciative of their service; those asked responded willingly that she was a good employer. She would listen to advice but did not always agree and though she was polite about it, she made her own independent decisions. She did not like unpleasantness and would not deign to argue, but simply turned the other cheek. She was very well read, but subscribed for pure enjoyment to *Punch* and the *London Illustrated News*, partly because she was at heart English. She was an enthusiastic bridge player and played regularly with good friends both in Newton and Cotuit. She loved small pets and always had several little dogs at a time, and generally a number of parakeets as well.

The vicissitudes of old age were a great trial to Mabel Louise Riley as perhaps with most people. Arthritis crippled her increasingly during her last years. She became more isolated from people, even to the point of becoming a recluse and somewhat paranoid in fear of being robbed. Several men were hired to stand guard over the house and grounds. But even to the end of her life Miss Riley remained most gracious and generous to those spunky enough to get by the guards to speak to her of the needs of their favorite charities. Her life came to an end after several years of real illness on June 23, 1971.

It is better not to end by recalling her at a time when she was not fully herself. Although her generosity was felt through gifts to many public charities, more typical were her thoughtful kindnesses to all kinds of people, important or not. Lovingly remembered by many a small errand boy grown to manhood was the silver dollar tip pressed into his hand. Equally well remembered by a certain Ritz-Carlton Hotel doorman are the paid hospital bills of his sick daughter. A favorite hairdresser, hands seriously impaired in an automobile accident, was treated to the surgery needed to correct the injuries. And a black lady remembers gratefully when Mabel Louise Riley saw to it that a room, said not to be available, was provided for her sick child and paid for as well.

While her name will long be connected to the trust established from her estate, it is hoped that this report will help preserve the memory of the fine person that was Mabel Louise Riley.

Note: In addition to news articles, directories and books, Jean Husher's bibliography lists the names of 18 personal friends and acquaintances of Mabel Louis Riley, some of them members of the Social Science Club, who were interviewed for information about her life and character.

Endnotes

1 The Stamp Savings Society of Boston, the first of its kind, was started in 1890 to promote thrift among school children. Similar programs, selling stamps for a penny and more to paste in individual savings booklets, spread slowly in schools through the country.

2 The pound was an enclosure where stray cattle were kept until their owner paid a small fine. The church sexton was often appointed pound keeper so the fees might supplement his income.

3 Quoted in *Society and Medical Progress*, Bernhard Joseph Stern, Arno Press, Inc. New York, 1970, p. 39.

4 Homeopaths referred to this traditional practice, and in fact any non-homeopathic system, as allopathy. (Wikipedia)

5 The full name is the Stone Institute & Newton Home for Aged People. It provided for 26 residents, most of whom were women in the years Miss Riley was on its board.

CHAPTER THREE

From the Arts to Outreach

The Fine Arts: The Club's Intellectual Foundation
by Duscha Schmid Weisskopf

One attribute the original six women brought to the table in 1886 when they decided to found a women's study club was a firm grounding in the arts. Music, playing and singing; canvas arts, drawing, painting and appreciating; writing poetry and journaling; to say nothing of needlecraft, a much neglected visual art, were intrinsic to a well brought up young lady's basic home training. While some of the first members could boast of a college education, it did not necessarily follow that they would be 'allowed' by the societal mores of their times to pursue careers outside the home; unless, of course, they were spinsters. The first group of college women "had considerable difficulty after they graduated finding a role for themselves which could incorporate their hard-won knowledge and new view of themselves," Jane Addams said, a poignant and pointed remark that Sylvia Skinner quoted in her 1992 paper on the social reformer. This expression of the need for validation of thinking women could as easily have come from the mouth of any of the Social Science Club's first members.

The SSC, thus, opened up a unique opportunity for the Newton women of the last decade and a half of the 19th century. With plentiful household help and time to call their own it is no surprise that their interest in the arts found intellectual expression in the Club, allowing them to take their knowledge of a socially acceptable subject one step further — the enthusiastic exploration of the lives and works of artists and composers, writers and poets.

From the earliest days of the Social Science Club the ladies were eager to 'study' the arts. It must surely have provided a comfort zone, an area of intellectual inquiry that they knew something about and loved, and that provided a level of immediate reassurance as they embarked on educating themselves to the level of conversational equality with their husbands. Besides, as these exceptionally bright women surely realized, the arts were a perfectly fertile and well suited jumping off point to the study of politics, sociology, psychology, world affairs, philanthropy, women's rights and the role of women in the home and the world. All were intrinsic at one level or another in what was so genteelly deemed areas of inquiry suitable to women, those of the visual and performing arts.

The passion for the arts and the ease with which most women embrace them has been the 'thread that runs so true' in the 125-year history of the Club. Music in particular has enthralled Club members from day one. Although the first official musicale, auspiciously enough showcasing the talents of the Arthur Fiedler trio, dates to December 1923, music was incorporated in study and appreciation well before then, indeed from the earliest meetings.

In 1897 Anna L. Goodrich presented a paper on "Music as a Social Force." She noted that, "Man has been controlled by the power of music ever since the morning stars sang together." At that time there were no American-born members of the Boston Symphony Orchestra although there were 1000 students at the New England Conservatory. Goodrich quoted Lowell Mason, a well known music educator, as saying, "In Europe every town and church has trained singers while in this country the musical awakening dates from the middle of this [the 19th] century. At that time [a commentator] said that there was "no organist in Boston who could play a first-class fugue by Bach." Mason had such high praise for the Boston Symphony Orchestra that he said it "is without a superior in the world." Mary C. Blakemore, a member of the Club, nevertheless worried that "a foreign musical education was often obtained at the sacrifice of morals," since there was as yet no way to receive an American education in music. Orinda Hornbrooke added a new element to the discussion when she asked Goodrich why Negroes had so much pleasanter voices than whites and was told it appeared to be partly a matter of temperament, but also that "American women were lacking in respect to placing their voice."

A special evening program in December of the same year, 1897, featured a quartet from the Hampton Institute. The Club had provided a $70 scholarship for an Indian boy attending the Virginia school since 1892 and was an occasional stop on the Institute's fund-raising trips through New England. The quartet performed plantation songs and spirituals, "their melodious voices ringing out in these Southern religious airs so musically that one could easily understand how the emotional nature of the Negro could be roused to ecstatic zeal," in the words of one enthralled Club member. Indeed this first concert given by Hampton Institute students may have sown the seed that grew into the Club's annual holiday musicales. For the Club's 40th anniversary Negro spirituals were presented in 1926, as well as a reprise of the Hampton Institute Quartet in 1929.

Music continued to play an important role in the early Club. In 1906 the Club celebrated its 20th anniversary with "live music and song." The afternoon concluded with singing Auld Lang Syne. Two weeks later Grace Van Dusen Cooke spoke on "The Voice," illustrated by anecdotes, whistling and singing. Many questions followed.

During World War I the custom was to sing patriotic songs at every meeting. The war continued to reverberate in women's consciousness. In 1919 the Annual Report states that "the [Boston] Symphony Orchestra concerts have been experienced by convalescent soldiers from the hospital in Boston through the generosity of one of our members."

After the war which so greatly changed the tenor of life, members of the Club asked themselves "whether time spent on literature and art is in accordance with the purpose of the Club?" The answer they arrived at was that "in these troubled times the . . . uplift of such subjects is what we most need."[3] Among the members engaged in this discussion might have been Rosalind Denny Lewis, remembering the famous words of Cicero in defense of the humanities from her classics curriculum at Radcliffe: "These studies sustain us in our youth and delight us in old age; they add to our joy in prosperity, they provide refuge and comfort in adversity."[1]

Music education was a natural fit for the Club. In 1920 when the Club was made aware that the West Newton Music School was $500 in debt, it contributed $25 to help out. In 1922 guest speaker Thomas W. Surette, a composer, organist and the director of music at Bryn Mawr, spoke on the teaching of music. He allowed that people must be trained to listen to symphonic music; otherwise their listening becomes "a drowsy reverie relieved by nervous thrills." He continued, "It is most unfortunate that the traditions of teaching music were inherited from England instead of France or Germany." Professor Surette also had high praise for the West Newton Music School, which he considered a great asset to the community. His talk was followed with "many questions and intense interest." By 1922 speakers asserted that "as genuine a musical education can be obtained in Boston or New York as in London, Paris or Berlin."

Elizabeth Fyffe, founder of the West Newton Music School.
(Courtesy of All-Newton Music School)

The musicale came to be a regular event beginning in December 1923 when it showcased violinist Arthur Fiedler's string trio. Later musicales highlighted a number of musical genres. In 1928 it featured a harpist and in 1930 the American String Quartet performed. In 1935 the musicale presented "Latin America's Contribution to the Musical Arts."

While Club members appreciated traditional forms, they were curious about modern music. In 1962 member Beverley Lovell spoke on "The Fine Arts Reflect the Modern Man: Art and Music in an Age of Turmoil." Lovell pointed out that

> We are dismayed and upset when contemporary art and music seem to be not only completely unrelated to our aesthetic standards but completely incomprehensible to

our intellect. The dismay and frustration of the layman confronted with avant-garde paintings and compositions show not only that the layman needs education on the intent of the present-day artists but also that the contemporary artist needs to feel a new responsibility to communicate with the layman.

Atonality is a new language, she explained, and there is a certain amount of loss of contact with the public. Lovell also asked whether jazz is or is not a real art form, something most of us 50 years later tend to answer in the affirmative.[2]

An event of some interest to the Club occurred in 1996. The music library at the Massachusetts Institute of Technology was rededicated as the Lewis Music Library. That name was chosen to honor member Rosalind Denny Lewis, the wife of Warren K. Lewis, a famous and beloved head of the

Rosalind Denny Lewis
(Courtesy of Lewis family)

M.I.T Engineering Department who spoke to the Club in 1950 on "The Energy Problem in the U.S."[3] (He warned of a shortage of oil!) Lewis had joined the Club in 1918 after graduating from Radcliffe in 1908 with a cum laude degree in Classics. She was extremely musical, a very good pianist and singer. All her children were taught music. Her son-in-law donated the money to refurbish M.I.T.'s music library. Her granddaughter Rosalind H. Williams, who is an M.I.T. professor in the Department of Science, Technology and Society, spoke at the rededication. Current member Duscha Weisskopf was the first music librarian at M.I.T. during the early 1950s, more than 40 years before the music library was renamed.

Drawing on proximity to Boston and Cambridge and on relationships through their husbands with prominent professors and leaders in religious and business circles, the SSC has always been able to tap knowledgeable guest speakers and gifted performers to further their understanding of music. Both Thomas W. Surette and "Doc" Archibald Davison from Harvard spoke on music education. Boris Goldovsky, head of the opera department of the New England Conservatory and Marylou Churchill, revered violinist at the BSO and Newton resident, addressed the Club as well.

Members, often music authorities in their own right, brought insightful papers on the subject before the membership. In 1997 Gretchen Friend presented one of the most original — in subject and style — papers about the world of music to come before the Club. Entitled "From Branches to Beethoven: The Life and Times of Carleen Hutchins, Luthier in the Light of Science," it is about a summer acquaintance of friends on Lake Winnipesaukee in New Hampshire. Hutchins distinguished herself by becoming a maestro in the art of handcrafting violins considered on a par, tonally, with the Stradivarius. The paper is excerpted at length at the end of this section.

In 1999 Jean A. Kennedy delivered a paper on "Amy Beach: Passionate New England Composer and Artist." Beach was a true musical prodigy. Kennedy describes her gift in this way:

> Amy's first piano pieces were composed at age four while spending the summer with her grandmother in West Henniker. She composed these in her head, as her grandmother did not have a piano, and then played them for her mother upon returning home. Her mother's reaction was to restrain herself from showing her real emotion (how properly Victorian!), and [her mother] encouraged her friends to react in the same way. Amy continued to compose mentally throughout her entire life.

Kennedy, who in 2010 could boast of being the only woman among the Boston Symphony Orchestra's volunteer archivists (a post she has held for 15 years and "would never give up"), was intrigued by Beach's struggle to be taken seriously as a musician while fighting ingrained and imposed Victorian mores. She noted that Boston Pops Conductor Keith Lockhart recently described Amy Beach as 'a central figure in American music history'; however, his efforts to have her name added to the already inscribed list of 86 other local composers were not successful until a year after Kennedy's paper was given. Amy Beach is the only woman to be so honored.

Kennedy also wrote a paper in 2003 about another abiding interest: Tanglewood, the summer performance center of the Boston Symphony, and how it came to be. Also that year, writing under the umbrella topic of "How the World Celebrates: Pageants, Parades, Fetes and Festivals," Tamara Bliss, an opera enthusiast, gave a paper entitled "Celebrating the Magic of Opera with Children." The next year, Emily Sullivan, herself an opera singer and coach, presented "Toscanini: The Conductor as Mastermind" which spoke of the most famous conductor of his time. The theme that year, 2004, was "Masterpieces and Masterminds." No matter the topic for the year, almost always a Club member finds a way to write about music.

The love of music and the vigorous pursuit of greater appreciation continues to this day. At almost every holiday musicale the headliner is a classical musician or group. As always the Club draws from nearby educational resources such as the New England Conservatory of Music, and from personal contacts. Eliot Fisk — a student of Andres Segovia, a founding director of the Boston Guitar Fest and a teacher at both the Conservatory and Universität Mozarteum Salzburg in Austria — suggested his student, the up-and-coming classical guitarist Steve Lin for the 2006 holiday musicale. A classical guitarist was a first for the Club and was enthusiastically received by members.

Many of the 2011 SSC membership are avid music lovers, with opera being perhaps the most popular subset. Operatic tenor Davron S. Monroe, for instance, was the eagerly anticipated musicale headliner in 2010. He presented an outstanding program of operatic selections, holiday songs and gospel music. String trios, Broadway songsters, pianists and violinists, duets and soloists — as often as not unknowns with bright futures ahead — add the Social Science Club of Newton to their roster of resume performance venues. Meanwhile Club members enjoy reveling in a budding young artist's career and the boasting right of, "I saw her/him when. . . . " On the other end of the spectrum, established musicians like Gillian Rogell have also performed at Club musicales. Rogell is the founder of the Aspinwall Hill Chamber Music Foundation and an internationally acclaimed violinist who played the viola for the SSC with her string quartet in 2004.

After music, a love of literature has accompanied the ladies of the Club through the decades. A popular approach to the culture of the day was through this lens. Perhaps most amusing, especially from a modern-time point of view, was Clarissa Smith's 1898 paper entitled "Effect of Good Literature Upon Character." Some years later, in 1904, Helen Clark spoke on "Modern Drama." She included the works of Ibsen, Maeterlinck and Yeats. In the discussion that followed, Orinda Hornbrooke "strongly denounced the presentation to the public of plays dealing with moral and mental disease and degradation." A year later Grace Weston headed a symposium on the novel. She spoke on "Tendencies in Modern Novel Writing"; Adelaide Blodgett, on "The Psychological Novel"; Mary Speare, on "The Religious Novel"; and finally Harriet McIntyre on "The Historical Novel." The papers covered the aims, trends and leading exponents in each genre. Orinda Hornbrooke, always outspoken, got in the mix in 1907, writing on "Poets Laureate of England," explaining the evolution of the selection process from Chaucer to the present day.

The interest in literature produced other noteworthy papers. In 1938 Gertrude Dennison lectured on "The Poetry of Thomas Stearns Eliot" and expressed her belief that "Eliot today is outmoded." Mary Montague Powers spoke on "The Origin of the Bible" and Louise B. Fuller about "Cultural Boston." Beverley Lovell considered "The State of the Arts a Century Ago" for the 100th anniversary of the Club in 1986. The paper included the lines, "Think your way back to 1886. I want each of you to consider that you are much as you are today, a woman of enthusiasm, compassion, integrity, [and] curiosity."[4]

In addition to the interest evoked by such broad subjects, there has been extensive curiosity about the biographies of famous people, especially of course famous women. In 1994–95 the year's theme was "Women in the Arts." Caroline Bloy spoke about Sarah Orne Jewett whose writing focused on the situation of women during the late 19th century. Jewett was a feminist and a mentor to Willa Cather. Jewett also was the first woman to be given an honorary degree by Bowdoin College. The critic Josephine Donovan states that, "Women were depicted as self-sufficient wives, independent widows and spinsters," and that the central concern in Jewett's work develops from her intimate awareness of the limited emotional, economic and social conditions of women; most of her stories deal with women's efforts to transcend their condition." Quoting Lillian Faderman, Bloy states that Jewett was a "conscious, articulate feminist." And Duscha Weisskopf contributed a paper in 1995 on Sigrid Undset, the Nobel Prize winning novelist who is best known for her depiction of the unusually determined and independent figure of Kristin Lavransdatter. The value place on literature by the Club continues to this day. Each meeting is begun with either a selection of poetry or philosophy chosen and read by one of the members.

Not far behind their love of books comes the Club's interest in the visual arts. In 1900–01 Mable Hall organized a class around the work of the British art critic and social philosopher John Ruskin (1819–1900) who had died the previous February. They had four meetings, with Miriam Pearce leading the discussions, to study "Ruskin in connection with the great movements of the 19th century; [Ruskin in conjunction with] social movements; [Ruskin in conjunction with] art; and [Ruskin as] Interpreter of Nature and the Religious Movement." The Club's interest in Ruskin and also William Morris (1834–1896), who himself was an artist, writer and socialist, continued for more than half a decade.

The papers in 1906, for instance, focused on the work of Ruskin and Morris. The interplay of the arts and social movements was of great interest to the Club, so that their study of the two Englishmen came naturally. As part of that season's presentations, Adelaide Blodgett spoke on "John Ruskin." A week later Eliza Hamilton took up "Social Theories of Ruskin." The season continued with guest speaker Maird Sommers' talk on "William Morris, the Craftsman" followed by Grace Burton's paper on "The Socialism of William Morris." Further evidence of the depth of interest in this area is the 1906 yearbook which contains a unique offering: a suggested reading list of eight books by and about Ruskin and Morris. The following spring Mary Montague Powers' 1907 paper on "Art Museums" covered the role, goals and history of museums as well as the timely observation: "We must regret the removal of our museum from Copley Square but, wherever it may be, let us give it support not only financially but in interest and appreciation."

As recently as the 1994–95 season the Club's interest in the arts again was worthy of a full year's consideration. "Women in the Arts" included Jean Husher's paper on "Mary Stevenson Cassatt" who — in addition to her outstanding, well known works —painted a mural for the Women's Building of the 1893 Chicago World's Fair. Emily Hubbs Scott followed with a presentation on "Women in Photography." She began by quoting Naomi Rosenblum who said that photography gives "women a chance to have a state of absorption and wonderment that nurtures imagination and enriches life" and gives them freedom since "photography is unencumbered by many of the conventions that restrict traditional arts."[5] Dorothea Lange, the well known photographer of the Depression, is quoted as saying that portraiture is "a profession to which women are especially adapted." Emily herself is a professional photographer.

The last presentation of that year was by Anita Abeles writing on "Anne Whitney: Her Life, Her Labors, Her Legacy." This distinguished 19th century sculptor created "Child With Calla Lily Leaves" for the 1893 Chicago World's Fair. A replica was cast for the city of Newton by a friend and installed in 1902 (the original was donated to the Children's Museum in 1932). But in 1991 a vandal removed the cherub from the fountain. Abeles became interested in Whitney when she spearheaded the restoration of the fountain in 1995. It is located in the island carved out by the intersection of Chestnut and Valentine Streets in West Newton.

Although we cannot know how many members had private art collections, we do know that in 1991 member Sarah Buchan Jewell donated 118 works of Qing Dynasty court art from 19th century China to the Museum of

Fine Arts in Boston. The collection was bestowed upon her grandparents, Mr. and Mrs. Edwin Hurdconger, first U.S. ambassador to China, by the Empress Dowager Cixi. The collection includes paintings, prints, ceramics, textiles, calligraphy, photographs and metalwork.

A natural offshoot of the members' investigation of their paper topics was support of the public library system, in Newton and well beyond. Up until the last decade of the 20th century Clubwomen were heavily dependent on doing research in libraries. Although Newton boasts that its first library, all 165 books, opened in 1798, that facility was private. By the time the Club was founded, the Boston Public Library, which pioneered the notion of 'book lending,' had been open 32 years, and the Newton Free Library just 16. It was dedicated in 1870. Its value as a community resource, especially to women with aspiring intellects who could recall a time *before* lending libraries, cannot be overstated.

Through the years interest in public libraries engaged members. In March 1892 a Miss Bullard of the South Boston Free Library spoke on the relationship between the public libraries and public schools. There was also a paper in April 1904 by a member on "The Use and Abuse of Libraries" and among the abuses listed was too much fiction! Most recently, in 2000, member Margaret Sudbey, herself a one-time librarian at the Newton Free Library, gave an overview of public libraries entitled "Librarians: from Dewey Decimal to .com." Sudbey wrote that, "Librarians viewed themselves as engaged in a program of social betterment among those less fortunate." This was also the sentiment when in 1920 a guest speaker acquainted the Club with the fact that libraries were an important factor in helping immigrants adjust to life in their new country.

Along with education initiatives, financial contributions to libraries far and wide across America constitute the Club's first acts of outreach. Anne C. Purple quotes from the 1903–04 Annual Report that "in many a lonely spot in the south, the earnest, intelligent but poor seeker after truth opens one or more of the 3000 books sent by the SSC and blesses the name written therein." The Club's involvement with library start-ups across the country probably began with their positive response in January 1896 to a petition from Everett, Washington to all women's clubs in America to help them start a public library by donating a single book. The Club complied, and in so doing it entered into a flurry of contributions to new libraries all over the country — North Dakota, Oklahoma, Indian Territory in Alaska. Thanks came from "the mountain whites of Tennessee." Because there is no indication in the Club records of an organized effort to identify communities that might need their (modest, always) assistance in getting a public library off the ground, it seems that they merely, and readily, agreed to help when asked.

The Club's dedication to the public library system came full circle in the late 1980s when the Newton Free Library acquired all existing Club records. Ever since then, the Newton Library has archived and preserved record books, papers, photographs, tape recordings and Club memorabilia in their Special Collections Room — in the vault, no less. The high regard with which the Club holds libraries was repaid with the highest tribute a public library can give — to hold in trust works deemed of enduring value to the community at large.

Note: This section is based on Club Record Books, volumes 11–14.

Philanthropy and Other Outreach

by Marie Baroni Allen

In the annual report for the 12th year of the Club, Ethie M. Howe, the secretary, reflected, "Let us not rest upon our laurels though we can scarcely avoid gratification in the past records of mental, social and practical work, but let these encourage and inspire us to higher ideals, broader range, more unselfish and impersonal views, more earnest philanthropies." The next fall the Club adopted its current motto, "privilege is obligation." As demonstrated throughout its history, the Club applied this obligation not only to Newton but also to the nation and the world.

In 1985 Club member Anne C. Purple presented a paper that summarized the Club's finances during the first 100 years. She wrote:

Many appeals for funds were made because of a special concern of one of the members and their interests were varied.

For example in 1890 an appeal was made for a contribution towards a monument in memory of Mary, mother of George Washington and they voted to give $2 from the Club funds. Through 10-cent subscriptions, $25 was raised for a proposed Medical Department for Women at Johns Hopkins University. There were a number of requests for books to establish libraries from across the country and they always gave generously. As the century turned, Berea College in Kentucky was the recipient of both money and reading matter.

The Club's giving reflected the times: in 1917, $200 was voted from the sinking fund to help the children in warring countries, $100 to Syrian and Armenian funds, $50 for Belgian Relief and $50 for French Relief. In addition, $50 was given to the YWCA for war work.

During this period the Club omitted some meetings and the printing of the yearbook so that those costs could be applied to the war effort, thus $50 was given to the War Camp Community Fund. In 1919 at least one meeting was held at the YWCA so the members could participate in 'war work.'

Although much of the relief giving was for international causes, the Club also addressed national crises. In January and February 1937 the Ohio River overflowed its banks causing a disaster that devastated five states. That year the Club sent relief funds to Jeffersonville, Indiana, which was particularly hard hit. Around this time Club members also supported the 'books for seamen' drive and individually provided hospitalized veterans with playing cards, books and other gifts.

According to Ida Clyde Clarke, author of *American Women and the World War*:

Women have had a large and a very important part in the success of practically all of the societies included in the Allied War Relief Organization. Many of them were organized and are operated by women, and there are none in which women are not working as auxiliary or active members. Many organizations of women devoting themselves to various lines of work, immediately upon the declaration of war in Europe, turned the full strength and power of their organization to war work, while numerous new associations were formed within a short time after war was declared.

This was true of the Social Science Club of Newton. Reports from 1938–1942 indicate donations totaling $175 for the support of the Chinese Relief Fund and the Chinese Industrial Co-ops. In 1940 a War Relief Committee was formed and Sarah Buchan Jewell was appointed chairwoman. The Club's practices mirrored the times — once again the number of meetings was reduced to save money toward the war effort: contributions were collected for the United Nations Relief Fund; $1780 was given to the War Bond Drive of the Newton Federation of Women's Clubs; $14.25 was sent to Fort Devens to refurbish the sunroom; and $14 was designated for seeds

Typical minesweeper's glove, World War II.
(Knitting and Sewing, H. Doran Co., NY, 1918, p. 95)

for Britain. In addition to monetary support the Club's women put their hands and backs into their philanthropic endeavors. They shipped close to 2000 books to army camps and four cases of clothing to British Relief. Throughout the war years they knitted and crocheted for the war effort, providing at least 50 pairs of minesweeper's gloves. In 1947 the women were provided free wool to knit items for American Aid to France.

The philanthropic efforts of the Club changed with the cultural changes of the 1960s. The finance committee report of January 3, 1968, states, "As philanthropic giving has fallen off considerably this committee has asked members of the Club to review our philanthropies." Thereafter the giving was focused on monetary gifts, primarily the annual scholarship.

Hawaii, the Hampton Institute and Newton
by Marie Baroni Allen

The students of the Hampton Institute in Virginia benefited from the philanthropy of the Club for many years. A review of Club financial records shows that the annual gift of $70 was for an American Indian scholarship. What led the Club to support this school in Virginia rather than one closer to Newton?

The founders of the Club were typical of Victorian women in that they were affiliated with religious institutions. Although we don't know the religious affiliation of all the founders and early members, we do know that their ideologies were steeped in Protestantism and that three of them had close links to two Newton Corner churches. Charlotte Grosvenor Whiton Calkins and Mary Whiton Calkins were respectively the wife and daughter of the Rev. Wolcott Calkins, pastor of Eliot (Congregational) Church, and Orinda Althea Dudley Hornbrooke was the wife of the Rev. Francis B. Hornbrooke, pastor of the Channing (Unitarian) Religious Society. An early member, Melissa Creegan, was the wife of the Rev. Charles C. Creegan, secretary of the American Board of Commissioners for Foreign Missions.

It was the American Board of Commissioners for Foreign Missions that supported the 1819 Boston departure of the ship *Thaddeus* en route to the Sandwich (Hawaiian) Islands. Eventually this Board sent 12 companies of missionaries that included ministers, teachers, printers, farmers and physicians who trained and prepared for their journeys at a school in Cornwall, Connecticut.

"Their presence was of tremendous importance in guiding the affairs of the Island-kingdom according to democratic, if somewhat Puritan, New England ideals. Their names, many familiar to Boston and the Social

Science Club, were to become prominent in the history of Hawaii: Bingham, Thurston of the original group, Judd, Dole, Castle and Cook, some of whom were not ordained ministers but were associated with the mission."[6] Although these families were important and many of the men became officials of the Hawaii government after the death of King Kamehameha III, one family that would have a 90-year connection with the Club was that of Richard Armstrong (1805–1893), Hawaii's Minister of Public Instruction from December 6, 1847 to July 1, 1855. While he was in Wailuka on Maui, his sixth child, Samuel Chapman Armstrong (1839–1893), was born. Samuel attended Oahu College before transferring to Williams College. After graduating in 1862 he went to Troy, New York, where he mustered a regiment of Union troops and was commissioned as Captain Armstrong. During his military career he was captured at the surrender of Harpers Ferry, fought in the Battle of Gettysburg, commanded the 8th U.S. Colored Troops, was part of the siege of Petersburg and was commissioned as Brevet Brigadier General in 1865. In that year, the Bureau of Refugees, Freedmen and Abandoned Lands, known as the Freedmen's Bureau, was made a department of the United States government. Armstrong was made a freedmen's agent providing for the needs of ex-slaves in 10 Virginia counties. In addition he was made superintendent of schools over a loosely defined area of Virginia.

Early on, Samuel Armstrong realized that, "The education of Freedmen is the great work of the day; it is their only hope, the only power that can lift them up as a people and I think every encouragement should be given to schools established for their benefit." In 1867 he suggested to the American Missionary Association, the greatest financial power at that time interested in the education of ex-slaves, that they fund a school in Hampton, Virginia. The Association agreed to purchase the estate "Little Scotland," and Armstrong was appointed headmaster of the new school[7] that within a few years also educated American Indians and was to become known as the Hampton Normal and Agricultural Institute and, much later, Hampton University.

Armstrong decided that the school needed to include the industrial and

Earth science class at Hampton Institute, 1899.
(Library of Congress, Frances Benjamin Johnston Collection)

traditional educational model used at the Hilo School in Hawaii. Since the school was to be tuition-free he needed to raise considerable funds. "As early as 1867 Armstrong foresaw the coming need for friends in the North and took several trips thither, quietly getting himself introduced to a few influential people here and there."[8] Among those from whom he garnered monetary support was Harriet Hemenway. It was through her introductions that

> he was able to approach and know charitable Boston. On January 27, 1870, his first public meeting was held in the Music Hall, Boston, under the auspices of the Hawaiian Club of Boston presided over by Governor Claflin and attended by many of the philanthropic people of Boston. This meeting marked the beginning of a two-month campaign that was the first of a series that extended over a period of twenty years. Hampton took its place in New England as a charity of recognized worth. Clubs or committees were organized which pledged themselves to send a fixed sum yearly; a scholarship or a small sum of

money which paid the tuition of one student for one year and established a personal relation between giver and recipient was a favorite means of giving.[9]

An additional mechanism for raising funds was his establishment of the Hampton Jubilee Singers who toured in the North from February 1872 to June 1875 to raise $200,000.

Just as Armstrong had hoped, he found he could count on support from the Greater Boston philanthropists among whom many were from Newton — the Channing Sunday School, the Eliot Church Sunday School, Ellen D. Jackson, Samuel S. Ward, Mrs. E. N. L. Walton, William Claflin, the Judson Mission Band of the Newton Centre Baptist Church, the Freedman's Aid Sewing Circle, the Women's Educational Club of West Newton and the Social Science Club of Newton.

Both of Armstrong's fund-raising methods attracted the attention of the Club. For many years the Club gave an annual donation of $70 needed for the tuition of an American Indian student at Hampton. The bond between the school and the Club was strong. On occasion the scholarship recipients would visit Newton and, as late as January 1929, the Hampton Institute Quartet entertained the Club with a selection of spirituals.

Note: Janice Morgan presented a paper, "The Newton-Hawaii Connection," on December 3, 1991. This is the story of John Palmer Parker and the Parker Ranch, the world's largest privately owned cattle ranch, measuring more than 250,000 acres. In 1809 at the age of 18, Parker left Newton and went to sea on a whaling ship. When he reached the Big Island, King Kamehameha granted him permission to remain on the island where he spent his adult life and was a central figure in the development of Hawaii.[10]

Returning to Nature — Again and Again

by Duscha Schmid Weisskopf

Expanding the Club's concerns to include conservation and the environment dates to the Club's earliest days. Beginning innocently as a love of nature, SSC members often wrote about — and therefore advocated for — subjects with serious political as well as social overtones. Motivated by a desire to 'spread the word,' they wrote about issues affecting the health and well being of the physical world. This was political outreach — first endeavoring to educate the membership and through them, consciously or not, they sought to influence their husbands and their cronies, that is, the voters.

Mary Lathrop Tucker spoke in 1903 about the Charles River with regard to the disposal of garbage, much of which was at that time simply dumped into the river. Over the years her devotion to the environment expanded greatly and the Club benefited — in 1910, she spoke on "Conservation and Waterways"[11] and in 1913 she asserted in a talk on "Inland Waterways of the United States" that "the first thing to be considered is the forestation of headwaters." Also in 1913 Tucker introduced a resolution, ratified by Club members and signed by the president and secretary of SSC, to be sent to President Woodrow Wilson. It protested the use of the Hetch Hetchy Valley of the Yosemite National Park as a water supply for San Francisco. It was to no avail — President Wilson gave in to developers and signed the bill destroying what John Muir had described as early as March 25, 1873, in a Boston newspaper, as "a grand landscape garden" of sublime beauty.

As head of the Club's conservation committee, Tucker continued over the years to fuel members' thoughts on the environment, giving a talk in 1920 on "The Land and the People." She warned listeners that, "The attitude of modern nations toward their natural resources, including our own, has been most inexcusably wasteful since the days when the pioneers were obliged to cut the trees." Incited, the Club members decided to formally enter the political arena in the only way they could — with their collective pen. A resolution was passed and forwarded to President Warren G. Harding demanding that the National Parks be left undisturbed, and in 1922 a letter from the Club was sent to senators and representatives in Washington concerning the protection of water rights in Sequoia National Park. As a keen advocate of conservation, Tucker seemed able to link almost any issue to her fervent feeling. In 1921 for example, Tucker spoke on disarmament, saying that "it underlies all conservation work in the broader sense."

As early as 1904 the Club became concerned about the gypsy moth, and from then on through 1948, there were frequent speakers from the Massachusetts Forestry Association. Guest speakers from the MFA addressed the Club concerning not only insect control but also the entire question of forest conservation. In 1920 the Club voted for a state and federal bill "to reforest 250,000 acres of idle lands in Massachusetts," while in 1922 a resolution was sent to Congress supporting the purchase of national forests by the federal government every year. In 1928 the Club gave $100 to the Society for the Protection of New Hampshire Forests to help in the purchase of land near Franconia Notch. Conservation continued to be the subject of concern for many years. In 1940 a guest speaker lectured on the "Northeast Timber Salvage Administration and the New England Forest Emergency"; in 1945 there was a special comment on the importance of victory gardens and in 1948 the chief forester of Massachusetts spoke once more on forest conservation.[12]

Concern with the environment motivated the Club to learn more about the earth in general. For example papers were written by at least two members on the subject. Mary Lewis Speare discoursed on "The Development of Life Through Geologic Periods" and Emma Moore wrote about Darwin, "that most profound and diligent seeker after truth the world has ever known." Moore quotes Darwin: "The main conclusion will be highly distasteful to many. But we are not here concerned with hopes and fears, only with the truth as far as our reason permits us to discover it."

Gardens on the other hand were a more domestic way of being involved with the earth. Gardening like music was a beloved avocation. Close consideration was given to "What Makes a Garden" and to "Garden Aristocrats." In 1937 the Club had the privilege of hearing Dr. Donald

Wyman, the head of the Arnold Arboretum in Jamaica Plain, speak on "The Greatest Garden of Them All," meaning of course the Arboretum itself. A discussion on Newton's activity against Dutch elm disease[13] was followed by a talk on "Conservation in Our Own Backyard" by Dorothea Harrington.

The subject of gardens continues to appear into the new millennium. In 2007 alone two papers dealt in part or full with landscape design when the year's theme was "Footprints in the Sands of Time." Then president Susan Kaplan wrote about "Mount Auburn Cemetery," noting

> In 1829 the Massachusetts Horticultural Society was formed, which resulted in bringing about the beginning of Mount Auburn Cemetery. Seventy-two acres of rolling woodland on the town line between Cambridge and Watertown was purchased. The property was a colonial farm named Stone Woods, but it was known as Sweet Auburn after a mythical place in Oliver Goldsmith's poem, *The Deserted Village*. It was frequented by Harvard students, neighbors, and others, including Ralph Waldo Emerson, who thought it "most picturesque . . . magical."
> The combination of cemetery and experimental garden gathered support, and in June of 1831 the Massachusetts Legislature issued the charter to permit the formation under the name of Mount Auburn.

Later that year Dyanne Ridill, herself a landscape design enthusiast and member of the Massachusetts Design Council (part of the U.S. Garden Federation), delivered a paper on "Beatrix Jones Farrand: Advancing a Landscape Career Through a Hub of Social Influence." This biography of Farrand, a landscape architect who studied the accomplishments of Charles Sargent and Frederick Law Olmstead before starting her own firm, could serve as a metaphor for the Club's own conservation inroads — observe the masters, use your circle of influence to aid in your mission, strike out and make a difference.

Orinda Hornbrooke, who served as president of the Club from 1903 to 1904, inspired the women to take a lively interest in the fate of birds (see

Chapter One). Hornbrooke, offended by the use of bird feathers in millinery fashion, embarked on a one-woman campaign to educate those around her to this abuse and so eradicate the harvesting of birds for their feathers. She remained an indefatigable advocate of "our feathered friends" to the end of her life. Other speakers on birds were Howard H. Cleaves, a nationally recognized member of the American Ornithologists' Union, who spoke on "Experiences with Wild Birds" and explained the valuable work being done by the Union's conservation committee in preserving forests, adding that "sometimes he felt that our whole wild country was in the process of being reduced to park-like territory." He was also one of various advocates of birds to warn against pet cats. A paper by Margaret J. Snider on Charles J. Maynard (1845–1929) of West Newton (*see* pp. 79–82) directs attention to him as one of the first conservationists of Newton. She cites him as writing that, "West Newton Hill is covered with houses, Oak Hill is being cleared of woods while the cedars in the cemetery have been cut down and the homes of the herons there were but a memory. Can we wonder that we are losing birds?"[14]

Of course not every paper delivered on the state of the environment was political. Some have simply been appreciations. In 2005 Marygrace Barber gave a paper on "The Honeybee Colony: A Masterpiece with Assistance from some Masterminds," a history of the beekeeping industry beginning in the U.S. in the 1800s, from primitive honey use to modern beekeeping. After all, where there are birds there must be bees.

Note: This section is based on Club Record Books, volumes 11–14.

From Branches to Beethoven. The Life and Times of Carleen Hutchins, Luthier in the Light of Science

This paper by Gretchen Friend was presented on March 12, 1997, under the theme "Out on a Limb." Carleen Hutchins was a neighbor of Gretchen Friend at her summer home in New Hampshire. Edited and abridged by Duscha Weisskopf.

Born in 1911 in Springfield, Massachusetts, Carleen Maley lived in Montclair, New Jersey [during her childhood]. Most of her playmates were

Gretchen Friend
(Photo by Emily Hubbs Scott)

boys and her favorite activities included camping, collecting leaves, insects and the like, and raising silkworms and snakes. She was given a bugle when she was eight and from the age of ten worked her way through Girl Scout camp as a bugler. While at camp she cultivated a strong interest in entomology. Carleen had also developed an interest in woodworking. When she was six years old she was given a plane, a saw, a hammer and a T-square. When it came time to start home economics in sixth grade, her mother enrolled her in shop class instead, very unusual for a young lady in the 1920s.

She played first trumpet both in the band and orchestra at Montclair High School and upon graduation entered Cornell University where she pursued entomology, graduating in 1933 with a degree in biology. During the summers beginning in 1931, she was an instructor in nature and woodcrafts at the National Girl Scout Leaders' Training School. One day at the camp she went out, chopped down a poplar tree and made a canoe paddle and soon afterwards made a pair of snowshoes as well as a pack basket from an ash tree.

Carleen became a student assistant at the Brooklyn Botanical Gardens and in 1934 started her career as a science teacher in private schools. In 1938 she moved to the Brearley School in Manhattan where she taught science and sometimes woodworking to elementary students.

Beginning in the early 1930s she started visiting Lake Winnipesauke. A couple of years after purchasing lakefront property there in 1941, she cut up 30 to 40 pine trees that had blown down in the 1938 hurricane and took them to a sawmill. She designed a house and hired carpenters who framed the house and laid the rafters. When she told them she wanted to build with them they laughingly dismissed her but when she returned with wood cut up to their specifications they were impressed and let her join the crew in laying the floors and putting up the paneling. It was in New Hampshire that Carleen Maley met Morton Hutchins and they married in 1943.

After working in a school in Hell's Kitchen, she returned to Brearley and it was during her last four years there (1945–49) that events led her into work as a luthier and acoustician. The music teacher at the school founded the Amateur Chamber Music Players. Carleen Hutchins loved chamber music and tried to play the trumpet with this group but the trumpet was too loud and they needed a violist. She learned to play the viola as she said, "adequately — they would tolerate me." As an accomplished woodworker she decided to make a better instrument since her viola was a cheap one.

In 1947 Hutchins bought blueprints, a book and a few instructions from a Russian violinmaker. She spent two years on the project and brought the instrument to the Swiss luthier Karl Berger. She asked his opinion of her viola. He took her question seriously and proceeded to dismantle her viola piece by piece. When he was finished he handed her the pieces and told her, "Now go and make it better." Thus began six years of study with Berger. She worked on a total of about 30 instruments between 1949 and 1955. Then in 1955 when Berger was slowing down he sold her the remainder of his wood.

During the time she was studying with Berger a friend introduced her to Frederick Saunders, a retired Harvard physicist who had been conducting research on violin acoustics since the early 1930s. President of the Acoustical Society of America, he tried her viola. After speaking with Saunders and reading some of his articles, she realized how she could help him. The only thing Saunders had been able to do was to work with musicians who came with instruments as they were. In his experiments he didn't dare change anything except to take a penny and put weight on the bridge. What she offered was to build instruments on which he could make actual changes, like the position and size of the f-holes or the height of the ribs. Hutchins pushed ahead with her plans to make experimental instruments and soon Saunders was writing her with advice on how to make instruments with flat tops and explaining the physics involved. They collaborated on more than 200 experiments. For many instruments made by Hutchins, Saunders plotted loudness curves, playing notes to their breaking point and recording decibel output to find out the power of the instrument in various ranges. Hutchins learned much about the physics of the violin as well as the acoustics.

In 1960 Saunders encouraged Hutchins' plan to set up an electronic laboratory of her own for testing instruments. This nationally known expert acknowledged that their relationship had gone full circle: he had been asked about his association with the work of Carleen Hutchins and she had become famous in her own right after her first *Scientific American* article, "The Physics of the Violin" in 1962. She made the cover of *Scientific American* with her 1981 article.

Hutchins had made the acquaintance of Rembert Wurlitzer and Fernando Sacconi, a fine Italian instrument maker and restorer and leading authority on the work of Antonio Stradivari. He joined the Wurlitzer firm in 1950. For Hutchins' first Guggenheim Fellowship in 1959, Wurlitzer wrote an encouraging letter of recommendation, saying her measurements "may quite likely lead to a scientific approach to the making of superior bowed instruments." Hutchins won a second Guggenheim in 1961.

Hutchins worked with Sacconi who urged her to follow as closely as possible the methods he had evolved from the work of Stradivari — the molds, the designs, the tools and the ways of using them. One of the biggest boons to her research was the opportunity in 1962 to test the plates of the Wirth Stradivarius violin which was dismantled for repairs.

An eminent physicist said about Hutchins, "Her greatest contribution to violin making is that she doesn't keep secrets. When she finds out something she tells the world about it. She is so willing, so anxious, to share her ideas and techniques." The traditionalists scoff at the idea of a scientist having enough feeling to create an instrument worthy of Mozart and the other masters. To some science and music seem too unrelated but they meet in the work of Carleen Hutchins — musician, violinmaker and scientist.

Note: Carleen Maley Hutchins, violin maker and pioneer in the exploration of violin acoustics, died at the age of 98 on August 7, 2009, in her home in Wolfeboro, New Hampshire.

Endnotes

1 Knox, Bernard, *The Oldest Dead White European Males*, W. W. Norton, New York, 1984.
2 Social Science Club, Record Book, Vol. 1, January 9, 1962.
3 SSC, RB, Vol. 15–16, February 1, 1950.
4 SSC, Papers, Vol. 23–25, February 12, 1986.
5 Rosenblum, Naomi, *A History of Women Photographers*, Abbeville Press, New York, 1994.
6 SSC, Papers, Vol. 3, March 27, 1946.
7 Talbot, Edith Armstrong, *Samuel Chapman Armstrong: A Biographical Study*. Doubleday, Page and Company, New York, 1904, p. 159.
8 Ibid., p. 162.
9 Ibid., p. 222–225.
10 SSC, Papers, Vol. 4, December 3, 1991.
11 SSC, RB, Vol. 9, March 30, 1910.
12 SSC, RB, Vol. 15–16, December 1, 1948.
13 SSC, RB, Vol. 15–16, March 12, 1947, and February 4, 1948.
14 SSC, Papers, Vol. 2, February 4, 1976, p. 5.

CHAPTER FOUR

DIVERSITY WITHIN AND WITHOUT

by Anne McKinnon Larner

From their earliest meetings, the women of the Social Science Club of Newton discussed the hot topics of the day. High among those topics were the issues of immigration and the status of minorities, particularly blacks and American Indians. While the discussions were civil and polite, they were sometimes pointed and the women were seldom unanimous in their views. On occasion those assembled would split into two or more camps; at other times a lone voice would make strong exception to the point of view presented. One must play detective to uncover the views of the membership in different years because few papers before 1960 have survived and the summaries in the Club's minutes vary in both the detail provided and clear distinction between the perspectives of the presenter, the recording secretary and the membership. As the Club matured more care was taken that the secretary record, not opine on, subjects discussed, but, unfortunately, less space was devoted to recording the reactions of the members.

Immigration: From Heated Debate to Personal Experience

In March and April 1889 when the first spirited discussions on immigration took place at Social Science Club meetings, the gathered women were all native-born citizens of the U.S. and of western or northern

European heritage. A hundred years later in 1989–1990 when the most recent extended series on immigration in the Club's history took place, the year-long program included a panel of four Club members speaking on their personal experiences as immigrants, and the roster of Club members included ethnicities not present a century earlier. But differences other than the change in Club makeup are most striking. Early papers more often voiced strong points of view and the audiences were seldom reluctant to challenge the presenter. In recent years papers have focused on educating the audience on a subject or issue and seldom take a strong position on a controversial topic. Discussion is restrained. The women of the 21st century are no less passionate than their predecessors but the role of the Club in women's lives has changed substantially, with members today having many other outlets for their strong advocacy and fierce debates.

In 1889 the issue at hand was the 'Chinese Question.' Club member Mrs. William Andrews [first name unknown] Brown, a defender of free immigration for the Chinese, was the first presenter in a series of discussions. She read a pamphlet to the assembled members. The broadside contained "an earnest defense of the Chinese, comparing them most favorably to other immigrants, praising their fidelity, industry and respect for age." Brown contended that the movement against Chinese immigration was led by labor organizations that feared the competition of less expensive labor.

No sooner had Brown concluded on that March day than Orinda Hornbrooke rose to oppose. She is quoted in the meeting's minutes as stating that there is "real cause for fear [the Chinese] would overflow the country." The real question is not "What will we do with the Chinese, but what will the Chinese do with us?" Hornbrooke then enumerated her concerns about "the spread of immorality, opium habit and the dreaded disease, leprosy." She also spoke of the Chinese enslavement of women and the cruelty of their men. She cited Archdeacon John Henry Gray, a former resident of Hong Kong for 20 years, as her authority. She ended by quoting a Bayard Gaylins that "the Chinese are 'the most debased people on the earth. Justice to our own race demands that they shall not have a foothold in our orb.'"

For three more meetings the focus on Chinese immigration continued. First a guest speaker who had lived on the west coast and had intimate experience with Chinese immigrants praised their cleanliness and ability as servants but questioned the Chinese ability to progress or to be 'amalgamated' with others. She supported limiting numbers immigrating. Pro-immigration talk dominated on April 17, focusing again on the pamphlet Brown had presented in March. Finally on April 24 Brown read her own fact-filled paper in defense of Chinese immigration, underscoring the rich history, high ethics and strong social values of the Chinese people.

The minutes note that Lucy Sawyer supported Brown's position, underscoring that contracts are not needed with the Chinese. Their word is their bond. Catherine Hobart read a letter also supportive of Chinese immigration.

The intensity of the discussion and the differences of opinion are not surprising, as the Chinese Question was a topic of much public debate at the time. In 1882 Congress had passed the Chinese Exclusion Act, the first major act to limit America's open door policy, which severely limited Chinese immigration for the next ten years. As the women gathered to hear the discussions that spring, the time was approaching for either renewal or rejection of the exclusion of Chinese immigrants.[1] Renewal in 1892 settled the question for another decade but a critical shift in the countries from which American immigrants originated was already occurring and would soon stir debate about additional limitations on immigrants entering the United States. That accelerating change would increasingly influence the discussions within the Social Science Club over the coming decades. Between the 1880s and the 1890s the percentage of American immigrants arriving from northern and western European countries was cut almost in half while those arriving from eastern and southern Europe more than tripled. In ten more years the numbers arriving from the east and south would be more than double the numbers arriving from the traditional north and west of Europe. This change unsettled many people.

The question of immigration returned in January 1892 as Clarissa Smith presented a paper on current policy and issues of concern. She summed up by asking, "whether the time has come for excluding immigrants?" The rambling discussion that followed ranged from debate about the wisdom of preventing emigration at the source to discussion of colonies of Swedes and Icelanders in Maine to how great an importance should be put on encouraging English-speaking immigrants rather than non-English-speaking newcomers. The minutes recorded no consensus but clearly the members were more open to restrictions for immigrants than in their discussions just three years earlier.

Even when not the explicit topic of the day, the topic of immigration bubbled to the surface entwined with other subjects. When guest lecturer, fellow Newton resident, and son of SSC member Ruth E. Ripley, Professor William Z. Ripley of M.I.T. spoke to the Club in April 1894 about the issues in the cities, he ended up advocating that the best approach for dealing with our out-of-control cities was to limit the less desirable immigrants from entering the country and, simultaneously, to disperse those who do come to areas outside the city.[2]

And on January 30, 1895, when the subject before the Club was "Strikes and Labor," the discussion following the presentation turned to immigration. Mary Lathrop Tucker stated: "If we should exclude the laborers who go into our sewers, who would be found to do such work for us?" Mary Stetson then invoked the name of Senator Henry Cabot Lodge, well known as an advocate of restrictions on immigration. Others advocated that newcomers should be restricted from voting, while yet another group worried out loud that our prisons and poor houses were filled with foreigners.[3] A growing sense of fear was evident.

In April 1896 the Club was back to a more formal look at the subject of immigration and Orinda Hornbrooke presented a paper, "A Study of Our Foreign Population." Her view was consistent with the nativist platform of the day. She defined all who came to these shores before the Revolution as 'natives' and all who came later as 'immigrants.' She outlined the problems triggered by the country's 'open house' policy. "The decline of the native stock in the face of foreign arrivals was noted." In concluding her presentation, Hornbrooke stated: "It is time we have a tarif [sic] to protect the citizenship of our country."

A lively discussion followed with Emily Potter, Ellen Sondericker, Mary Billings and Harriet Bowman each supporting some restrictions against undesirables or at least denial of suffrage to certain immigrant groups. Emma Merrill looked at both perspectives but her 'Christian duty' pushed her compassion to the fore. Lucy Sawyer in turn stated, "Charity should be subservient to order." The minutes note Mary Tucker "held independent views, wishing to encourage immigration, while believing in the restriction [on] citizenship and [serving in elective office]." She believed better legislation would allow us to cope with existing evils.

It was more than ten years before the subject of immigration surfaced again in Club records. On April 21, 1907, Maud Sommers, a guest, presented a paper titled "Immigration." Sommers made the case that America's role in the world was to harbor people from many places and provide them the opportunity to "achieve material and moral well-being." She stated that immigration had been a blessing, allowing tremendous growth in our industrial life. But there had also been a dark side. She complained the penalties were too low for steamship companies who ignore the laws that prohibit transporting "idiots, imbeciles, the feeble-minded and those afflicted with epilepsy, consumption and tuberculosis." She also believed that conditions must be upgraded in steerage accommodations on transport ships and also in the congested factories and slum districts where newcomers worked and lived.

Between 1911 and 1919 there were many presentations and discussions at the Club about immigrants, but the focus was consistently on how to improve assistance to the newcomers. The questions were about what type of educational and social services best served the populations. During this period the issues of restrictions and exclusions did not surface or at least were not recorded in the minutes. This puts the Club squarely in the period's progressive sector, following the lead of the Settlement House movement on this issue.[4]

In March 1911 Ella Hobson of Dorchester came to speak and strongly advocated for both compulsory education for all and manual training for immigrants and Negroes. Later that month Mabel Frost of the Women's Municipal League spoke on issues in the city of Boston with its high volume of immigrants and the difficulty in properly assisting them. That December Edith Guerrier, a guest speaker, described terrible conditions in the Jewish and Italian quarters in the city with young mothers in need of instruction and assistance and a critical shortage of public nurses. In early 1912 Jeannie Hamilton gave a paper on the vulnerability of young women who in unprecedented numbers were working away from the protection of their homes and open to exploitation. Two years later A. E. Dodd told how his North Bennet Street School was started to address the need of immature boys and girls who were primarily immigrant and who were required by law to be in school but who also were required by need to contribute to the family earnings. He stated that so far this experiment in schooling had been very successful.

In this period (1885–1915) foreign-born residents comprised between 27% and 32% of Newton's population. Since the children of immigrants were often born in the United States and thus not counted among the foreign-born in the census, immigrant family members comprised a significantly higher

Newton school children on Chapel Street in Nonantum, c.1900.
(Courtesy of Jackson Homestead and Museum)

percentage of the city's population than the census figures record. In the early years Newton's immigrants were mostly from Ireland, Canada, and England — English-speaking countries. Beginning in the 1890s Italians began arriving along with Scandinavians, followed by Russians and Poles. This change in Newton's make-up must have had an effect on the city and its institutions.

But Club members gave no presentations about immigrant life in Newton. Their discussions don't mention the countries from which immigrants migrated to Newton nor is there reference to specific immigrant issues in Newton. It is only from a few quiet references by guest speakers that it is clear that much of the Club's work with the Nonantum Vacation School, the Nonantum Day Nursery and the Newton School Department's work through the Stearns School was with the children of immigrant families.[5] In the many references to the Vacation School and the Day Nursery, there is little detail on the background of the families. A short report by Grace Weston in the 1911–12 yearbook on behalf of the Social Service Committee indicates that the Nonantum Day Nursery is "able to reach out a helping hand to the hundreds of Italians who are moving into our city." It is one of the few recordings by the Club that mention the ethnicity of the local families being helped by the Club's good works. The distinction that does surface a number of times is class.

By 1919 Americanization programs were sweeping the country. There were subtle but distinct changes in presentations to the Club. Of the ten presentations given to the members between 1919 and 1925 on immigration, just two were papers from members. The other eight were talks by outside experts, seven of them on Americanization. The focus was on assimilation, conveying American values to the newcomers and building loyalty toward the United States. Education was still front and center but discussion of what contributions immigrants brought to this country had receded to the background. Literacy was a top concern as was counteracting propaganda from either subversive groups (especially anarchists and Bolshevists) or from unscrupulous vendors out to earn a buck at the expense of too trusting newcomers. Representatives from libraries, the University Extension Service, the Open Forum National Council and the North American Civic League for Immigrants spoke to the Club.

All provided either services or opportunities for immigrants with those listed being the most sympathetic to the heritage and values the immigrants brought with them.

One of the two members' papers in this period was read on March 30, 1921, by Ethel Dow Stubbs. Her topic was "Racial and Economic Effects of Immigration." The recording secretary quotes Stubbs' description of various waves of immigrants as follows. From 1783 to 1880 they came "for the most part sturdy Northmen — Irish, Scotch, Welsh and Norwegian"; later "hordes of Jews and Poles came"; and finally "the people from the southern European countries." Stubbs shared her concern that there were so few restrictions on immigration that "any Bolshevist or criminal finds little difficulty in entering the United States." She presented data for 1920 of the number entering with 'loathsome diseases' or 'mental deficiencies,' about 2900 daily.

Today we bristle at Stubbs' insensitive descriptive language contrasting "sturdy Northmen" with "hordes of Jews and Poles" but in 1921 such descriptions were mainstream and readily recorded in the Club record with no evidence of anyone's discomfort.

Stubbs stated that the approach of immigrants had changed since the war — they now came with an attitude, looking for high pay and easy hours. She continued that about one-third of the U.S. population was currently of foreign birth. The forecast was for 2.5 million more in 1921.

The second member paper in the 1920s on immigration was presented by Emma Merrill, "The Immigrant: An Asset or Liability?" presented February 18, 1925. Merrill repeated the theme of earlier presenters that immigrants came in waves, those coming earlier being far superior to those coming after 1880. "These latter immigrants have failed to assimilate, coming to gain money and living any way in order that a return to the homeland may be made as soon as possible." She too stressed the need for education, spoke of the brotherhood of man and that it's up to us to make our country what it can be.

There were no further papers or guest speakers on immigration again until after World War II. This is not surprising since the restrictions enacted under the Immigration Act of 1921 and the National Origins Act of 1924 triggered a dramatic drop in annual immigration to the United States to a rate less than 10% of its previous level. But there was an extensive series of papers and guest speakers on both China and Japan in those intervening years. The emphases were on current political and social struggles in these countries as well as glimpses at their histories and cultures. From the records of the meetings the discussions on China in 1927 were most respectful and had no charged language or stereotyped vignettes as the turn-of-the-century Club discussions had.

In a similar vein the paper in April 1930 by Alice Cary on the "Women of Japan" presented a broad summary of Japanese history and traced the emergence of women from "positions of ignorance, servitude and surveillance to lives of freedom and usefulness." In conclusion she asked her audience to pay attention and give "sympathy to the Japan of today, that rising power which politically is at our gate."

In November 1935 Professor Bruce Hopper of Harvard University, speaking on "The Far East from the American Point of View," traced Japan's rapid change from feudalism to industrialism and stated that for the first time "we have in Japan a potential enemy." He spoke about what we should be doing to meet the challenge Japan presented. He believed in outreach, student exchanges and general social engagement to break down stereotypes. Despite his basically positive approach he did paint the old stereotype of the Japanese as lacking originality while being "the world's masters in making copies superior to the original."

Hopper was followed in December by Mabel Fitts on "The Roots of the Japanese Character" and in February by a paper entitled "Japan Discovering the World" that focused on Commodore Perry's opening of Japan and the years since. Although none of these talks or papers on Japan painted an exaggerated picture of a menacing people, they did underscore the rising political and social tensions in that part of the world.

In addition, in the same period of time a Mrs. Andrew J. George, a guest speaker, several times presented lengthy synopses of the political situations in both Japan and Germany. She expressed concern regarding developments in both countries.

On February 25, 1948, Club member Margaret Bacon Ambler writing on "Other Minorities" spoke of Jews, Southwest Mexicans and the Japanese.

Between 1900 and 1929 a large number of Mexican laborers, uneducated, underpaid and indigent, came into the U.S. "This second generation of Mexicans in this country has not been assimilated and their maladjustment breeds violence and open warfare." She spoke of attempts in Texas through the services of the Extension Service and Good Neighbor Commission to address discrimination against people of Mexican heritage.

She went on to discuss the issues of Japanese immigrants. Despite discrimination and the exclusions under the 1924 Immigration Act, the Japanese on the West Coast had been remarkably adaptable:

> The Americans tried to assign them a fixed inferior position
> of a caste nature, but the Japanese refused this inferior place
> and strove for equal opportunity on the basis of merit. Pearl
> Harbor and the consequent mass evacuation of the Japanese
> only served to stiffen their loyalty to their adopted country.

In conclusion Mrs. Ambler said that prejudice and fear which leads to animosity against these minority groups must be overcome in order that we, as a country, may profit by their contributions and they, as individuals, may benefit through our understanding and tolerance.

It would be 40 years before the topic of immigration surfaced again. The 1989–90 year was devoted to the issue. Not all the papers from that series have survived. It is clear in reading the papers of three that are preserved — Jean Husher's "Emigrantin Fra Norge Til Amerika" (excerpted at the end of this section), Doris Blake's "Portuguese-Speaking Immigration" and Elizabeth Everett's "Armenians" — that the frame of reference of the Club members in 1990 was significantly different from that of their predecessors 100 years earlier. In the late 19th century the women of the Club, whether supportive of immigration or not, wrote and spoke about groups of faceless, nameless people with little reference to the impact on individuals and families of the strain and hardship of their starting a new life in a new country. Portraits of individuals, when they existed, were stereotypical and lacked much humanity regardless of whether the speaker intended to favor or disparage the particular immigrant group. The perspective taken was to focus on the impact of the new arrivals on their country. Descriptions were broad generalizations about the character of various nationalities. In contrast the women of the Club in 1989–90 were very graphic about the experience of the immigrant: what it felt like and how they managed. They made the stories personal even when they were not about their own families. They also spoke of the positive contributions made, even though certain groups such as the Portuguese-speaking immigrants came with very limited levels of literacy and significant poverty, and did not have an easy time.

The highlight of the 1989–90 series on immigration was a panel of four members in March 1990 telling in their own words their experiences as immigrants. Duscha Weisskopf (at the time Duscha Scott) came to the

United States in the 1930s as a young teenager. She told the harrowing story of having lived in Munich with her family at the time of Hitler's Roehmputsch when approximately 2000 people were killed. An opposition leader, Wilhelm Schmidt, had a similar name to Duscha's father.[6] Although her father was a musician and music critic and not a political activist, he was arrested by the Nazis and shot before they discovered the mistaken identity. Duscha's mother emigrated to Austria where she remarried and was eventually able to migrate with her whole family to the United States.

Duscha Weisskopf
(Photo by Garrow Throop)

Dorothea Jeanloz arrived in Montreal, Quebec from Switzerland in 1946 with the thought of returning home after a while. She stayed in Montreal for a year, moved to Maryland and eventually to Boston. She moved to Newton in 1954. Another member, Lilo Willoughby, came from Germany in 1952 to study democracy at the University of Wisconsin. Before coming to the U.S. she had been very active in the Labor Movement in Germany. She met and became engaged to her future husband while studying here. They returned to Germany, settled there and Lilo began teaching. Eventually however, they came back to America. She loves the United States, especially its political system. To her democracy is the basis of all else.

And finally Thelma Fleishman outlined her journey with her husband and children from South Africa in 1964 after Jews and Catholics had been declared second-class citizens in their homeland and their sons had reached the age for being inducted into the army. At the time immigration from South Africa was strictly limited and Thelma's husband had to find a job in the U.S. that no American would take in order to qualify the family for the move. He became the medical director of Tewksbury State Hospital. A major difference she found between South Africa and the U.S. was that in South Africa she found herself very often faced with moral decisions. For example, back home she depended on the police for her personal safety yet knew they were responsible for terrible abuse and discrimination. This presented a constant issue about whether and/or how to use their help. Life in the U.S. presents few such decisions.[7]

Emigranten fra Norge til Amerika

This paper by Jean M. Husher was presented on October 18, 1989, under the theme "United States—A Nation of Immigrants." Edited and abridged by Anne Larner.

Jean Husher
(Photo by Emily Hubbs Scott)

The four nations that make up Scandinavia — Norway, Sweden, Denmark and Finland — are very closely tied together in history. The social, economic and religious conditions that generated widely felt unhappiness in the early 1800s were nearly identical in each country. All four countries were Christianized, more or less by the sword, before 1200, becoming Lutheran before 1550. Lutheranism, originally a dramatic departure from the Catholicism of the Renaissance, had by 1800 turned itself into a highly bureaucratic, authoritarian and conservative arm of the Scandinavian states. The church through its local pastors controlled every aspect of the peasants' lives. No dissent of any kind was tolerated on pain of severe fines and jail sentences. However Lutheranism requires that every person be able to read the *Bible* in the vernacular language, so every parish provided a schoolmaster to teach the children to read, and often to write and to do simple arithmetic. Once anyone can read the *Bible*, however, it is really impossible to control how he might interpret it. Consequently dissenters appeared on the scene from time to time in all four countries. They were systematically banished, fined, deprived of property, jailed or committed to insane asylums. This worked until news of a free America filled with opportunity spread from valley to valley and village to village.

In addition to a rigidly reactionary state church, there was in each case a large landed aristocracy which from time immemorial had allotted the peasants specific plots on which to grow food for their families in return for service of various types. Peasants were allowed to graze their horses and cows on the common land and to cut wood for their fires in the forest. Later than elsewhere in Europe, the wealthy Scandinavian landowners discovered more efficient ways of farming than the medieval practices in use. Landowners dismissed peasants, usually giving each outright the land allotted his family for generations past or an equal amount elsewhere. In the course of this, grazing and woodcutting rights were cancelled. Further, under the law in all Scandinavia, upon death of the father, all of the peasant's property must be divided equally among the surviving children, male and female alike, with a widow allowed but a room in the house where she had previously been mistress.

For reasons not fully understood, population grew rapidly all over Europe during the 18th and 19th centuries in spite of little improvement in sanitation and no shortage of wars and plagues. The resulting larger families caused multiple land division in each generation so that in only three generations farms were often too small to support a family and the peasant became a cotter or outright pauper. While England was able to absorb many who were forced off the land into its busy factories, the industrial revolution came late to the Scandinavian nations. In 1800, 90% of their populations remained on the land. By 1840 most peasants were living marginally with no hope whatsoever of improving their lot however hard they worked. Two years of poor harvests due to drought in the mid-1840s was the final push to desperation. Although some had already left for America earlier, the numbers became enormous in proportion to the population from that point on.

And now we turn to look more closely at Norwegian immigration. More than 900,000 of its people left for America between 1845 and 1930. That total is not large in the vast story of the greatest folk movements in history but it is larger than Norway's whole population in 1800.

In 1800 Norway's population totaled only 885,000, of which 90% lived in rural areas. Two percent of the people were government officials, wealthy landowners and mine operators; 48% were middle-class farmers, artisans and small merchants; with the remaining 50% servants, day laborers, cotters and large numbers of paupers.

The following article appeared in New York City's *Daily Advertizer* on October 15, 1825:

> A vessel has arrived at this port with immigrants from Norway. The vessel is very small, measuring as we understand only about 360 Norwegian lasts, or 45 American tons, and brought 46 passengers, male and female, all bound to Ontario County where an agent, who came over some time since, purchased a tract of land. The appearance of such a party of strangers, coming from so distant a country, and in a vessel of a size apparently ill calculated for a voyage across the Atlantic, could not but excite an unusual degree of interest. They have had a voyage of 14 weeks; and are all in good health.

The little sloop was called the *Restoration*. The leader of the little band of immigrants and part owner of the ship was Lars Larson. They sailed up the Hudson River to Albany on one of America's earliest steamboats and then traveled by barge on the newly opened Erie Canal.

From the beginning many immigrants wrote home about their experiences and what life was like in America. Such letters were passed from family to family and village to village and sometimes were published in the newspapers. They were called "America letters" — enthusiastic advertisements for emigration that spread America fever all over Norway.

About ten years later most Norwegians from Kendall settlement [in New York] moved west to Fox River in Illinois to rich semi-prairie land with fewer trees to root out, but a few families remained behind, their homes serving as welcoming way stations for newcomers in the best Quaker tradition. Whenever immigrants arrived in New York without money, friends or work, the Norwegian counsul would pay their fare to Rochester, counting on Lars Larson, his wife and other Quakers still there to do the rest. Martha Larson, a busy mother of half a dozen small children by 1835, wrote wearily:

> Twelve Norwegians came here today and are now sitting at the table eating their supper. About two weeks ago there arrived from 90 to 100 people. They stayed at our house and my brother's house about a week and we furnished meals for nearly all of them. Most of them have gone to Illinois. There are still five families at our house of the first immigrants who arrived.
>
> Practically all of them came to us and we cannot help so many. We, of course, do what we can for them all. I have gone around town looking for work for them and Lars has taken many of them into the country. We spare no pains to make them satisfied.

Gjert Hovland was among those to sell his land in Kendall and move to Illinois. In 1835 he wrote:

> Six families of the Norwegians who had settled in this place sold their farms last summer and moved further west in the country to a place called Illinois. We and another Norwegian family have also sold our farms

132

and intend to journey this May to that state where land can be bought at a better price and where it is easier to get started. There are only enough trees there to meet actual needs. Cattle can be fed there at little cost, for one can cut plenty of hay. The United States owns an untold amount of land which is reserved by law at a set price for the one who first buys it from the government. It is called public land and is sold for $1.25 per acre.

The Fox River settlement was about 70 miles southwest of Chicago and it proved to be a fine choice. The land was very fertile and not forested, making it easy to cultivate. New settlers flocked to the entire Illinois River Valley over the next several years — Norwegians, too.

Johannes Nordboe wrote home from Fox River in 1837:

The land in the state of Illinois is largely prairie, with little woodland except along the rivers and creeks. The summers are extremely beautiful. Then the whole country, both woodland and prairies, is bedecked with grass and flowers of all colors. The summer may be compared to an earthly paradise, but the winter, on the contrary, may be likened to a mountain climate.

A few years later a sad chapter unfolded at Beaver Creek, south of Chicago. There an unscrupulous developer sold land that appeared dry at the time, but was actually marshy and malarial, to a group of 80 led by Ole Rynning. Most of the settlers died of malaria within two years including the 27-year-old Rynning.

In the 1840s Wisconsin became the new center for Norwegian settlers. The first to arrive came from Telemark and Numedal in south-central Norway, sailing from Drammen, 40 miles south of Oslo. One of the most important settlements was at Lake Muskego, south of Milwaukee, a location that also proved to be malarial with a number of deaths in 1843. Nevertheless the settlers prevailed and in time built a prosperous community.

Crossing the Atlantic was often a harrowing experience. Few Norwegians could afford other than steerage passage. Families were packed into the hold of the ship with bunks three tiers high and almost no room in between. Often they were expected to bring all or a major portion of their food, enough for eight to 12 weeks. Water was in short supply and often bad. If disease such as cholera broke out, daily burials at sea were the rule. The captain and crew often treated emigrants cruelly, with beatings and rapes common. English ships had the worst reputation on all counts and were avoided by many.

The first of four major surges of Norwegian immigration began immediately after the Civil War. Most in this wave consisted of families from rural Norway. They usually had a reasonable set of expectations based on widely circulated letters home from early emigrants and abundant advertising by newspapers of the provisions of the Homestead Act (160 acres if settlers stayed on the land for five years and provided improvements).

The second wave began in 1883 after several years of limited immigration due to a sharp depression. It continued until the early 1890s. Instead of families, almost two-thirds of those emigrating from Norway in this wave were young, single and adventurous. While most were ordinary laborers, this wave also included engineers, technicians, artists and other trained persons reflecting that Norway itself was changing but not fast enough to absorb the trained and the skilled. Those who were unskilled and poorly educated continued to go to the midwest and west to homestead or to work in lumber camps or mines.

A third surge began around 1900 and continued until the beginning of World War I in 1914. During this period Norway established its independence but Norwegian industry could not expand fast enough to absorb its ambitious people. The result was the United States gained Norway's best-trained youth.

The last and smallest wave from Norway followed World War I and tapered off quickly when immigration restrictions were enacted in 1924. The Great Depression not only ended immigration from Norway all together but prompted 32,000 to return from the United States.

Although homesteading in the west continued to attract some Norwegians, most newcomers arriving after the turn of the century went to the cities. By 1930 there were more than 63,000 Norwegians in Brooklyn and on Staten Island, New York. They worked in shipyards, in construction, were merchants and businessmen or engineers and technicians. For the most part they were solidly middle class and well paid. Others went to Chicago following similar pursuits or working as seamen, ship captains or ship owners on the Great Lakes. Still others settled in the Minneapolis-St. Paul area, working in the saw mills and flour mills or as merchants, bankers, bakers or businessmen. Seattle also attracted Norwegians, located as it is at the end of a deep fjord and surrounded by mountains.

Norwegian immigrants started their own Norwegian-language newspapers very soon after their numbers began to swell. The earliest was *Nordlyset* (The Northern Light) first printed in 1847 in Even Heg's log cabin at Muskego. By 1880 the number of Norwegian language newspapers swelled into the hundreds with communities from New York City to the northwest coast hosting such a paper. As late as 1940 there were still some 570 Norwegian language papers being published in the United States.

In spite of the fact that the early immigrants left Norway with bitter memories of a homeland where they could not earn enough to eat no matter how hard they worked, where no opportunity to change this was possible or where they were persecuted for their religious beliefs, their descendants are truly proud of their heritage and feel a closeness to Norway.

The Ladies and the Negroes: Advocacy, Ambivalence and Moments of Grace

From the very beginning the women of the Club had a very different relationship with blacks and the 'Negro Question' than they had with immigrant. The women had students and teachers from Hampton Institute as their guests at meetings and receptions in their homes and invited Booker T. Washington to speak to their Club. No immigrants received that respectful treatment until 100 years after the Club began. Yet side by side with a certain amount of respect was a decided ambivalence. And side by side with empathy and political support there was distance, a tendency to sentimentalize and a hint of fear or discomfort.

At the March 12, 1886, meeting Lucy Sawyer presented her paper on the "Political Status of the Negro." The paper itself no longer exists and the minutes are sketchy. There is a reference to the "present state of things in the South," verifying the wisdom of Charles Sumner's strong objections to actions during Reconstruction. Also mentioned is "the attempt of the whites to keep the colored race still despised" and concern about freedom of the ballot box in the south. Following the paper, debate arose about the effect of "hybridism upon the intellectual and physical vigor of the offspring." This subject resurfaces again and again over the next 40 years, underscoring the members' discomfort (and probably that of society in general at the time) with intimate relations between black and white.

Two weeks later a Mrs. Allen of the Club led a discussion on fraud at the ballot box in the south. While those gathered agreed that there was widespread fraud, especially efforts to keep Negroes from voting or to discount their votes, opinion was split on what might be done about it. Some counseled silence as the wisest course, believing that the situation would self-correct. Others strongly stated that silence unwittingly supports "the supremacy of the current tyrannical or oligarchical element in the South."

This was a post-Reconstruction period when white backlash resulted in social and political actions in southern states to return blacks to subservient roles. Meeting minutes indicate that Allen used the example of South Carolina's Eight Box Law to illustrate efforts to subvert the Fifteenth Amendment that had guaranteed all males of age the right to vote. Mississippi, Louisiana and South Carolina all had black majorities in the 1880s and led the way with 'creative' legislation to disenfranchise minority voters. The Eight Box Law was enacted in 1882. Its author General Edward McCrady stated bluntly in a *New York Times* interview several years later that "[T]he eight-box law was the result of an earnest and honest effort to secure the control of the government to the intelligence, education, and property of the state as against the ignorance and robbery of the Negro rule, without resort either to fraud or violence." [8]

The gist of the law was to require a separate ballot box for each contest and to disallow any distinguishing symbols on the ballots or any election worker to read a ballot to a voter. Getting the right ballot into the correct box and checking the desired name all necessitated being able to read. A wrong ballot in a box for a different office gave election officials the right to disqualify a number of ballots in that box. Voting by blacks fell dramatically following enactment of this statute. [9]

While the women focused primarily on election laws and efforts to throw out black votes, the issue of interracial marriage came up in discussion as it had earlier in the month and the minutes note that such marriage was noted by some at the meeting as "a thing quite against nature."

In early 1888 Club members spent time at a number of meetings from January to March discussing the state of education in the south for blacks and whites across all economic classes as the Blair Bill, then being debated in Congress for its third attempt at passage, became a subject of interest to the women. On January 4 Orinda Hornbrooke read a letter from Reverend A. D. Mayo, a national advocate for the Blair Bill, outlining the sorry lack of literacy in the south. The minutes note that in the south there were as many poor whites as Negroes at that time and it was stated that the whites "were much more degraded." On January 11 discussion continued but focused on the Blair Bill itself. The bill was the first attempt to provide federal aid to education by state, allocating aid based on comparative rates of illiteracy. Details of the discussion are sketchy but a series of meeting minutes make it clear that views questioning the constitutionality of the bill dominated that day and Anna C. Hardon is noted as stating that some southerners just want "to be left alone to take care of themselves." On February 1 supporters of the Blair Bill presented their arguments. Reverend Mayo was again quoted as the authority on the state of southern education. He is quoted as stating:

> The illiteracy of the southern states is absolutely appalling.
> [N]ot only is the illiteracy confined to the colored people
> and the poor whites but there is a great danger, unless

something can be done soon, that great numbers of the children of the better classes of the white people of the South, will be plunged into illiteracy — while the blacks and poor whites are better off in educational affairs now than before the war, the children of the better classes are absolutely worse off.

Discussion of education in the south died down, but through much of the rest of the year the women did focus on education of poor children closer to home, with particular interest in manual training.

In November of the same year Booker T. Washington, founder and head of Tuskegee Institute in Alabama, addressed the Club at its November 21 meeting. The professor spent from late October to mid-December that year in the New York/New England region both visiting schools and cultivating potential patrons. His topic for the members was recorded in the minutes as "The Condition of the Colored People in the South." He described how the post-war mortgage system in the south kept blacks tethered to their former masters via ever increasing debt. He closed by telling about Tuskegee and his efforts to unite "manual training and mind culture." While Professor Washington's full remarks are not available, his collected papers do contain an address made in Boston to the Unitarian Club during the same trip north that has an uncanny similarity to notes of his speech in the Social Science Club minutes.[10] It's reasonable to assume that Professor Washington gave pretty much the same speech in Newton as he did

Booker T. Washington in 1895. He was a guest speaker in 1888.

(Library of Congress, Frances Benjamin Johnston Collection)

in Boston. His references to the importance of manual training as part of the journey toward integration into full citizenship must have resonated with the women who were already becoming involved in that issue right in Newton. His strong support for his own *alma mater*, the Hampton Institute — and the importance of northern sponsors to sustain its students — may well have laid the first seeds of the Club's later financial support for that institution.

In February 1893 Emma Merrill presented a paper on "The Attitude of the Constitution towards Slavery." While the meeting minutes give no sense of the content of the paper, they indicate that discussion focused on "how the count of slaves was made for taxation and for representation." Given the ladies' fairly consistent support for education and civil rights for blacks, it seems odd from a 21st century perspective to have had a focused discussion on the accounting metrics for slave taxation and representation. But this is part of a pattern of support versus denial that existed for many years.

In February 1894 two papers at back-to-back meetings focused on "What the United States Contributed to the Moral Progress of the World" and the "Moral Development of England." Augusta Ballou saw the "lifting of slavery" in the U.S. as a "moral triumph because [it was] brought about by the people," while Fannie B. Coffin saw England's action to abolish slavery before the United States as a challenge for the U.S. to take stronger leadership on critical moral issues. Discussion following Coffin's presentation focused on our moral obligation to educate blacks.

A March series of four papers focused on "Mixed Races." The topics raged from Eurasians in India and 'half-breeds' in South America to "Mulattoes in the United States." "[I]n the brief discussion which followed [the last paper] it was shown that mulattoes are a weak race; that pure blacks had an instinctive horror of a mix with white blood and the idea of sending the Negroes back to the Indies had been superseded by the belief in a true education as the one solution [to] the problem."

At that same meeting Cornelia Jackson read a letter from Booker T. Washington answering the question, "Does a mixture of white blood improve the Negro?" Professor Washington's answer was affirmative. Summing up the meeting Club president Lydia Wellington stated that although the study subject was depressing, she had high hopes for the mixed races. "[R]eminding the Club that it is too early in our national history to form an opinion of the outcome of this great question, we should trust nature more, and believe that it is not working against the Great Original Plan. That it is too early to fully understand the laws of heredity, and that while waiting for the wheat, we should not be blinded by the chaff."

In December 1897 at the home of a Club member, the membership gathered to listen to Rev. Dr. H. B. Frissell, principal of the Hampton Institute, speak about the mission of the school and the importance of the financial support from women such as those gathered for this occasion. He brought with him two former Hampton students, one an American Indian and the other a black, who reported first hand on their schooling at Hampton and their subsequent work as both tradesmen and teachers for their own people. The talks were followed by entertainment by the Hampton Institute Quartet who lifted spirits with a number of very well received spirituals. Following the entertainment the members held a reception for their visitors from Virginia.

In February 1900 the women of the Club agreed to support a scholarship to Berea College, a co-ed college in Kentucky that had been open to both blacks and whites since 1869. Meeting minutes don't provide much background on this social action. The Club continued support for a few years. Interestingly, in 1904 Kentucky outlawed integrated schools. At that point Berea provided money to set up Lincoln Institute for black students and continued to support Lincoln for a number of years. Why the Club discontinued support to Berea was not noted in the records.

In the 1890s the Social Science Club became increasingly active in the Federation of Women's Clubs both as part of the state organization and by participating in the General Federation at the national level. The General Federation meeting in Milwaukee in June 1900 caused a stir that in turn enlisted the women of the Club in an extended action to redress what members saw as an egregious wrong.

In 1893 a Boston woman named Josephine St. Pierre Ruffin founded a club for black women called the Woman's Era Club. Its motto was "Make the World Better." There were black women's clubs throughout the country similar to the growing number at that time of women's clubs in general. In 1899 the Woman's Era Club became a member of the Massachusetts State Federation of Women's Clubs without incident and in 1900 Ruffin sought participation in the General Federation of Women's Clubs at their biennial conference to be held that year in Milwaukee. Prior to the conference, she was granted credentials through the Federation's normal process. Upon arriving in Milwaukee, Ruffin found herself barred from participation by the leadership of the Federation. The large Massachusetts delegation with strong support from Illinois, Utah and Iowa delegations worked hard, though unsuccessfully, to get Ruffin seated and recognized. *The Los Angeles Times, The Chicago Tribune, The New York Times* and *The Atlanta Constitution* along with the *Boston Daily Globe* carried prominent stories of the convention's 'color line' controversy for several days running. The president of the Federation, Rebecca Davis Lowe of Georgia, was cited by reporters as both expertly wielding the gavel and "outgeneraling" the New Englanders to keep Ruffin from being recognized.[11]

> The south is as determined as ever against the colored clubs, and the north is solid for them....
>
> The reorganization subject was disposed of this morning, when by a vote of 498 to 298 it was decided not to reorganize the federation.[12] The session was the most spirited in the history of the body, and so heated were the arguments and debates that hissing was indulged in at times, and on more than one occasion 50 women were on their feet shouting for recognition.

Mrs. Lowe broke a gavel trying to maintain order and finally appealed to her sisters to preserve order not only for the dignity of the body, but also that their husbands could not point to them with words that women cannot come together without quarrelling.

The detailed vote by state, for and against reorganization, respectively, included the following: Connecticut, for 0, against 1; Maine, for 6, against 0; Massachusetts, for 63, against 19; New Hampshire, for 7, against 0;

Rhode Island, for 3, against 1; Vermont, for 1, against 0.[15]

The Massachusetts delegation left for home disappointed and already strategizing how to gain support against a color line within the Federation. Lowe, on the other hand, had no intentions of being a gracious victor. The *Boston Daily Globe* of June 10, 1900 reported the following:

> It will be recalled that two months ago [Mrs. Lowe] congratulated Mrs. Ruffin upon joining the federation.
>
> This is what [Mrs. Lowe] had to say on the color question today:
>
> "Mrs. Ruffin belongs among her own people. Among them she would be a leader, and could do much good, but among us she can create only trouble.
>
> "In the South I have done considerable to assist in the establishment of kindergartens of colored children, and the colored women who have them there directly are all good friends of mine. I associate with them in a business way, but of course they would not think of sitting beside me at a reception or standing with me on the platform of a convention.
>
> "Mrs. Ruffin should go to them. She could become a leader among them. Among us she can never be more than what she is now, and if she is the cultured woman everyone says she is, she should put her education and talent to good use as a colored woman among colored women. It is the high-caste Negroes who bring about all the ill-feeling."[14]

Back in Boston Ruffin resumed her club activity and also took opportunities to explain in person exactly what had happened in Milwaukee.[15] As avid readers of newspapers and as well connected members of the Massachusetts Federation, women of the Social Science Club were no doubt aware of the controversy in Milwaukee soon after it occurred. But due to the lack of formal Club meetings between May and November, there is no record of discussion of the June events until

November 1900. The first inquiries noted in meeting minutes have Emma Barstow Bates asking for a report on the events in Milwaukee, referencing the published letters of Ruffin and a Miss Winslow, with the chair deferring the question to a later meeting. The issue was raised again at the next meeting and the chair stated that it would be discussed at the first meeting in January.

The evidence indicates the chair was buying time both to meet with other club presidents within the federation and also to figure out how best to keep this heated issue from dividing the Club. At the January 2, 1901, meeting, Club president Charlotte Calkins read a statement from a Mrs. West expressing concern over a lack of facts regarding the controversy. She also reported the views expressed at a prior meeting of club presidents that she had attended in Boston. She stated:

> [I]t was hoped that every club in the Federation would
> express condemnation of the judicial action of the
> [General Federation]; deliberate action on the part of
> *this* and every club in the Federation was advocated as it
> was thought the next Gen. Fed. meeting may be held in
> Boston in 1902, when representation by state, as favored
> by Massachusetts, may be the outcome of the meeting.

Discussion followed and it was agreed that the chair would set up a committee to formulate a solution satisfactory to the membership. The committee of Charlotte Calkins, Orinda Hornbrooke and Mary Lathrop Tucker reported back to the Club on February 6 requesting support for the following resolution:

> Whereas the Board of Directors of the GFWC refused to
> admit to membership the Women's Era Club of Boston
> previously accepted by its Executive Board,
> Resolved: that we the Social Science Club of Newton
> believe this action to be wholly unconstitutional and
> contrary to the spirit in which the federation was founded
> and as such to be condemned.
> Resolved: that the Board of Directors of the GFWC be

requested to acknowledge the constitutional rights of the
Women's Era Club by receiving to its membership said
club at the first opportunity.

Resolved: that a copy of these resolutions be sent to the
President and to the Board of Directors of the GFWC, to
the President of the Massachusetts State Federation and
the President of each federated club in Massachusetts.

Club members debated at length the language in the resolution,
particularly the use of the word 'condemn.' At the end of the discussion
the members accepted the strong language and the resolution passed as
originally presented. The Club followed through on sending copies across
the state to other clubs as confirmed by the many notations, meeting after
meeting for the rest of the year, of responses from other clubs and copies
of similar resolutions from throughout the Massachusetts Federation.

The skill of the president in selecting a committee that spanned the
political spectrum of the membership and included revered leaders is of
particular note as is her strategy and wisdom to align with other clubs.
The Club's initial silence on the issue suggests the membership was not of
one mind and the leadership needed time and some outside peer pressure
to bring about a united response. That Ruffin, who lived so close by (and
gave many papers before various clubs in the Federation), appears not to
have been invited to speak to the Club adds to the suspicion that the issue
was controversial within the Newton membership.

To offer some perspective on how divided opinion was at the time
regarding biracial socialization, Booker T. Washington did not support
Ruffin's position in the summer of 1900 despite the efforts of many
mutual friends to get him to speak in support of her. And 1901 was the
year Professor Washington himself caused a storm by dining at the White
House at the invitation of President Roosevelt, a social and political move
which made headlines and was criticized by many across the country. By
the yardstick of the time, both the members of the Social Science Club
and the Massachusetts women of the Federation were pretty valiant and
persevering in their actions.

While Massachusetts Federation activity continued fighting against a color line, Ruffin appears to have pulled back from active pursuit of the issue sometime in 1901. Up until a month or so before the 1902 biennial meeting of the General Federation, it appeared that Massachusetts would press the issue to let the states decide who would be seated from their state at the national meetings. Late in the game Massachusetts reversed that position. Club minutes note that the Newton delegation to the national gathering was "uninstructed" on April 12, 1902, to support the Massachusetts Plan, noting that some compromises were in the works.

In November 1903 Nellie Follett presented an emotional paper on her conversion from "a hater of the Negro race" to an admirer of its "noblest son, Booker T. Washington." She told of her visit to Malden, West Virginia, and Washington's early home. She met with a Madame Ruffner, the widow of the owner of the salt works where Washington had worked before he attended Hampton Institute. She also met with Amanda Johnson, Washington's half-sister.

> Booker Washington has proved a wonderful leader of his people, and has evolved the best method for solving the race problem. He has found that the black man may be raised from degradation . . . not by the franchise nor by political endeavor, but by making him a man. He was freed but lacks freedom.
>
> [Professor] Washington's plan for the uplifting of his race is impressed in three ideas as follows: Industrial education for the masses; the higher education for the few. The conciliation of the South so that respect shall be joined with desire for black labor. Submission and silence as to civil and political rights until such time as education and property shall be franchise essentials for both black and white.

The minutes report that, "By her stirring words the hearts of all were turned to the black brother struggling under the burden of oppression and hatred, made still heavier by his own ignorance."

The minutes also note a "slight discussion" and a "standing vote of thanks." The recording secretary clearly was moved by Nellie Follett's conversion and elaborate praise for Professor Washington, but it's unclear how others reacted. By 1903 a standing vote of thanks had become a routine response to presentations.

On February 11, 1914, Mary Evans Wilson, wife of Butler Roland Wilson, then the secretary of the Boston branch of the National Association for the Advancement of Colored People and a practicing attorney, was a guest speaker. The Boston branch of the NAACP was one of the few integrated branches of the NAACP across the country at that time and Wilson was one of its most prominent black leaders.[16] Club minutes over the years rarely described a speaker's race (and did not in this instance) but it seems likely that Mary Wilson was the first woman of color to address the Club. The meeting minutes outline her presentation:

> [Wilson] said segregation was the absorbing topic before the world today, and the Negro suffered most therefrom . . . . [She] asked for equal rights with other nationalities.
>
> She cited numerous instances to prove that the colored people were discriminated against in government departments in Washington, and she gave a severe [assessment] of the present administration, asserting that race prejudice and segregation were sanctioned by the government, and were rapidly growing.[17]
>
> In the favor of the race [she said] they had fought in all of the wars for the flag, that they spoke the same tongue, and that the hope of any people was in its best, not its worst element.

At the meeting of April 15, 1914, Club president Laura Drake spoke of her trip to Washington, D.C., and the opportunity she had to visit Hampton Institute in Virginia to view in person the good work being done there. Meeting records include almost annual letters from Hampton describing successes of each scholarship recipient the Club supported over the years. Members always enjoyed the first-hand reports of fellow members who were able to visit the school.

The January 24, 1917, guest Mary C. Palmer, president of the Newton Federation, spoke on the Sea Islanders of South Carolina. She described the town of Beaufort, which was "nine-tenths colored," as having delightful relations among the races, a feeling that could not be replicated in the North "for lack of understanding." She read several poems and Negro songs accompanying herself on the violin, and then delivered two dialect sermons "in an amusing manner" according to the meeting minutes. The only hint of how Palmer's performance was received is the language used by the recording secretary who termed the presentation as "delightfully interesting." It is difficult to interpret the lack of recorded comments. It is unclear whether the description of race relations struck the women as off-key or whether the dialect sermons made them uncomfortable. In any case, from the vantage of almost 100 years later the contrast among the various presentations, talks and discussions about blacks during the first two decades of the 20th century is very sharp, leaving unclear the perspectives of the members of the Club regarding black-white relations.

On February 9, 1921, Rosalind D. Lewis[18] read her paper entitled "The American Negro Problem." According to Lewis it was difficult for blacks in the north to find work but they had no trouble exercising the vote. In the south, on the other hand, there was plenty of work for blacks but they had no opportunity to vote. After Reconstruction, southern whites eliminated the blacks from active politics, "making the Fifteenth Amendment a dead letter. Even now the Negroes are not allowed to vote in sufficient numbers to influence legislation, and the great majority are not really fit to exercise the suffrage."

According to Lewis, education in the South was problematic for blacks — too few schools and a school year that was too short (from three to five months). Facilities were better in the cities than in the rural areas but the schools were very crowded.

Lewis spoke of Dr. W. E. B. Dubois, editor of *The Crisis*, and reported that he was opposed to the ideas of Booker T. Washington.

[Dubois] urges the colored people to fight for their rights

and not consent to be merely 'hewers of wood and drawers of water' to the whites.

Mrs. Lewis spoke of the evil of lynching and its demoralizing results, and said that swifter and sterner justice by the courts would tend to decrease it. There is now an anti-lynching bill before Congress, the first serious attempt to stop lynching by the federal government. One hopeful fact is that in 1920, there were 22 fewer lynchings than in 1919.

She also spoke of the 1919 start of a Boston chapter of the Urban League in which people of both races worked together to try to eliminate trouble between the races. She indicated that a labor shortage in the north in 1916–1917 drew a migration of blacks from the south to northern cities. Those blacks remaining in the south found themselves receiving more consideration than in previous years since the northern migration made labor more scarce in the southern states.

On February 24, 1923, Mary C. Merritt presented her paper on "Reconstruction and Adjustment." According to the minutes, she stated that some minds were bent on humiliating the south. The north was in turmoil as soldiers returned; roads and bridges were a mess from neglect. "Several million Negroes became free: ignorant men who wandered about the country knowing not what they wanted. [It was] a chance to test their freedom. Poverty was the lot of men reared in luxury for Virginia had been a battleground for four years."

Merritt suggested Andrew Johnson was not a good match for the challenge such times presented. "The Negro problem was immense. Homeless, master-less, ignorant blacks were everywhere. Those who did not work came under the laws of vagrancy, and death sentences for some of the worse crimes were enforced where insurrections were feared. Negroes were office holders, men who could not write their own name."

She continued that vast debts were being piled up for future generations to bear. There was at the same time economic disruption in northern markets. In 1871 President Ulysses S. Grant declared the South 'reconstructed' even though relationships between the races were "as far off as ever."

On April 23, 1924, Edward Murray East, professor of experimental morphology at Harvard, gave the one guest lecture in this period on immigration that did not focus on Americanization. It was entitled "Race Problems of the United States." First he spoke of the seriousness of the issue of Japanese on the west coast, with a birth rate much higher than that of the U.S. in general and their holding a very significant percentage of the irrigated land in the area.

He went on to state that the issue of the Negro race was "no longer of great importance." On the one hand he predicted that the race would decrease and end in another 100 years. On the other hand he saw mulattoes as an issue — higher intelligence, higher birth rate. "Mulattoes will become an issue." He underscored the value for the white race of the study of eugenics. The limited meeting notes state that he saw the solution as education not legislation.

Dr. East was an interesting choice as a guest speaker. Given their connections and breadth of reading on current issues, at least some of the Club members must have been familiar with the professor's views. East's original expertise was in plant genetics. His experiments with in-breeding and cross-breeding corn led to radical new methods of propagating that plant. After several decades focusing on plants, he began in the 1920s to apply his knowledge of genetics and heredity to the social and political arenas. In 1923, the year before he spoke to the Club, he published his first of several books in this area, *Mankind at the Crossroads*. In it he argues that there is scientific proof of qualitative differences among the races, especially between the black and white races. "And the situation that actually confronts is this: the Negro race as a whole is possessed of undesirable transmissible qualities both physical and mental, which seem to justify not only a line but a wide gulf to be fixed permanently between it and the white race."[19]

He states that all of his conclusions were based on scientific proof. The 1921 publication of results from tests performed on black and white army recruits was the primary proof he cited. He concluded that the pure

Negro was 60% as mentally efficient as a comparable white and a mixed blood Negro approximately 75% as mentally efficient.[20] Professor East saw himself as a scientist and not a racist. He came out strongly against miscegenation and saw it as not in society's interest. Unfortunately, although the record indicates that Professor East's talk stimulated many questions and comments, no detail about the audience reaction is in the record of the meeting. To have been a fly on the wall for that discussion would have been fascinating. One suspects the professor fanned the flames of some of the ladies' fears but also left more than a few Club members uncomfortable.

On January 16, 1929, the members of the Club and their guests gathered to listen to the Hampton Institute Quartet sing Negro spirituals. In addition to the entertainment, William Waddy, a 1928 graduate of Hampton, spoke of his time there and the importance of the strong relations between faculty and students. Another Hampton representative also spoke of the school's mission to train teachers to meet the growing needs of schools for Negroes.

A year later on March 23, 1930, Elizabeth Mitchell presented her paper, "The Contributions of the Races to American Civilization: the Negro." The summary by the Club secretary in the minutes includes the following information: "Imported [as slave] by the North as well as by the South, the Negro has always been a disturbing element in the [history] of the country. Neither in his own country nor in America has [the Negro] been a producer. He has shown no capacity for government, has exerted no strong influence on other races, and has been unable to stand alone."

Mitchell went on to make some sentimental comments about plantation days and stated that she "regretted the fact that although Negro servants still exist, these old relations are no more. [She] felt that miscegenation and low standards of morality have been most detrimental to the true progress of the Negro race and that the only remedy would be a social awakening."

Contradicting her earlier statements, Mitchell concluded that the Negro's contribution to our civilization has been "great." She named individuals from Phyllis Wheatley and Paul Lawrence Dunbar to W. E. B. Dubois and Booker T. Washington who had made significant contributions. She noted there were many younger members of the race who had gained prominence in various professions. "In closing Mrs. Mitchell expressed her belief in the church as a recognized power in uplifting the Negro and pleaded for tolerance for that race and gratitude for the many gifts which it has laid on the altar of our civilization." Again the notes give no indication of discussion or comments.

It was more than 15 years before the subject of black-white relations returned to the Club. On March 20, 1946, Rabbi Beryl Cohen of Brookline's Temple Sinai spoke to the Club on "Racialism and American Democracy." He stated, "Racism has brutalized men and nations. [It is] another atomic bomb hanging over us." He analyzed how physical differences can lead to beliefs of inferior and superior races and actions by one race to subjugate another. He stated his belief that racism threatened our freedom in the United States. He cited the enforcement of the color line in the armed forces. He advocated a return to the Bill of Rights and the principles of freedom, equality and justice. "[Rabbi Cohen] said that intolerance and arrogance have caused much trouble among peoples. 'We are sick, having a high temperature.' Now our one hope of liberty and justice toward all is in a better understanding of all races and a feeling of goodwill among nations." His talk was well received and inspired a lively discussion.

In February 18, 1948, Rosalind Lewis, who had spoken on the "Negro Problem" in 1921, presented another paper titled "Peace in Relation to Minority Groups: Negroes." She stated that the Negro problem had been with us constantly since the Civil War but that the nature of the problem had changed over time. Lynchings had steadily decreased. In the North there was residential segregation but easy access to schools and colleges and scholarship opportunities. Employment opportunities had improved since the war. There had been a number of successful experiments in interracial cooperation. Examples include the Springfield Plan; Johnson, Vermont; and Hopkinton, Massachusetts. The audience provided more examples during the ensuing discussion.

The last and most recent Club paper on blacks in the United States was delivered on January 28, 1970, by Lavina Chase Tomb. It was entitled "Black Power." From the vantage point of the early 21st century, we associate 'black power' in 1970 with an aggressive, edgy political movement and social action. Tomb had another perspective for her paper. She looked at a variety of philosophies and styles within the existing mainstream black political arena. She compared and contrasted Adam Clayton Powell's use of power (Big Daddy will take care of you) with that of Senator Ed Brooke (the Negro must win allies, not conquer enemies) and Carl Stokes (treat everyone the same). She went on to state that "America is the blacks' battleground. The revolution will have succeeded only when Black Power is *invisible* [sic] in this land."

There is no record of discussions or guest speakers on any of the tougher issues of racial tensions between white and black America since the late 1940s: Brown v. The Board of Education in 1954; Rosa Parks and the Montgomery Bus Boycott in 1955; Alabama Governor George Wallace's inaugural address in January 1963 with its infamous "segregation now, segregation tomorrow, segregation forever"; the murder of Medgar Evers in June 1963; Martin Luther King's "I have a Dream" speech in Washington, DC, in August 1963; the September 1963 bombing of the 16th Street Baptist Church in Birmingham that murdered four young girls; the murders of civil rights workers James Chaney, Andrew Goodman and Michael Schwerner in Mississippi in 1964; the murder of Martin Luther King Junior in 1968; widespread urban rioting and the subsequent 1968 *Kerner Report*; and Boston busing violence in 1974.

The Ladies and the Indians: From the Dawes Bill to Cjegktoonuppa (Slow Turtle)

In the past 125 years the women of the Club have discussed issues related to American Indians at 24 separate meetings. A few of those discussions took place in the early years of the Club but most (in fact 17) took place in the last 40 years. Race and ethnicity were often topics of heated conversations among the women from the Club's beginning in 1886 until World War II but the plight of American Indians was not usually included. Ironically in the modern era (post-1960) American Indians have been the one racial/ethnic group the members have researched, analyzed and reported on. It may be that the absence of a significant indigenous population in the Boston area made it easier to question and discuss without bruising sensibilities or creating disagreements among the members that might have been challenging to handle.

"The Indian Question" was the topic of the second paper ever presented to the Club (February 19, 1886). Harriet Stone wrote a puff piece extolling the good works of the federal government in dealing with what she termed a challenging issue. The paper does not survive and the minutes give scant detail but they do indicate that she praised the administration of President Grover Cleveland for having done more for the natives than any predecessor. Members of the Club objected to her conclusions since she presented no comparative data to support her statement and their personal opinions differed. In fact this discussion set the tone of feisty but civil give and take on controversial issues which was the rule for the early decades.

At the next meeting a week later Ellen Weston read an abstract of the Dawes Indian Bill and requested support for the measure that was then before Congress.[21] The discussion revealed a number of Club members more sympathetic to the plight of the American Indians than Stone had been the week prior and more than a bit skeptical of the just administration of laws or treaties with the Indians.

> [T]he question arose whether there was any more reason to believe that this law would be executed [more justly] than had been . . . the numerous solemn treaties with the Indians in the past. . . . . [A]t the time these treaties were made, there was as confident an opinion among the people of the U.S. that justice . . . was finally to be done the Indians [as there seems to be now about the Dawes Bill].

The women requested that the bill be reread at the next meeting. A blank page in the book of minutes and no further mention of the Dawes Bill in subsequent weeks leaves the outcome of the request for support unknown. The Dawes Bill did become law the following year, setting incentives for tribes to accept allocation of Indian lands to individual tribe members at a set number of acres per adult male and a lesser amount for others, with surplus land being sold on the open market.[22]

It was six years before the subject of 'Indians' returned with Alice Farquhar giving a paper on "The Indian Question" in January 1892. She traced subsequent problems after initial Indian encounters with colonists to a failure back in the early 1600s of colonists to define relationships with the natives.

> And then for forty years there was a gradual effort to give to the Indians the place in the country which justice demanded, but the European settlers as they increased in numbers grew reckless and drove the Indians before them into the interior. Then followed an account of the gradual development of the policy that treated the Indians first as allies, next as foes, then as subject nations and finally as people to whom we owe everything we can give in the way of civilizing and Christianizing influences.

She went on to speak of Indian rights under U.S. law, the work of the Bureau of Indian Affairs, the role of philanthropists and the progress in Indian education in recent years. Farquhar finished by quoting from the Mohawk Conference regarding the needs of the Indians.

A lively discussion followed, centering on political corruption in government management of Indian Affairs, the need for greater funds and the importance of education. It was from this presentation and discussion that the proposal came for the Club to sponsor a student at Hampton Institute which at the time served both black and Indian students and served as a critical teacher-training center for both black and Indian schools.[23] The many thank-you letters from Hampton students and from the staff at the Institute recorded in Club records indicate that the scholar supported each year for the first several decades was an Indian. His name, tribe and background would usually be described in the correspondence. The

Institute was forced to drop the Indian program in 1923 due to dropping enrollment but the annual scholarship support continued into the 1980s.[24]

Club interest in Indian political and social issues was sufficient in 1892 that in subsequent meetings during the winter, Club members brought attention to newspaper articles about Indians and the news alerts were noted in the meeting minutes.

In March 1894 the members held a series of discussions on "Mixed Races." One paper focused on Eurasians in India, another on the issue of blacks and whites 'amalgamating' in the United States and two papers focused on Indians. Almira Etta Crosby wrote "Indian Half-Breeds in South America, especially Brazil" and Susan Baker wrote about "French and Indian Half-Breeds in Canada and Northern Maine." There is little record of the contents of the papers and the meeting notes record that the discussion centered on black-white liaisons.

It was 32 years before the topic of Indians surfaced again. In 1926 Caroline H. Leeds spoke on "The Growth of the West." Her focus was the white settlers. She gave a traditional white person's description of Indians' menacing frontier families and named the native tribes as a challenge for settlers along with wolves, bears and forest fires. "Slowly the Indians were quelled and finally General Wayne marched to battle and brought about the first lasting peace on the frontier."

It's worth noting that in 1929–30 the theme for the year was "The Contributions of the Races to American Civilization." The groups covered by members' papers or by guest speakers included the Spanish, Italian, English, Dutch, Scandinavian, East Indian, Japanese and the Irish, as well as Jews and Negroes, but no mention of any indigenous peoples.

It was not until 20 years after Leeds 'paper that another Club member would speak on Indians. In January 1946 Christine Jameson presented a paper on "Land of the Amerindians," the first paper in a series on territorial expansion of the United States.[25] She began with a general history of Indians in North, Central and South America, noting their advanced cultures and lamenting that "the priceless records of that civilization have been generally destroyed." She went on to focus on North America. Her perspective as reported in the Club's record book was generous, respectful and sympathetic to the Indians:

> These Indians were not aggressive. But the treatment they received taught them much. Perhaps the men who settled in New England and Virginia were not as cruel as Columbus in the Bahamas or Pizarro in his conquest of Peru. But it is not a record to be proud of. And the Indians retaliate[d] with King Philip's War and the French and Indian War. Only the Quakers treated them with kindness and fairness.

She ended by noting how Indians had served with great honor in the recent world war.

Twenty-five years later Club members returned to the topic of American Indians. In 1970–71 "The American Indian" was the topic for the year. Six papers and a guest speaker comprised the year-long program.

The 1960s and early 1970s were times of much unrest and political agitation in the U.S. — student teach-ins and political action over Vietnam; civil rights marches, racially motivated murders, urban riots and the assassination of Martin Luther King; and the increasing aggressiveness of the newly founded American Indian Movement (AIM) that focused on poverty, housing, treaty issues and police harassment. It is in this context of fairly steady political action that the women again took up the issue of the Indians in America.

In December 1970 Virginia Horne began with an historical piece on the highly developed civilization of the Aztecs, lamenting the destruction of a "great civilization" by Spanish greed and cruelty. Patricia Ingersoll then focused on an early view of North American Indians by French Jesuit missionaries, using diaries and papers of several missionaries: "In summary, the early French Jesuits found more than they realized at the time: a well-developed society, struggling against a harsh climate, which had a definite social system and customs and a religion that was varied but strong."

A month later Margaret Ball brought a personal touch by focusing on local Indians and bringing in her family's history of encounters with

Indians in Deerfield. Margaret Snider then spoke of the iniquities inherent in white settler expansion westward, broken treaties and the forced migration of Indian tribes, concluding: "The Indian has never recovered from the degradation of his defeat by the white man."

Two remaining paper writers and a guest speaker all focused on understanding the then-current call for redress of grievances against the native peoples and what might be done. Anna Perkins in February 1971 spoke of the historical misunderstandings and frustrations between Indians and whites as the cultures clashed. Laws passed with one intent were often administered by the Bureau of Indian Affairs with another. "The Indians gave in with passive resistance not really understanding what was happening to them. Now they are trying to come into their own with many plans for self-help programs. To quote from the weekly newsletter of the Boston Indian Council, 'I hurt. I do not want to be a little you. I want to be a big me.'"

While the following month Dorothy Jeanloz, in her paper, critiqued the Bureau of Indian Affairs as being run by Indians who were not in touch with the reservations, she did see slow progress. She stressed the need for leadership training as the key to speeding up progress. She clearly supported self-determination for the Indians. "The Negro wants a fair share of the white man's world. The Indian wants to be left alone with recognition as a separate nation. Instead he has to take his grievances to the [out-of-touch] Bureau of Indian Affairs."

From the New England Hobbyist Association,[26] Mrs. W. Ronald Head ended the series, speaking on "The Place of the Indian in Contemporary America." She spoke of fragmentation within the 'red power' movement with half-breeds and white radicals taking over and pure bloods deserting the group. She agreed with several of the paper writers that Indians do not want to be a part of white culture. "What our society has to offer is very inferior in their minds. They are happier in their way of life than we are in our cluttered and messed-up one: they see us from the underside."

She also spoke of Indian values. "The Indian [is] peaceful. He is not above nature. He is part of nature. He does not compete with his friends and relatives as it might embarrass them if he advanced ahead of them.

The white man gets. The Indian gives. The Indian comes and goes as he pleases even if it slows down the process of earning and learning."

Unfortunately, throughout the series of papers and speakers, meeting notes record no flavor of the discussions although several times notes do state that lengthy discussion followed.

In 1988–89 "The North American Indian in the 20th Century" was the program topic for the year. Alison T. Umbsen began the series in October 1988 with a paper on "Background on the North American Indian in the 20th Century." With the perspective of being able to look back over 100 years of history, Umbsen criticized the effect of the Dawes Act that the very first members of the Club debated during the Club's inaugural year. She wrote that the legislation had a negative impact on American Indian culture, language, traditions, art, identity and spirituality by attacking the underpinning of the tribe, communal land.

> The Dawes Act of 1887 was supposed to at least start the [Indian] nations on their way to citizenship. It was instigated by a Massachusetts senator who was a member of the senate committee in charge of Tribal Affairs. This act was to provide for the allotment of lands in surety to the various tribes. In essence the act was really meant to force the Indians to cease their tribal ways, especially their feelings of ownership of the land which had been theirs for centuries. In return they would be given [individual tracts of] land for farming. Anything left over would go to the white man.

At other meetings Mary Baker spoke about contemporary native artisans and Carolyn Bloy presented "The Native American Church." In the spring of 1989 Nancy O'Brien wrote about the Plains Indians — the Blackfeet, the Crow, and the Cheyenne — and Thelma Fleishman and Duscha Weisskopf, respectively, wrote about "The Five Civilized Tribes" who ceased operating as tribes by the early 1900s and the Pueblos who remain true to their traditions today. The variety of topics taken together gave the members a sense of the varied experience of Indians in America and the social complexity and long history of the many Indian peoples. But even more important were the guest speakers who spoke to the members from their personal experiences.

In November Jimmy Sam, a Choctaw Indian and executive director of the Boston Indian Council, spoke to the members about both his own personal story and his work with the Council. He showed a video on the Council's program providing social services to Indians that spoke to their culture. Urban Indians, he reported, are at a distinct disadvantage when far from the tribal supports found on the reservation. He indicated how difficult it is to generalize about Indians because the tribal experiences and cultures differ considerably.

In December following her presentation on several Indian leaders of more recent history, Emily Hubbs Scott introduced her guest speaker, Slow

Slow Turtle, a Mashpee Wampanoag medicine man.

Turtle (also known by his tax name John Peters, Sr.) who was the executive director of the Massachusetts Commission on Indian Affairs and also a supreme medicine man, one who tends to the mental well being of his tribe.

Slow Turtle's formal name is Cjegktoonuppa. "Slow Turtle called white men 'the original boat people' and observed that we were actually Europe's outcasts. He said that white people had brought rum with them in order to confuse any people they encountered and that the Bible has been used to manipulate Indians.

He noted that the word 'Indian' is derogatory because it describes a location that is not his spiritual homeland. He prefers to be called a Wampanoag."[28] He continued,

> Each person is an individual and must find his own special gift, path and ideas. It is critical to know your own thoughts rather than to adopt another's views, because all decisions are made by the group. Problems are discussed extensively until a consensus is reached, and the discussions stress sharing rather than controlling.

Slow Turtle does not like America's education because it encourages 'tunnel vision' in children rather than an opportunity to explore their own paths, and because it is used to gain power over other people rather than to share knowledge.

Other Minorities: The Rabbis and John Smith

In addition to discussing the 'problem' or 'question' of Negroes and American Indians, the members of the Club also discussed the followers of several religions in a similar manner. The message was that the women of the Club and the society of the period (1886–1945) perceived these religious peoples as outsiders, in some way suspect, and in the instance of Mormons clearly their moral inferiors. Jews and Mormons were the two groups discussed in this fashion in some depth in the first 60 years of the Club's history. While Catholics were also mentioned briefly in a few discussions, the comments were more benign and there were far fewer references.

While Club records at no point indicate the religious affiliation of each member, a review of the records up to World War II provides a consistent and strong sense that all members during that period were practicing Protestants. A number of long-term Club activist were wives of ministers; Protestant clergymen were often quoted as authorities on subjects — on both political and moral issues; terms such as "Christian duty" and "Christian charity" were sprinkled throughout discussions; and conversations about Jews, Mormons and Catholics consistently projected a frame of reference that the members were discussing outsiders, not their social peers.

The subject of Jews surfaced in a number of ways. The first was an invitation to Rabbi Charles Fleischer of Temple Israel in Boston to speak to the Club on "Facts and Fictions about the Jews" in February 1905. Fleischer was not your average rabbi but a very well known activist and ecumenist in the Boston area who counted among his friends Harvard President Charles Eliot, painter John Singer Sargent and writer and

Unitarian minister Edward Everett Hale among others.

In 1905 no members of the Club were Jewish. That the rabbi would title his talk "Facts and Fiction about the Jews" indicated how Jews were viewed by the general public and probably by the membership of the Club. There were myths about Jews that called for correction. That the ladies invited a well known rabbi to speak to them about Judaism instead of a Gentile academician indicates willingness on their part to learn as well as a certain respect for Rabbi Fleischer himself. They did not invite Mormon or Catholic authorities to speak to them.

An announcement in Club notes several years later in April 1913 underscored a different consciousness that existed simultaneously with the desire to learn more: "maids available for gentile families."

In March 1930 Gertrude Dennison gave a paper entitled "The Contributions of the Races to American Civilization: the Jews." She began by sketching the history of Jews in Palestine and Spain and their persecution.

> Many of the Spanish Jews migrated to America, bringing with them the pride and glory of rank and intellectuality which had produced Ferdinand and Spinoza. The second migration of Jews came from Germany and Austria [and] produced great merchants, financiers and philanthropists and many of the prominent families have descended from them. During the Civil War, they showed great patriotism. [Then] came a large influx of an entirely different type. They were largely Polish and Russian political refugees, members of an outcast class, the victims of cruelty and the objects of massacre, leaving the fetid European ghettos to dwell in the cities of America.

Dennison went on to name many prominent Jews in art, music, literature, science and invention. "Mrs. Dennison believed that the Jew has many admirable characteristics, a lofty idealism, a capability accentuated by years of struggle with adversity, a loyalty and a love of peace which will meld the world together and which may break down racial barriers and

FROM HEARTH TO HORIZONS

result in a homogeneous humanity."

It is ironic that in 1930 Dennison foresaw Jews as melding the world together and breaking down racial barriers at a time when Hitler's dark shadow was already spreading in Germany. But most portentous was the lack of feeling of connection between Jews and the membership. This sense of distance would continue as the situation in Europe deteriorated during the next decade.

From 1932 to 1936 there were periodic reports to the Club about evolving political tensions in Europe and the Far East. While there are glimpses of an early enchantment with Mussolini and even some positive comments on Stalin, those who reported on Hitler in March 1933 saw him from the beginning as a menace and as stating he was going to rid Germany of the Jews as well as "the Reds." Despite this insight, the plight of the Jews in Europe during this decade received relatively little attention in meeting records.

Unfortunately meeting minutes are silent on whether any discussion or comments followed. There is a clear recognition of an evil political force built on anti-Semitism but no hint of the personal toll on Jews in Germany and surrounding countries. The picture painted is eerily antiseptic. This contrasts sharply with the compassion and emotion usually recorded when the women discussed blacks, Indians and immigrants.

In February 1948 Club member Margaret Bacon Ambler presented a paper on "Other Minorities" that included a section on Jews in addition to sections on southwest Mexicans and the Japanese. "[T]he Jews in this country were a religious, ethnic and economic minority and the prejudice against them was due to ignorance and fear, and has led to their continued persecution. They came in greater numbers between the years 1880–1914 and anti-Semitic agitation reached its height with World War I."

The next mention of Jews found in Club proceedings was in the minutes of March 20, 1990, when member Thelma Fleishman as part of a panel on immigration told the members that one reason she and her family left South Africa was that they were Jews and Jews had been relegated to second-class citizenship. By 1990 Newton, the home of the Club, had changed.

Jews were no longer curiosities to be studied and analyzed and many of the members, like Thelma, were Jewish.

Between 1888 and 1908 the women of the Club had a number of discussions about Mormons. Initial conversations revealed mostly curiosity about a religion few of the women knew anything about. This was at a time when Utah was seeking statehood and polygamy was still an official practice of the church. Later discussions reflected a growing national bias against Mormons (tied to their practice of polygamy, outlawed in 1890) and fears that Mormon beliefs were incompatible with fealty to the nation.

On February 15, 1888, Emma J. Sheppard presented a paper on "Mormonism." She had visited an elder and his five wives and 26 or more children in Salt Lake City. "Seven-eighths of the Mormons were foreigners lured here from their own homes by great promises of wealth and power. Boys and girls at the age of eight voted on church matters, also the women. The women were more devoted to the faith than the men. They were hard workers and believed in polygamy. The Gentiles were obliged to pay towards Mormon schools." Members expressed surprise and interest in Sheppard's remarks.

At the following meeting on February 29, Anna C. Hardon read a description of Salt Lake City (which some members found "shocking to listen to") and proceeded to sound off on what she saw as unsettling, growing support for the Mormons. "That a people are allowed to live peacefully in our country, who by most solemn oaths pledge themselves to do all in their power to overthrow the government seems strange, and still the Mormons have great power in Congress and dare seek to have Utah admitted as a state that they may extend their influence still farther."

The subject did not return again until 11 years later. Meanwhile a growing concern about Mormonism was being voiced from the pulpits of Protestant churches. On April 26, 1899, Club member Emma Barstow Bates advocated against the seating of Representative-elect Brigham Roberts of Utah because he was a Mormon and a polygamist, "it having been hoped that the united action of women's clubs might bring moral influence to bear against the seating of a Mormon legislator." The Club went on to order and distribute 100 pamphlets on Mormonism published by the Social Service League to help promote the petition against the seating of Roberts.

Brigham Roberts was elected in November 1898 as a member of the U.S. House of Representatives from Utah. He appears to have won strong support from non-Mormons in Utah as well as fellow Mormons. "The *Salt Lake Tribune* and Protestant churches in Utah led the fight to prevent him from being seated. Polygamy was the center of the campaign against him. The House refused to swear Roberts in, referring the case to a special commission. On January 25, 1900, the House voted 268 to 50 to exclude him. While it is true that Roberts was the husband of three wives, and the father of eleven children, there was no proof that he had married any wife since Statehood or since the Manifesto of 1890 discontinuing polygamy."[28]

In late 1899 Bates reported on her work helping the petition of the Anti-Polygamy League and won approval of a motion asking Club members to write their representatives and urge them to deny Roberts a seat.

Again in 1903 the question of seating an elected official who was a Mormon came before the Club. The official this time was Reed Smoot who had been elected that year by the Utah Legislature to serve as U.S. Senator. Smoot was an Apostle for the Church of the Latter Day Saints, one of the highest church positions. The Senate allowed Smoot to be seated while his status was being considered. Hearings commenced in 1904 and did not end until 1907 when he won a substantial majority vote to be seated.[29]

In December 1903 the Club president read a circular from the Interdenominational Council of Women for Christian and Patriotic Service seeking support for their drive to prevent the seating of Smoot. The March 2004 Annual Report notes the matter was "laid on the table" and died. It also notes that a petition to exclude Mormon clubs from the General Federation of Women's Clubs also died for lack of action.

Smoot had never been a polygamist. This may have been the deciding factor why the Club did not seek action against him. As for barring Mormon clubs from the Federation, it's likely the members and other Massachusetts members of the Federation remembered their own unsuccessful struggle in 1900 to prevent a color line in the Federation and wanted no part of a faith line in that organization either. While not embracing Mormonism, the women separated the moral issue of polygamy from the minor discomfort of having a senator of a faith to which they felt little connection.

Several years later Club member Pauline Patton gave a paper on Mormonism. While the minutes note a lively discussion, the level of controversy and calls for action of a decade earlier had disappeared. In the last 102 years the subject of Mormons has not been broached and there is no record of whether or not a Mormon has ever been a member of the Club.

Diversity Within

From the beginning in 1886 the members of the Club expressed interest in learning about others, especially those of whom they had little knowledge or to whom they felt little connection — Negroes, American Indians, Chinese, Japanese, Jews, Mormons, etc. The women asked pointed questions and fearlessly waded into delicate areas. Many members traveled throughout the U.S. and abroad, reporting back what they saw and whom they met. While opinions about immigrants and various ethnic and religious groups differed widely, most members were open and generous in their research and discussions about races, religions and ethnicities that differed from their own.

Despite their gracious hospitality to minorities (they welcomed minority speakers, students and musical groups into their homes), the women of the Club in the years up to World War II lived their lives pretty much in social isolation. They were all white, Anglo-Saxon Protestants, most of whom came from wealthy families or at least families who had deep roots in this country over many generations. Many depended on servants at home to free their time for Club work. As the Club looked to expand, members naturally recruited their neighbors, fellow congregants, and women from their own social circles who were interested in discussing and acting on pressing political, social and educational topics. While their vision of opportunity for diverse groups of people was broad, their daily social experience with diversity was limited.

During the 20th century the Club matured, the world changed and women's horizons broadened. After World War II Newton's demographics changed, bringing into the city more women from diverse backgrounds who shared common interests with existing members. But at the same time the widening of opportunities for women in the professional world left a decreasing pool of women with time to participate in Club activities. The clearest change to the Club that occurred as a result is that the average age of members increased substantially. Retirees became the most fertile ground for recruitment as younger women chose employment. And slowly but surely recognizable Italian, Irish and Jewish names appeared increasingly on the membership lists and a trained ear could pick up occasional faint traces of non-native accents among the members.

One factor that has not changed over time is the racial makeup of the membership. No record could be found of Club discussions about diversifying the membership, but not all discussions get into the record. A conversation with Emily Hubbs Scott, a 50 year member, and at her suggestion a review of records from the late 1960s through the 1970s indicate efforts by several members during that period to change the all-white façade of the Club. Guests of color attended numerous meetings but without the hoped-for result of expanded membership. Emily's best recollections are that meeting hours and the inconsistency in the quality of papers and programs were significant hurdles. Most potential members were often employed and only consistently strong programs could justify taking time off during the normal work day. In addition a review of the annual reports for 1968 through 1979 indicates that it was difficult in those years to recruit any new members.

In the winter of 2010 a provocative question by a new member about the process to join the Club sparked lively discussion about the process itself possibly being a barrier to diversification. Following considerable discussion a new application based on self-selection was developed and approved by the membership. This replaced a process of nomination and secret ballot for each candidate proposed — a process uncomfortably reminiscent for some of offensive former practices of country clubs and elite social clubs of 'blackballing' to prevent minorities from becoming members. Whether this new process will make a difference is yet to be seen. Breaking through racial barriers is hard work and usually takes more than good intentions. It's likely now, as always, that members will recruit from their own social circles. Change may well depend on more members taking steps to broaden the diversity of their own social circles before we can successfully broaden the diversity within the Club.

Endnotes

1 Hing, Bill Ong. *Defining America Through Immigration Policy,* Temple University Press, 2004, pp. 28–50. In 1870 Congress had prohibited Chinese immigrants from becoming naturalized citizens, at the same time it allowed African immigrants citizenship, confining them to second-class status.

2 Ripley, a political economist who dabbled in sociology, published an influential volume, *The Races of Europe: A Sociological Study,* in 1899. Shortly thereafter he joined the Harvard faculty.

3 Henry Cabot Lodge served several terms in Congress before taking a seat as a senator from Massachusetts in March 1893. He worked for more than 20 years to see a literacy test implemented as part of the Immigration Act of 1917, a bill passed over the veto of President Wilson.

4 Kennedy, David. *Over Here*, Oxford University Press, 2004, pp. 63–66.

5 For example in February 1914 Alice Taylor, former school matron of the Nonantum Day Nursery, spoke to the Club and indicated that help had been provided to approximately 5000 through the office at the Stearns School and most of those families were foreign born.

6 Duscha's father was named Willi Schmid without a "t" while the opposition leader was Wilhelm Schmidt.

7 Unfortunately no recording of this panel discussion exists and the meeting notes are quite brief.

8 *New York Times*, November 27, 1888.

9 http://en.wikipedia.org/wiki/disenfranchisement_after _Reconstruction_era.

10 *The Booker T. Washington Papers,* Vol. 5, open book edition, University of Illinois Press, 1976, pp. 499–504.

11 *Boston Daily Globe*, "Out of Place," June 10, 1900, p. 5.

12 Re-organization was the Massachusetts strategy to gain a voting seat for Ruffin.

13 *Boston Daily Globe*, "Stole a March," June 8, 1900, p. 4.

14 *Boston Daily Globe*, "Out of Place: Mrs. Lowe's Free Advice to Mrs. Ruffin," June 10, 1900, p. 5.

15 Articles in *Boston Daily Globe*, including June 20, 1900, "Indorses [sic] Mrs. Ruffin," p. 11, and August 11, 1900, "Work for Colored Women," p. 10, gave detailed accounts of the controversy.

16 Schneider, Mark, "The Boston NAACP and the Decline of the Abolitionist Impulse," *The Massachusetts Historical Review*, Vol. 1, 1999, pp. 95-114.

17 Woodrow Wilson was president and his bias against Negroes is well documented in Kennedy, *Over Here*.

18 The same Rosalind Lewis for whom the M.I.T. music library is named.

19 East, E. M. *Mankind at the Crossroads*, Charles Scribner's Sons, 1923, p.133.

20 Ibid. pp. 133–138.

21 The Dawes Bill was passed by Congress in 1887 and while it

purported to insure land ownership for Indians and aid in developing Indian farms, it had the detrimental effect of breaking down tribes and Indian culture and decreasing Indian land holdings from 138 million acres in 1887 to 48 million acres in 1934 when it was repealed.

22 Carlson, Leonard A., "The Dawes Act and the Decline of Indian Farming," *The Journal of Economic History*, Vol. 38, No. 1, Mar. 1978, pp. 274–76.

23 Hampton Institute opened in 1869 initially to serve black students. In 1878 it opened a special Indian program that ran until 1923 to train young men and women as teachers or in manual arts. Indian students were housed and schooled separately from black students. Declining enrollment, poor graduation rates, low rate of Indian graduates getting jobs, the death of General Samuel Chapman Armstrong, the founder of the program, and tensions between black and Indian students all contributed to the demise of the Indian program. While the Club's initial interest appeared to be in the Indian students, records indicate no expressed racial preference for scholarship recipients. And the Club continued its support of Hampton students for many years after the Indian Program ended.

24 See Donal Lindsey, *Indians at Hampton Institute 1877–1923*, University of Illinois Press, 1995.

25 The term Amerindian was coined to identify Indians of the American continent.

26 A hobbyist is defined as "a non-Indian who has a wide range of interests in American Indian subjects but mainly, arts and crafts, Indian dancing and singing." In the 1960s and 1970s there were one or more hobbyist groups in every major city in the country. The New England group put a special emphasis on education, working with school systems to advise on curriculum regarding American Indians. *The Handbook of North American Indians: The History of Indian-White Relations*, Vol. 4, William Sturtevant, Smithsonian Institution, 1988, pp. 557–561.

27 The standard used in this chapter is based on data indicating most indigenous Americans prefer to be identified by tribe. When referred to collectively, the majority prefer the term American Indian; a smaller number, the term Native American.

28 Whitney, Orson Ferguson. *History of Utah*, Vol. 4, George Q. Cannon & Sons Co., 1904, p. 693. This book was sponsored and published by a company set up for the single purpose of supporting a multi-volume history of Utah. Whitney was a bishop in the Mormon Church and clearly takes a pro-Roberts perspective. His mother Kimball was married at 14 to Joseph Smith, founder of The Church of Jesus Christ of the Latter Day Saints. After Smith's death she married Horace Whitney, Orson's father. Even this author does not dispute the fact of Robert's three wives.

29 Http://en.wikipedia.org/wiki/Reed_Smoot_hearings.

CHAPTER FIVE

OPEN TO THE WORLD

by Marie Baroni Allen

Early on, the founding women determined that theirs was not to be a literary club. Perhaps more unconsciously it evolved that the Club ought to be as expansive in scope as possible, allowing them to broaden their knowledge and understanding in a great number of directions. And enlarge their horizons they did. The women had an overarching need for intellectual stimulation, discovery and expansion. As their understanding grew, the world they embraced became broader and wider.

Within this chapter each section represents a theme that has been identified in the Club's records. While studying these records it becomes apparent that the women have been citizens of the world since the Club's inception and taken note of the world's changes and eventual globalization.

Citizens of the United States and the World

Local Nobel Peace Prize laureate Emily Green Balche often would announce, "I am a citizen of the world." It is apparent that the Social Science Clubwomen had and have this same philosophy, always looking outward from Newton to the nation and the world. Throughout the Club's history the members have recognized themselves as citizens with the attendant duties, rights and privileges. To this end the civics committee, the legislative committee and the international relations committee were formed.

In January 1888 the Club meeting focused on an important national issue, the Blair Education Bill. Since the Bill provided for funds to be distributed based upon illiteracy rates, the south would have been highly favored by its passage. The Club's efforts in support of this bill were in line with its support of the Hampton Institute.

When the Club became a member of the Newton Federation of Women's Clubs, the legislative committee often presented the state federation's arguments in favor or against endorsements of legislative bills. By 1902 the women's interest in legislation was significant enough to form a legislative committee. The committee brought forward such topics as opposition to giving the Spanish American War veterans a special status (1904) and control of liquor traffic (1904). In 1910 the Club worked diligently in support of the Child Labor Bill. Although the bill did not pass they continued with their efforts. In 1916 Club vice-president Laura Drake "read extracts of the report of the Child Labor commission giving portions of the Keating-Owen Bill soon to come before the legislature, which is designed to protect the American child." This bill was enacted.

Around 1912 public health became a focus of government and in 1914 the Massachusetts State Board of Health focused its attention on the spread of typhoid fever and learned that a significant number of cases of the disease was caused by milk-borne typhoid. In 1915 the Club's attention was drawn to the support of Senate Bill number 78 that made it illegal to sell milk produced under unhygienic conditions.

When in 1937 President Roosevelt proposed enlarging the Supreme Court, some Club members attended a hearing at the State House and asked other members to write to their congressional representatives regarding the proposal. That year the Club unanimously voted against the proposal.

In the late 1940s the members favored a bill supporting jury service for women. They also petitioned the U.S. House and Senate in favor of the Marshall Plan. In 1950 when State Senator Lee spoke about current legislative issues he focused on the Alternate Death Penalty Bill that he favored. This bill would give jurors three options in capital cases — death penalty, life imprisonment or not guilty. Prior to this time there was no life imprisonment provision. There is no record of the support the Club may have offered this bill but it is clear that Senator Lee's appearance was meant to gain support since the Newton Chief of Police was against the bill.

The last record of formal presentations regarding legislation was in 1953 when Howard Whitemore, a member of both the Massachusetts Legislature and the 'Baby Hoover Commission' spoke to the Club. In 1949, 12 bipartisan members were appointed by the governor to streamline the state legislature. This issue had last been tackled in 1921. By 1950 the commission had "formed an outline of procedure and undertook to analyze, through the help of researchers, each [governmental] department. Whitemore noted that the 'Commission had saved an estimated 106 million dollars. There have been 119 recommendations: 41 adopted, 55 pending and 23 rejected by the legislature.'"

The civics and legislative committees were merged in 1962 and then, with the Club's major administrative restructuring in 1976, all three committees ceased to exist. After this time only informal reporting about political issues occurred at meetings, although it is clear from topics of papers, comments and announcements that the members remain interested in politics and worldly events and pursued these through other avenues that did not exist in 1900.

There was, however, another aspect of the phrase 'citizen of the world' and it was part of the Club's culture. Many members were fortunate enough to experience other societies and share their knowledge and impressions with the Club. Two papers, "A Foreigner in Angola" and "Out on a Limb — Chinese Style," are presented here as examples of the women's expansive and experiential world.

A Foreigner in Angola—A Different Way of Life

This paper by Doris N. Blake was presented in October 1991 under the theme "Personal Choice." Edited and abridged by Marie Baroni Allen.

Doris Blake
(Photo by Emily Hubbs Scott)

We were Methodist missionaries in Angola (Portuguese West Africa) from May 1948 to January 1957 — nine years with the year 1951–1952 in the States for furlough. When we arrived in Angola we had two children: Paul, almost five, and Sue, two. While in Angola we had three more sons — John, David and Stephen.

In preparation for missionary service, besides [my husband] Melvin's ministerial training and six years' experience as pastor of a church, we'd had a semester at the Kennedy School of Missions in Hartford, Connecticut, and eight months of Portuguese language study in Lisbon — a story in itself. We took with us a Chevrolet Carryall, three beds, a refrigerator, a wood-burning kitchen range with reservoir, a folding organ, a sewing machine, two bicycles, a 100-roll carton of toilet tissue and 27 barrels, trunks and packing boxes. At the dock in Luanda we were met by Ralph and Eunice Dodge, older graduates of our college.

Our first daytime impression of Luanda was the glare of sun on cream-colored buildings and red-tiled roofs. Some said that Luanda at that time was perhaps the most beautiful city on the west coast of Africa with a population of 65,000 of whom 50,000 were African. The modern art of the city, built around the curve of the bay, was indeed beautiful— nice shops, two cinemas, large commercial houses, private homes with walled yards, many of the walls covered with red bougainvillea. It is a very old city and a great fort built by the Dutch in 1648 stands on a headland overlooking the harbor.

A cliff rose sharply above the commercial port of the city and up on the edge of that cliff the Methodists owned 30 acres of land. They had had it for 75 years and the Portuguese wanted it very much. In fact, one old city plan envisioned a Catholic cathedral in the middle of the Methodist property. On the 30 acres there was a big church, an elementary school, the church parsonage, some African teachers' homes, two new missionary homes, a small office and a carpenter shop. In the African section of the city there were 18 small chapels under the care of the central church where people gathered for weeknight services. There were also four primary schools. Scattered over a wide semi-circle around Luanda were 16 village churches, many of them with outlying chapels and primary schools.

Our house was six months old [and] built for the tropics, that is, all cement to be termite-proof. Some of the floors were red cement, some tile. It had very high ceilings and enormous window panels that slid back to let in the breeze. Windows and doors were well screened so we didn't need mosquito nets, but the kids slept in screen cages.

Two months after we arrived in Angola, I took over the house so the Dodges could pack and I could learn the ropes. The biggest part of my work was to run the house as a stopover for missionaries of all denominations when they came to Luanda — on business, on vacation or on their way to and from the States or England. Sometimes for long stretches we would have a dozen people at the table. That's why there was such a big house and an upstairs living room, a place where the family could get away from the guests and be by themselves.

To help run our house I had a cook, a washwoman or two, a girl or boy to watch the smaller children and two or three school boys who washed dishes, served the food and dusted. Of these the cook was the most important. He was responsible for boiling all our drinking water as well as water to clean our teeth and wash whatever vegetables and fruit we ate raw. He had to go to the market every day to buy fruit, vegetables and meat and prepare them from scratch. Chickens were sold with the feathers on and fish were just as they came from the sea. I was lucky in usually having a cook who could read recipes. I taught them to make bread, pies, layer cakes, yeast doughnuts and cookies. I tried to show one cook how to taste the food using a small spoon so that he wouldn't put the stirring spoon in his mouth, but he showed me how he did it by just dropping a bit of food from the big spoon onto his wrist and licking it. Later when I discovered he had TB, I was glad he had done it that way.

I learned about buying food from Eunice. Meat was usually beef, lean and no choice of cuts. If we got liver they always insisted in putting in a piece of spleen since the Portuguese used to make it into gravy. Usually there was fresh fish. The vegetable we had most often was collards, that I have since found out are very nutritious, but we had enough other vegetables too. We had a variety of bananas, oranges, avocados and large thick-fruited papayas that we ate for breakfast with a little lemon juice. I used green papayas to make 'applesauce' and 'apple butter.'

When we got 100 pounds of flour I personally sifted it through a silk screen, put it in the oven to get very hot and then stored it in five-pound milk cans. Otherwise it would get weevils in it. When we had beans I insisted on sorting them myself, after they had been soaked. I didn't trust the cook to do it, and it was easier to see the weevils after the beans had been soaked. When tomatoes were at their best Paul and I took baskets and walked down to the market in the cool of the early morning to pick out a lot of good ones. Then we came home in a taxi and the cook helped us can tomatoes. One year we had 100 quarts.

Another job I took over from Eunice was teaching English, not to Africans but only to Portuguese: conversation classes with high school students, a group of doctors and their wives, a group of young working people, plus private lessons. Later I exchanged English lessons for Portuguese lessons with a businessman who bought trucks in Europe and needed help writing letters. One time I said something to him in Portuguese and he said, "Don't say that, but don't ask me why." Something risqué, no doubt.

Missionary mothers taught their children through the eighth grade and then sent them to the States for high school, unlike the English who sent their children back to England when they were four or five years old. I used very good Calvert course materials to teach my children and we had school every morning. Eventually I taught Paul all of his elementary school except third grade, Sue through fifth grade and John through second. Mothers had birthday parties for their children and invited other English-speaking children and their mothers — American, English, Dutch and Scottish. Usually our children's playmates were the American and Portuguese missionary children and the little Africans whose parents worked around the mission. Naturally our kids learned Portuguese.

The kids said something interesting happened every day — an enormous centipede found in a basket of onions; a scorpion fell out of some old magazines and scurried down the hall; a crazy man ran in off the street and raced upstairs; a very sunburned English woman rode in on a bike and we found she had ridden, by herself, all across Africa; the church ceiling fell in; a young man from Kansas came out to be the bookkeeper and lived with us. Much later John had his tonsils out with only local anesthesia because Luanda did not have a good anesthetist. A Portuguese friend took Sue over the city in an airplane. A British warship came for a good will visit and English-speaking mothers and children were invited on board for tea and a tour.

Angola was still governed by Portugal and was called a province. The Africans suffered great social injustice. Contract laborers were taken from their villages and forced to work for years on sugar plantations. One day in the middle of a downtown street, I saw a Portuguese man slap an African on the face and the African dared offer no resistance. Even our African pastor, a fine man, was addressed by "tu," the form for servants and their children rather than the adult form of "O senhor." I felt that, in contrast to this sort of thing, the church offered people an opportunity to develop as human beings of worth and dignity. Quite possibly it also helped them later to develop the confidence and courage they needed to free themselves from Portuguese rule, although we did not consciously promote revolt.

Because of the children and my work I usually didn't go with Melvin on his trips to villages. But when he went to Nova Caipemba for several days I left the three kids and went. Maria Julia, an African woman, stayed in the house with them, and the Edlings were nearby. Melvin and I and two African ministers went in an open Jeep, starting very early in the morning. Most of the traffic into the interior was large trucks and they were always loaded high, with Africans riding on top of the cargo. Those trucks were the only means of transportation inland except along the rail line. For the first 30 miles we were on blacktop. After that it was dirt roads built and kept up by gangs of men and women with baskets of dirt on their heads, and often with babies on the women's backs. Gas stations were just drums of gasoline with a pump attached. No rest rooms! From time to time we stopped beside the road and men went in one direction and I went in the other. The rainy season had already begun. Long stretches of the road were very rutted and in some places the ruts were under water.

Along in the afternoon we stopped at a government post to greet the official and present our credentials. Later we began to ask how far it was to Nova Caipemba. A fellow said it might be 50 kilometers but he knew it was a two-day trip on foot. Another said it was a long way but we would get there that day. Then one said "near." Yet another said "two curves of the road." Finally we came to the village of Nova Caipemba and, on the far side, its huge mud-and-stick church, equally large school and a big parsonage. A bedroom off the living room had been cleared for our camp cots. It smelled of creosote that perhaps was used to kill the bugs. They brought me a pan of water and, after I had washed off the dust, served us eggs, fruit, bread and butte,r and hot milk with dishes better than I had at home. I thought that was supper and after a bit was about to go to bed when we were served another meal, this time soup, meat gravy, rice, mashed potatoes, fish and lemon grass tea. Breakfast was liver and onions and a thin gravy along with boiled manioc and coffee. Of course Angolan villagers don't eat like that. Their main food is manioc mush with palm nut gravy, greens and some fish or meat when they can get it.

In the early evening of the second day the men gathered for a final meeting to solve a particularly knotty problem. Dusk had fallen and a single lantern lighted the big church only dimly and cast shadows on the high thatched ceiling. It was a special time and, as I watched from the back of the church and listened to each man give his opinion, I felt that I would rather be there in that mud-and-stick church with Melvin and those men than working in the biggest church in the United States.

On July 4, 1951, we boarded a freighter headed for the States for a year's furlough. A freighter is allowed to carry only 12 passengers and has no doctor on board but it's ideal travel if you aren't in a hurry. We weren't. We needed a vacation. The trip home took us six weeks. We appreciated the good American food that we ate with the officers.

A year later we went back to Luanda, this time on a Belgian freighter. After we'd been back in Angola more than three years we moved to the Dembos hills 225 miles north and east of Luanda. This was the beautiful coffee-growing area of low, tree-covered mountains. The mission owned a plantation up there near the village of Mufuque. It was a base for the supervision of a wide area of churches and schools. Fred, an agriculturist, and Margaret, a musician, lived in one of the two houses and we would have the other.

Food was more difficult in Dembos. The local people had nothing to sell us. We had to be sure to order everything we needed when the truck went to Luanda. We started a garden in a valley a long way from the house. A few times a hunter brought buffalo or antelope meat to sell. I froze some and ground some to make buffalo burgers. Buffalo was a little strong for me but the rest of the family liked it. Antelope was really good. We ate lots of Spam, tuna and canned hotdogs. In season we had more avocados than we could eat. Sometimes we'd get delicious pineapples but the monkeys were often quicker than we were. We usually had bananas and lemons. A boy came from a distant village to sell eggs.

Living in Dembos was my best experience of real African village life. We were within sight of the village of Mufuque and by using binoculars I could see quite a bit. Besides, we were over there every Sunday for church where we sat on small half-logs and listened to the sermon in Kimbundu. From our front porch we saw the village women going to their gardens, children on their backs, baskets on their heads, and sometimes even a few chickens along with them. We often saw monkeys sitting in the trees 'talking' to us as we went to the garden. I carried a snake-bite kit and one day a green mamba raced across the path ahead of me but I never needed the kit. A few times we saw buffalo on a distant hillside, and Fred brought in a dead aardvark, a leopard and a wild hog.

Just before our second Christmas in Dembos, Melvin came back from Luanda to report we were leaving Angola. We had known that it might happen. He had been asked to take a job in the New York office overseeing Methodist work in Europe and Africa. I was glad that I had had time to consider this possibility; it made leaving easier. There was at least one good thing about it. Paul was ready for high school and, by returning to the States, we would not have to send him back by himself.

In New York I forgot myself and spoke Portuguese to a store clerk. That was only a small adjustment of the many I had to make upon return to a different way of life.

Out On a Limb — Chinese Style

This paper by Leila F. Sobin, a frequent visitor to China, was presented on October 16, 1996, under the theme "Out on a Limb." Edited and abridged by Marie Baroni Allen.

In all the history of China, people have been watched, reported on and recorded in government files. Family members and friends as well as the culprit have been punished. Surveillance was and is part of daily life in China and one is always aware of it and fearful. Guilt is assumed until innocence is proven, even in court. This has never changed and, in fact, during the recent Cultural Revolution people became more mistrustful, more fearful than ever and less apt to try anything new or daring that might attract attention. This suspicion even follows Chinese persons to the United States and in a seminar on a Chinese subject in a university you will rarely if ever find them participating. If you corner them alone and ask why not, they will tell you that they just don't know who is sitting in the room.

If a foreigner came to call, the Chinese equivalent of the French concierge reports to his superior and the potentially guilty person would be called to the security bureau to be grilled about the conversation and the reason for the visit. This would probably be followed up with three or four more visits to ascertain the truth of the story previously told, and more often than not entered into the person's file. At some later date, if that person or their children or grandchildren or even friends had trouble, out would come the file and the old relationship with a foreigner would come back to haunt the person in trouble. Upon departure [of a guest] they were expected to report the details of the visit, word for word. One can imagine the problems this would create — or maybe one cannot. Developing a friendship is dangerous and nearly impossible even now.

One would suppose that this would preclude any foolhardy activities in China and yet the undaunted desperation and the lack of anything to lose drove some people to daring economic feats. Daniel Bell, eminent sociologist at Harvard University, concluded that it was "the poor, the less educated and the relatively uncivilized part of American society," those who had nothing to lose, who contributed most to the economic wealth of our country during the Industrial Revolution.

In China the elite technocrats believe their managerial skills and their leadership have made possible the economic boom. But one wonders whether they are out of touch with China's reality and their expertise instead may drain the treasury and deplete the economic well being of the population. The vast Three Gorges Dam project may be a perfect example of this, uprooting over a million people who live in the area from their homes, villages, jobs, friends, etc. So who did create the economic miracle? In Sunan, the region where industrialization of the rural areas originated, agriculture only accounts for 8% of the total output value in the region while industry accounts for 92%, whereas in the past the figures were just the reverse. Although there must be more than one factor, one wonders what or who contributed to this economic explosion?

Could it have been 'peasants-turned-industrialists' who played a vital role in China's great industrialization revolution, one of the greatest revolutions in human history? Similar to Daniel Bell's findings, these peasants too were from the poor, less educated and underprivileged part of the society. Historically there has never been a time when so many people made so much money in a single generation as the coastal peasants of China. During the past several years my friend Jie has met several dozen wealthy rural industrialists, visiting them and hearing their stories. Each time she felt like she was listening to the stories of a Carnegie or a Rockefeller and was impressed by both the hardships they endured and the tremendous successes they have achieved.

One of the former peasants whom she met, Mr. Chen Jinhai, was a factory director in 1984 in Suzhou. Five years later Jie found Mr. Chen's hometown to be unrecognizable and she told me that the elegant restaurant where her sister had had the dinner party was now only a canteen for ordinary meals, while many newer and more elegant restaurants had been established. Glamorous modern luxury hotels with exquisite traditional gardens had been built and the modern Wujiang Hotel was one of the most glamorous that she had seen either in China or abroad. The GNP had increased by 52% since the year before. In 1993 there were 900 foreign-owned enterprises with a total foreign investment of $1.3 billion. The head of the Public Administration department told my friend that some of the entrepreneurs had become "incredibly rich by [the] standard in any country."

At lunch Mr. Chen told Jie that he would be willing to tell her his story. It is a story of a self-made Chinese entrepreneur born to a peasant family in 1949 in one of the poorest villages in China. The family lived in a straw shed for more than 20 years, planting rice that they could not afford to eat and catching crabs that they sold to the government. For the most important holiday, once a year, his mother made a new suit of clothes for him only because he was the oldest son, and his old suit was passed to the number two child. Once he was invited to go to the town banquet for the spring festival and his parents allowed him to go with the admonishment not to eat too much. Nevertheless he was so hungry that he ate almost an entire pig and was sick for weeks thereafter. Poverty and hunger were the standard for people of his class and in this environment.

Leaving school after two years of junior high, Mr. Chen went to work full time on the farm. By the time he was 20, he was married to a young girl from the village with the same background and who also worked on the farm. Together they earned about $25 a year. Ten years passed during which he performed backbreaking labor, all the time thinking of what he could do to work his way out of this seemingly dead-end situation. Finally he concluded that the only solution was to leave farm work and become a factory worker. With the threats of his leader that he would receive neither money nor grain from the village if he left, he sold his pigs and all his furniture and, at age 24 in 1973, he left the farmland and went to Suzhou to apprentice in a fiberglass factory.

For two years he lived in a public bathhouse, subsisting on six cents a day for food. During those two years Chen learned the technical skills and procedures for manufacturing fiberglass until one day he heard that a factory in Shanghai was looking for experienced workers and would pay $12 a month. The interview went well and his knowledge of the production was much admired, but he lacked a junior high school diploma and thus did not qualify.

Mr. Chen was bitterly disappointed but he began to think about trying to help the village or nearby town by starting a small factory in the countryside. He believed that the living standards of the country people could not be raised unless small factories were developed. This was a difficult concept for the local officials and they did not agree with Chen at the time.

Eventually Mr. Chen was able to persuade officials in a village not far from his home village to establish a workshop with Chen himself appointed as director. Now they were in business and in the first year the profit was about $2400, which was a great success for a little rural business with meager funds and untrained workers. But as often happens in China, [jealousy] the green-eyed monster reared its ugly head in the form of a person who wrote the people's commune that Mr. Chen was not "tending to his proper occupation and was engaged in dishonest work." He was held in custody for several weeks while the accusations were investigated.

Nothing improper was found by the investigatory team and in fact they found that Mr. Chen was a capable man who created jobs and brought wealth to the village. When he was released Mr. Chen was invited to come back to his home village to establish a fiberglass workshop there. The officials gave him a small advance of $240 and told him they would be satisfied if he could make a profit of $360. This would be just enough to pay the salaries of the officials and thus relieve the farmers of this burden.

When they started the workshop in 1976 there were only four workers including Mr. Chen and the work place consisted of two very small rooms. By the end of the first year the business became a real factory with "several dozen" workers. Mr. Chen produced quality products in order to survive the competition and at the same time signed contracts for air conditioning systems with institutions doing research on the building industries in the big cities. As time went on, he established air-conditioning systems in the new Shanghai subway, the Nanjing airport and the factories under the Bureau of the Shanghai Textile Industry. Scientists and engineers joined the factory staff as consultants and were well paid. Each of these projects brought several million in profits to Mr. Chen.

By now Mr. Chen is both chairman of the board and general manager, keeping a close watch over the seven factories that the group now owns. He has appointed his brothers, sister-in-law and brother-in-law as directors. Meanwhile the workshop is completely modernized and there is a big demand for the fiberglass-reinforced inorganic composites widely used in air-conditioning systems and exported to Japan and South East Asian countries.

All these developments have had a strong impact on Mr. Chen's personal life. Having become a rich industrial entrepreneur from a poor peasant background, Mr. Chen has accomplished a feat that was almost unthinkable in the past. He has moved his family permanently to a country town. Having divorced his first wife (settling 50,000 yuan, about $6000, on her), he married a peasant girl named Xiao Wang who is 16 years younger than he.

When Jie asked him how he felt about the changes in his life, Mr. Chen said that 20 years ago people had scorned him, looked down upon him and generally had no use for him and now he regularly contributes more than anyone else to town development. He has created several hundred jobs, built bridges and flood-free roads, has given 100,000 yuan (about $12,000) for commercial development in the town and donated money to the elementary schools and clinics in the county. After giving only about 20,000 yuan (about $2300) annually to the village as agreed with officials, he could either reinvest his profits back in the business or keep the rest for himself.

As in any country, resentment and admiration abound toward him and other people who have suddenly become rich beyond their wildest dreams and discrimination by officials is widespread. It is believed by the general population that entrepreneurs like Mr. Chen have had a negative effect on the society and many people believe that some of the money was made in a questionable way. Jealousy appears once more. By daring to go into a small business and daring to develop it step-by-step, Mr. Chen ignored the danger to himself and his family from officials and neighbors who may have wanted revenge for something they could not accomplish for themselves. It was interesting that Mr. Chen concluded the interview with a charming brief story: "I went to Shanghai one time about 20 years ago," he said, "looking for a job as a contract worker but I was turned down because I did not have a junior high school diploma. A few months ago the general manager of that same factory came to my office to discuss a cooperative venture between his company and mine."

The Changing World — Moving Toward Globalization
by Marie Baroni Allen

As early as 1897 the Club minutes reported an interest in the changing world. During that year noted as "the 60th of Queen Victoria," discussions on global concerns included comments such as these: "Plucky Greece shows a splendid impulse in facing the Great Powers" and "Japan who retains her supremacy says little but is building a powerful navy." When the observation was made that "the danger [to the world] lies in the character of the rulers today; their mental, moral and physical capacity is a menace of the world," Mary M. Billings went on record saying that Queen

Victoria should have the "glory of her reign without criticism."

In 1903 the Club members discussed the impact of immigration on civilization, focusing on the Huguenots, the Dutch, the Scotch Irish, and the Puritans. By 1905 they had spread

Guest speaker, Catherine Breshkovsky, "grandmother of the Russian Revolution," in 1914.

(Bibliotheque Nationale de France)

their view wider when Madame Breshkovsky was a guest speaker. A Russian socialist and revolutionary, better known as Babushka ("Grandmother") or, more solemnly, the Grandmother of the Russian Revolution, Catherine Breshkovsky was exiled to Siberia in 1878, founded a socialist-revolutionary group and escaped to the United States in 1900. As the world continued to change, socialism increased in impact and importance, resulting in its study during the 1912–1913 Club year. As World War I raged, studies were undertaken about colonialism, including Holland in the East Indies, England in India and the French colonies in Africa.

From 1914 to 1918 while World War I was causing havoc in Europe, many meetings and guest lectures focused on world problems and the need for cooperation among nations. In 1915 Jay William Hudson, professor of philosophy at the University of Missouri, delivered a lecture, "The American Contribution to the New Internationalism." The meeting minutes summarize his position as follows:

> Making a strong plea for greater cooperation between nations he said no nation could make war upon another without disturbing international peace for the national welfare has its roots in cooperation. He spoke with contempt of the aggrandizement of our nation at the expense of smaller countries, and pointed out that smaller countries have contributed most proportionally to the worlds [sic] welfare.
>
> His four closing points were: American democracy stands for settlement by reason and [for] the value of

the individual; American civilization stands for social obligation; America stands for cosmopolitan culture. The harmonious relation existing between the United States of America and the melding of our foreign born population into our national life, he characterized as an American contribution to the new internationalism.[1]

During 1915 and 1916 the focus of study was peace. The members looked closer to home with a guest speaker on Pan-Americanism and a discussion of the American contribution to the new internationalism. As early as 1916 George Nasmyth, secretary of the Massachusetts Branch of the League to Enforce Peace, spoke to the Club promoting the concept of a World Federation, stating:

> The great reconstructive remedy is a World Federation under which lie four great principles — the U.S. should ask other countries to establish a World Court of Justice; they should be asked to create a Council for investigation of questions not justicible [sic]; the bank of the World Court should have economic sanctions and forcible sanctions; international law should be codified.[2]

In the years following World War I the Club invited guest speakers to inform them of the ways in which change was occurring. In 1919 Mary E. Woolley, president of Mt. Holyoke College, recognized that the present period looking forward was more critical than the one just passed.

> [We] now face the greatest opportunity in history to shape and re-create the new world. We are standing at the parting of the ways with two roads stretching before us; the one founded on a frightful war-program that would mean a world cataclysm; the other established on principle and laid out on the broad foundation of justice. Miss Woolley made an appeal for an earnest and educated womanhood and a lifting of its standards, an appeal that the same spirit and brain-power [that] was applied to the problems of war may be applied to the problems of peace.[3]

In 1924 Alden G. Alley presented the Club with a view of a peaceful world. Alley was a Harvard graduate and president of the League of Nations Nonpartisan Association, an organization set up to promote world peace, educate the public about the League of Nations and mobilize support for U.S. entrance into the League. His presentation outlined the accomplishments of the League, the precursor to the United Nations.

The women remained well aware of the broader, wider world throughout the 1930s. The year 1934 was pivotal with the focus on "The Challenge to the Old Order in Europe." The members noted that the world was changing and they therefore studied Germany, Italy and Russia, in particular. In 1935, realizing that their world was affected by both European and Asian countries, they turned their heads toward the east. In April of that year Rev. Dr. David Brewer Eddy, secretary of the Congregational [Church] Board of Foreign Missions, spoke to the Club on "A Study of International Relations," the observations from an eight-month trip around the world. Then in November, Bruce Hopper, a Harvard professor of political science from 1931 to 1961, discussed "The Far East from an American Point of View." The following March, Evelyn S. Rolfe spoke on "Conflicting Currents in Japan." She presented the perspective of Toyohiko Kagawa (1888–1960) a Japanese pacifist, Christian reformer and labor activist. Kagawa wrote, spoke and worked at length on ways to employ Christian principles in the ordering of society and differentiated between 'Japanism,' Communism and Christian socialism.

By the late 1930s the topics of study indicate that the women sensed the world was getting smaller. World social issues and systems were investigated, with Mary W. Clark presenting "American Cooperation in Some Social Problems Abroad" that included those in Turkey, India, Europe and the Philippine Islands. Later in the year papers presented by Charlotte Calkins and Caroline B. Hollings discussed social experiments: "Denmark, A Cooperative Commonwealth" and "Public Welfare of Norway and Sweden," respectively.

A frequent guest speaker, Mrs. Andrew J. George, reviewed current events in 1936. She spoke of two Japans — one is associated with "artistic expression, exquisite courtesy and prodigal hospitality; the other with increasing industrialism, insidious propaganda, and a determination to attain complete dominance over the Pacific. There is a conflict of principle within the country. If the army influence becomes paramount, Japan will probably seize the present moment when Europe is divided into two camps."[4]   She believed war with Russia was bound to come.

Turning to the European situation George said,

> Twenty-five years ago a move as provocative as Hitler's occupation of the Rhineland would have undoubtedly caused a war. Today with an organization like the League [of Nations] where opposing parties can sit around a table and with England firmly united behind leaders pledged to collective bargaining rather than the balance of power, there is still hope of peace. If war comes, the isolation of the United States can only be theoretical. To attain it we should be forced to accept a very much lower standard of living. On what is decided in London during the next weeks rests the future, not only of Europe but of America.[5]

And so the women understood that the global nature of society was increasing.

In 1937 Frederick L. Schuman, professor of political economy at Williams College, spoke of "The Challenge of Fascism," the current social experiment in Italy. He indicated that,

> Fascism, in the long run is a more serious danger to Democracy than is Communism. Fascism repudiates Democracy in theory and practice — as a means and as an end. Communism repudiates Democracy only as a means, not as an end. To achieve a communist revolution extraordinary conditions are necessary. To produce a Fascist revolution, the required elements are far less. The menace of Fascism, then is the menace of war.

The inevitable collapse of Italy, Germany and Japan

will certainly result in war, and the United States will as certainly be drawn into that war. The democratic countries must give up the cult of irresponsibility. They must show a united front, and say to Fascism 'Thus far, but no farther' if they wish to keep out of war, they must be willing to fight.[6]

As the war drew on Pennington Hale, a vice-director of the League of Nations, came to the Club through the courtesy of the Newton Trust Company. Speaking on the topic "Total Victory," Hale noted that World War I was the war to end all wars but since that had not happened it was clear that after that war the task was not completed. He said, "This time winning the war is a double challenge, meaning more than a military victory."[7] He proposed that, "The needs of the world must be organized with the United States taking its ratio of responsibility in proportion to its great power," [8] and he concluded with the idea that the world must be organized at an international level with a system that must produce a decent standard of living for all people. These sentiments rang true with the Club's motto — privilege is obligation.

The women of the Club not only were interested in the consequences of communism and fascism but also those of Nazism. In December 1943 Herbert Gezork, a professor at Wellesley College and Andover Seminary, spoke on the subject, "What hope for Germany's youth after Hitler?" He explained that the German youth were drawn into political organizations that turned them into "fanatical devoted followers of nazism." But, he said, "The awakening is already faintly beginning. Gezork quoted from a manifesto issued by students in Munich, cradle of Nazism, calling for rebellion against Hitlerism."[9] Miriam Drury, recording secretary, noted that the most important idea put forth by Gezork was "that of a United Europe which is integrated for purposes of war by the Nazis."[10] There was recognition that the union of Europe was advantageous although at the moment the union was being used for the wrong purpose.

After World War II the Club studied the territorial expansion of the United States and the defense outposts of America. In the next decade the defensive posture changed to one of needed cooperation. In April 1949 the women were fortunate to have as a guest speaker Monsieur Albert Chambon, French Consul in Boston. Chambon stated,

> France is looking for a new economic social system by which the worker will receive a proper share of the profit in accordance with his efforts and quality of work rather than as a gift or charity. Solid steps in building economic elements on which the European Federation must be based have developed recently. This Federation has become an irresistible movement which will succeed despite efforts to stop it. If economic union is established within nations and between nations, political union will follow and a stable and prosperous continent will be constructed.[11]

Little did the women know that a year later Robert Schuman, Foreign Minister of France, would initiate what became the European Union.

The women continued to increase their understanding of the wider world and in 1951 Robert Norton, a world affairs analyst, emphasized the fact that we are one world. He made the points that the public mind is turned toward decent human relations and that discrimination between the sexes must end so that the world can take advantage of "a great woman power."[12] Then, only about a decade after its founding, the United Nations became the topic of study in 1957. The focus of the women's papers was on the U.N. as a replacement for the League of Nations and its purpose of stopping wars between countries and providing a platform for dialogue.

In 1961 the Club joined the World Affairs Council, currently known as WorldBoston. The Clubwomen used the membership as a mechanism to keep abreast of the changing world since the mission of that organization was to educate, inspire and engage the people of Greater Boston in international affairs and the critical global issues of the times.

During 1962 three meetings addressed the continued need for global cooperation and communication. The Club's committee on international relations invited Jeanette Bailey Cheek, a Radcliffe College historian, to speak. Cheek emphasized the changing world saying, "The rising of new nations has reduced our [United States'] importance. We must not impose our ways and institutions on these new nations. The importance of the Peace Corps is what its members will learn from those countries. We are no longer able to command a majority of the United Nations; and will not in the future. The world cannot live without a World Organization, the United Nations or otherwise."[13]

Once again, peace and cooperation were emphasized. At a second meeting of significance Anna K. Merlino presented her paper, "Communication in One World." After giving some historical background she highlighted the need for "intercommunication in a shrinking world."[14]

The third meeting of note was also presented by the Club's committee on international relations. The panel of Clubwomen who spoke on the topic of "The Common Market" consisted of Esther W. Gleason, Elizabeth Lee, Margaret B. Haskell, Florence Glasgow Johns, Margaret Ball, and Margaret M. Gerrity. It is clear from the meeting report that these women foresaw the eventual development of the European Union. They spoke of the "importance of the European Economic Community's (EEC) influence on social security, wage standards and political unity. Information was presented on the composition and structure of the EEC as well as the possibility of Great Britain entering the group. Ball remarked, "We [the United States] support EEC as a strengthener of Western Europe and an aid in ending old rivalries."[15] Clearly, the women were aware that globalization was on the horizon.

As the role of guest speakers and committees diminished so too did the focus on the changing world and international relations. Although there were years in which the annual theme was focused internationally, the papers presented usually were directed toward one country and its culture. It wasn't until 1999 that a paper acknowledged the current state of globalization and its impact. Marie Baroni Allen's paper titled "The European Union: Reforming Europe in the Twenty-First Century" was presented on April 7, 1999, just three months after the fusion of the currencies of 11 of the EU countries with the introduction of the Euro. And so, as the world grows smaller and the women's span continues to broaden, the Club continues to be in tune with the changing world.

Reflections on a Changing Club

by Kate Stout

Growing pains have dogged the heels of the Social Science Club since the 1970s when society's attitude toward women in the workforce really began to change in earnest — and membership took a nosedive. Having time to 'do it all' — wife, mother, career woman — often required cuts in other activities. Many Clubwomen had to rein in leisure activities, including membership in the SSC. Further the Club's insistence that meetings be held in the middle of the work week, in the middle of the morning — in spite of the periodic efforts of a valiant few members with courage enough to suggest this practice be changed — has excluded potential members necessarily. The early members were required to be over 30 years of age, so that they might be seasoned enough by life and free enough from household duties to be good members; now most incoming members are newly retired.

Here is what one current Club member recalls:

When I first joined the Club in the 1970s most of the members were not career women. They were involved in their community: volunteer work, philanthropic work, the PTA, and garden and bridge clubs. They relished expanding their knowledge; giving a paper was a very serious obligation. But the role of women in the outside world was changing dramatically. In the 1980s it was difficult to get women to join the Club. They were working outside their homes and they began having too much

Nancy O'Brien
(Photo by Emily Hubbs Scott)

on their plates. Club membership dwindled so much I was alarmed.

But Newton was changing also. It became a more multi-cultural city and as the older members retired, moved away or passed away new women arrived to fill the gap. It was slow at first, but word got around that this club was worthwhile. It was wonderful to witness it becoming re-energized 10 or 15 years ago. Meetings, as well as the ladies themselves, became less formal and more relaxed. No longer were there two greeters by the door decked out in hat and gloves to meet you as you came in. During role call I was no longer Mrs. William O'Brien or Mrs. Nancy O'Brien; I was finally myself, Nancy O'Brien.

Lest you think that I am favoring today's member over yesteryear's, I want to be clear that the earlier women were no less educated, interesting or aspiring. It was that their 'world' was more insular and expectations were different. Perhaps in a way they had it easier. But we have it broader.

—Nancy O'Brien, SSC member since 1977, in 2010

A past president who wished to remain anonymous submitted a list of milestones as part of her response to a 2010 questionnaire polling members on their Club and life experiences. Many of these milestones can be found in the Club timeline (see Appendix I). But what she reports otherwise reflects two significant evolutions within the Club as it strives to stay both current and vibrant.

The first was the maturing of the Club into the 'Information Age,' particularly as regards recordkeeping and communication. Member histories, formerly kept by hand on 3x5 cards, were painstakingly computerized, transferring every member's details — papers written and offices held — from the cards to spreadsheet software which can now be easily updated annually. This advance did not take place until 2008!

The file cards are now part of the Club's archives at the Newton Library. The same past president also remembers when Club presidents began communicating with members by email. Not until 1998, however, were email addresses first listed in the Club's annual yearbook, and it was well into the 21st century — 2007 — before all active members had them to list.

The second change involved throwing a wider net for members and responding to the Club's other growing pains. The need to keep the Club viable meant opening up the membership to interested women well beyond Newton. While membership in 2011 is still comprised primarily of Newton residents, many other communities are now represented, among them Watertown, Framingham, Brookline, Wayland, Jamaica Plain, Lincoln and Concord. As part of a 1991 rewrite of the bylaws, paper lengths were reduced from one hour to 40 minutes, while by the end of that decade the reception, held after each paper was given, was expanded to encourage more social time. Both moves reflect efforts to foster increased participation and engagement. Further, member introductions became more detailed and inclusive as Club members' accomplishments grew. And most recently, in the spring of 2010, the policy for suggesting and electing new members was simplified, replacing an age-old secret voting system with a more modern — and welcoming — invitation to join.

Endnotes

1 Social Science Club, Record Book, vol. 11, April 14, 1915.

2 SSC, RB, vol 1, November 8, 1916.

3 SSC, RB, vol. 12, January 15, 1919.

4 SSC, RB, vol. 14, March 14, 1934.

5 Ibid.

6 SSC, RB, vol. 14, April 14, 1937.

7   SSC, RB, vol. 14, December 16, 1942.

8   Ibid.

9   SSC, RB, vol. 15, December 15, 1943.

10 Ibid.

11 SSC, RB, vol. 15, April 13, 1949.

12 SSC, RB, vol. 15, February 28, 1951.

13 SSC, RB, vol. 19, January 3, 1962.

14 SSC, RB, vol. 19, January 24, 1962.

15 SSC, RB, vol. 19, December 5, 1962.

Tradition continues to play a role in the Social Science Club. At a season-opening welcome tea Margaret Sudbey (SSC president 1994–96) presides over the Club's treasured sterling silver tea service.

CHAPTER SIX

THE CLUB AND WOMEN'S ISSUES

Changing Roles for Women

by Elizabeth Everett

Mrs. J. Bernard Everett, known by fellow members as Betty, joined the Club in 1979 and found herself giving a paper in the fall of that year. Was she perhaps a guest speaker immediately converted to membership? She belonged for a further 12 years, dropping out in 1992. This paper was presented on November 7, 1979. Edited and abridged by Vivi Leavy.

Betty Everett
(Photo by Emily Hubbs Scott)

How has American society, from the earliest day, traditionally controlled the role of a woman's life? What have individual women done to change the controls society has held on them? What obstacles to women's freedom of choice have been removed? What obstacles remain? What do today's shifting sex roles reveal about oppressed women? What are their chances of changing the basic conditions of their lives? This paper will endeavor to answer some of these questions. It will discuss the ways American women have reacted to traditional ideas about their 'place.' It will report the ways in which women have helped to lift the controls with which society has restricted their freedom, both in the past and in the 20th century.

When an American clergyman mounted his pulpit in the early colonial days he was likely to survey a sober congregation, each member secure in his precise social station. Frequently cited by clergymen then (and by Phyllis Schlafly[1] now) was the biblical passage: "And the Lord God said, it is not good that man should be alone, I will give him an Help-meet for him." The word 'help-meet' gave the colonial woman her role: "She must be so much and no less, so much and no more." Of course there is another story of the creation. When God created the heavens, he stood back and said, "I am very pleased." When he decided he needed something else he created man and then his reaction was, "I know I can do better than that." And then God created woman.

Colonial women had no right to property, no legal entity or existence apart from their husbands. They could not sign contracts; they had no title to their own earnings or to property, even when it was their own through inheritance or to their children in case of legal separation. Divorce, when granted at all, was given only for flagrant abuses.

The question of equal status for women was first raised by two Quakers, Anne Hutchinson and Mary Dyer. Anne preached the religious freedom of the individual conscience and also the principle that women should have a voice in church affairs. She and Mary discussed these ideas in evening meetings with other men and women in Anne's home. Because of these meetings, they were both brought to trial by the church and by the civil court. They were condemned as heretics and were banished from Massachusetts Bay Colony.

Abigail Adams, a forerunner of women's right, wrote in a letter to her husband John (May 1777):

> In the new code of laws which I suppose it will be
> necessary for you to make, I desire you would remember
> the ladies and be more generous and favorable to them
> than your ancestors. Do not put such unlimited power
> into the hands of the husbands. Remember all men would
> be tyrants if they could. If particular care and attention
> is not paid to the ladies, we are determined to foment a

rebellion, and will not hold ourselves bound by any laws
in which we have no voice or representations.

However, her husband termed her request "so saucy" and he added the further comment, "We men know better than to repeal our masculine system." So Abigail was ignored. Neither the Declaration of Independence nor the Constitution of the United States elevated women to the status of political beings.

All major religious groups at that time relegated women to the role of silent participation in church affairs, and none admitted women to the ministry. The only exception were the Quakers who believed in the equality of men and women before God. They gave boys and girls the same education as well as the same chance to speak at worship. From the Quakers came some of the leaders and supporters of the feminist movement.

On colonial farms, where the labor of both sexes was equally necessary, men and women were partners. The family was a primary economic unit throughout the 1800s for the farm families and those who had settled in the west. Among the new middle class, however, home and family came to be seen as separate from the world of work and money which men inhabited. Middle class women's housework and motherhood was no longer considered 'real work' because, unlike men, they earned no money. No longer partners with their husbands, the women became 'dependents.'

Women and blacks were and still are considered by some people the great outsiders in western culture. Their subordinate positions and efforts to change those positions parallel each other in a number of ways. But it was only when Elizabeth Cady Stanton and Lucretia Mott were refused admittance to the World Anti-Slavery Conference in London in 1840 because they were women that they suddenly perceived their own political existence as similar to that of blacks. They raised the issue with the radical American men and were denounced furiously for introducing an insignificant and divisive issue into the abolitionist movement. The men said in effect, "let's win this war first and then we'll see about women's rights." The women saw the truth about their own lives and knew that "first" was *now*; there would never be a time when men would willingly address themselves to the question of female rights.

Thus was born the original women's rights movement, which became known as the women's suffrage movement because the single great issue became legal political recognition. Lucretia Mott and Elizabeth Cady Stanton, after being barred from the London conference, set up the first women's conference in Mrs. Stanton's hometown, Seneca Falls, New York, in 1848. The question was, if all men are equal why not women? If a woman is equal, why should she not do anything a man might do — speak in public, vote, hold office, even lead organizations? Once these questions had been raised it was only a very short step to the next one. Why should not women organize to help themselves and gain the rights denied them?

More than 300 women (and men) gathered at Seneca Falls and passed a paper called The Declaration of Rights and Sentiments, modeled after the Declaration of Independence. This statement put the women's rights movement on a broad and sturdy foundation. It is regarded as the birth of the women's movement. Those responsible were fully aware of the nature of the step they were taking. Today's debt to them has never been fully acknowledged.

The Civil War touched the lives of women in all areas — family, home, work, politics. After the war many women gladly returned to the tranquility of their pre-war lives as soon as they could. Yet society had seen women in new and unaccustomed roles, as breadwinners, educators, reformers. In this as in so many other ways, the Civil War marked a watershed in American history. Women would never be quite the same again.

During the war feminists had subordinated their own interests to an all-out effort on behalf of emancipation. Afterwards they expected the full support of abolitionists for inclusion of women's rights in civil rights legislation. They were bitterly disappointed. The Fourteenth and Fifteenth Amendments did not outlaw sex discrimination. Many feminists thought they actually worsened the status of American women. The Constitution had never contained any specific restriction on female suffrage; the matter was left to the states. However, the Fourteenth Amendment guaranteed "male inhabitants" the vote, thus enshrining sex discrimination into federal law. The Fifteenth Amendment said that voting should not be denied because of race, color or previous servitude.

Gas lighting, municipal water supplies, plumbing, canned and packaged foods, improved laundry and cooking equipment, as well as the sewing machine — all these improvements gave numbers of women leisure time at the end of the 19th century for other pursuits. Soon women's groups were starting up all across the country. The largest and best known was the Women's Christian Temperance Union started by Frances Willard. She was able to turn a small group of zealots into the most dynamic women's organization the country had ever seen. Willard's slogan was "Do everything," and the members did. You have all heard stories of the exuberant Carrie Nation who burst into saloons without warning and broke every bottle in sight. Another vigorous organizer was Julia Ward Howe. She is mainly remembered now for the *Battle Hymn of the Republic* but she actually made her major contribution as a clubwoman. In 1868 with other Boston women, she founded the New England Women's Club and was president for many years. Similar organizations sprang up all over the country, as did the Social Science Club of Newton in 1886. The General Federation of Women's Clubs started in 1890.

In the early 1900s the influx of poor people into the city from rural America and from abroad led to the growth of slum areas, crime, corruption and vice. In response Jane Addams started Hull House, the first settlement house in the country. It marked the beginning of the settlement house movement which provided a training ground for future leaders of various reforms. Also at that time Margaret Sanger defied law, tradition and all notions of propriety and advocated birth control as a basic right of women, an issue which still provokes heated argument today.

Women's suffrage, which had lagged as a result of a split into two groups, one wanting state approval and the other federal, came together in the early 20th century to try again to gain the vote for women. The movement gained momentum as increasing numbers of reformers of all kinds saw in female suffrage a cure-all for the evils of society. Susan B. Anthony, Carrie Catt and Dr. Anna Howard Shaw were some of the presidents of the

National American Women's Suffrage Association which united women of all social classes to a common cause. In January 1918 Jeannette Rankin of Montana, the first woman representative in Congress, introduced the Nineteenth Amendment guaranteeing women the right to vote which was passed by a very close margin. The amendment was ratified and became law in 1920, culminating a 72-year struggle.

But contrary to expectations, women's suffrage did not decisively alter the status of women in America. The promised female bloc-vote failed to materialize. Instead, class, race and ethnic backgrounds proved to be decisive. Even today, 60 years later, women have achieved no more than token political representation.

Many remember how the depression of the 1930s cut off whatever economic gains women had made in employment as men were given priority in the competition for scarce jobs. In the 1940s World War II seemingly reversed this trend and once again brought large numbers of women out of the home and into industry. Many a joke was told and song was sung about Rosie the Riveter and her friends in the war factories. But when the war ended, as at the end of the Civil War, returning veterans quickly reclaimed their 'rightful place' in the economy and displaced female war workers. Millions of women voluntarily retired to domesticity and to motherhood which had been deferred by the war. The 1950s saw earlier marriages and a dramatically rising birth rate.

And yet the position of these women was different. The persistent urbanization of American society, the availability of birth control information, the reform in divorce laws, the more lenient societal attitudes toward divorced women and greater economic opportunities all changed women's place in society. These changes meant greater freedom in the event of marital unhappiness, but they also imposed greater emotional demands and psychic stress, as both marriage partners now expected to find personal fulfillment through marriage.

For working women there was little change. More and more women entered the labor market and participated in trade union struggles together with men. But the only gains made in employment for women were a larger number of low-paid, low-status occupations now designated informally as 'women's jobs.'

The resurgence of feminism in the 1960s represented the third incarnation of a dynamic women's rights movement in American history. The first, started in 1848 at Seneca Falls, grew out of the abolitionist struggle. The second developed from the social reform ethic of the early 1900s and crested with the battle over suffrage, but women's enthusiasm succumbed to factionalism and public indifference in the 1930s. The contemporary movement, like its predecessors, grew out of generalized social ferment; however, it differs from its forerunners in at least three ways. It is moving in the same direction as the underlying social trends today; it has developed a diverse and decentralized organizational base; and it is pursuing a wide range of social objectives that strike at the root causes of [gender] inequality. No previous feminist movement has attempted so much or been better situated to make progress toward the goal of equality.

In contrast to the happily married housewives and successful career women, in the 1960s, many women were living under severe oppression. They felt they had been 'put down' by their fathers, their brothers, their lovers, their bosses. They felt that in their families, in their sex lives and in their jobs they counted as nothing; that they were being treated as second-class citizens, that their minds had been deliberately stunted and their emotions warped. Many of them found respite in small, informal group meetings, much like the women who met with Anne Hutchinson in colonial days. The modern meetings were called 'consciousness-raising groups.'

The contemporary women's movement was under fire from the beginning. Its enemies and detractors were many, although often they posed in their own minds as supporters, saying things like, "Yes, there is much justification in what you are saying, but what awful women you put on TV!" or, "I've always believed in women's liberation — I take my wife out to eat all the time. But what's going on now is just incredible — those strident man-hating bitches you have for spokesmen!" It's true that some of the early groups were radical both in structure and in purpose. One, an offshoot of Students for a Democratic Society (SDS), burned their bras at an Anti-Miss America pageant. Another (called SCUM) regards men as biologically deficient and dangerous. Some of those who started consciousness-raising groups call themselves "Redstockings"; and Feminists — with a capital F — denounce love, sex and marriage. They say all men are the enemy.

The book which had the greatest influence on the contemporary feminist movement was *The Feminine Mystique* written in 1963 by Betty Friedan. She called on women to escape what she called "the enclosure of suburban domesticity" to a more fulfilling life. She did not decry the roles of wife and mother; she just contended that in modern times such roles were too narrow for healthy, intelligent women. With a group of professional women in 1963 Friedan started the National Organization for Women, now the oldest and largest feminist group. In 1969 NOW had 3000 members. By 1978 membership had grown to 90,000, with 800 chapters in the U.S. and abroad. NOW has many men in its ranks and works within the system to bring about "truly equal partnership between men and women." Its leaders are devoted to the idea that America is a reformist country that ultimately will respond to the justice of their cause. With other organizations NOW worked to [achieve] the *Roe v. Wade* decision in the Supreme Court in 1973, making abortion a federal right for women. Since then it has concentrated on the ratification of the Equal Rights Amendment (ERA) for which feminists have been working since 1923. When this amendment is ratified, the employment and marriage laws of more than 40 states will be affected. In conjunction with this effort, NOW has also been demanding that child-care facilities be established by law on the same basis as parks, libraries and public schools.

In the middle of the 1970s it seemed clear that changes in behavior and attitudes among American women would continue to shape the social history of the country for the remainder of the 20th century. The birthrate continued to fall, each year setting a new record low. The fertility rate of women 15 to 44 years old was only half of what it had been 20 years earlier. This decline coincided with a trend toward later marriages. The number of unmarried women in the 20–24 age bracket had climbed from

28% in 1960 to 37% a decade later. Simultaneously the greatest increase in the female labor force occurred among younger women of childbearing age. By 1973, 61% of all women aged 20 to 40 were working outside the home. Among college women in that age group the employment rate was 86%! But the fastest rise of all took place among women with young children. From 1959 to 1974 the employment rate of mothers with children under three years old more than doubled.

Poll data as well as professional school applications suggest a new commitment on the part of women college graduates to carve out careers and to view family life as only one part of their multiple interests. Between 1968 and 1980 the number of women college graduates was expected to increase by two-thirds, twice the rate of increase for men, providing a growing pool of potential career women. The women's movement continues to register a significant impact on the expressed values of young people, men as well as women, encouraging a cultural consensus that equality between the sexes is a good thing. A Roper poll which showed women supporting the movement toward equality also showed a majority of men endorsing change. In fact one survey of college students indicated that 86% of men, as well as 92% of women, believed fathers should spend as much time as mothers bringing up their children.

When women graduated from college in the '50s, they hoped to add a 'MRS' to their name; it was their security for the future. Today women graduates are desperate instead for a 'JOB,' feeling that will provide security. Most of them are anxious about starting a career, getting set in the right job or the right graduate school. A decade ago, in the late '60s, students wanted to change the system; today they just want to get into the system. Young women find themselves living in a time of greater choice than ever before. They have almost unlimited options in their lifestyles. They can choose to marry or not. They can choose to have children or not. They can choose to be housewives or working mothers or part-time working mothers. They can drop out of the work force and re-enter. They have more choices than any previous generation of women in history.

Nevertheless, women do not have economic parity. They do not hold a proper proportion of jobs in the professions or in government. They make up a high percentage of the workforce but too many are in clerical or service jobs, with only 4% in skilled positions and 5% in managerial or administrative jobs. Sixty-two per cent of women workers are heads of households, yet many do not receive wages or salaries commensurate with their abilities and needs because of discriminatory pay schedules far below those of males.

Women of both major political parties met this year [1979] in Cincinnati to secure equal representation as an "independent political force" at the 1980 presidential conventions. More than 1000 members of the National Women's Political Caucus heard once again the complaint that women do not have equal representation in political power. Founded in 1971, the NWPC has developed from a small special-interest group to a 40,000-member organization.

For the first time in history women are acting to support other women and men. Women are turning out in impressive numbers to call for rights for women. Men no longer have to put on the mask of a competitiv,e macho male. Women no longer have to depend on a husband for financial support and for societal recognition. Women are actively involved in the political process: seriously searching out issues; assuming positions of influence as women. They are working hard to convince politicians that they must make democracy work by opening their minds to the needs of all Americans.

Betty Everett's last word:

In 1985 when the theme for the year was "Study the Past and Shape the Future," Betty Everett returned to her earlier topic. Her new paper was called "Roles for Women: An Update." It reflected a changed reality for the women's movement. In 1979 the expectation was that the Equal Right Amendment would soon be passed and the legal position of women would be clarified for all time. By 1985, not only had the amendment failed to be ratified, but opposition among more traditional women to the feminist movement had coalesced and become effective. In the light of that, the way forward for women, Everett explained, was through education. Many universities by then included Women's Studies curricula; Title IX of the Education Amendments of 1972 required that women be treated as equal with men in any federally supported education function; many more women were enrolled in graduate schools, training for traditionally male professions like law or accounting; the community college system supported the return to the classroom of older women. There was to be no legal watershed but a continuation of the long trudge of women to expand their choices.

Everett concluded her paper with a strong call for continuing social change:

First, it is essential to view women as different from men in their psychological makeup and to fight harder to have these differences valued by this society. We must continue to listen to the different voices of women's development, acknowledging and valuing their connectedness to others. The woman who stays home and nurtures her family must not be denigrated for that choice. The woman who chairs the annual company meeting must be supported in her efforts. Our society must support working women by providing good, accessible day care, maternal and paternal leaves, job sharing options and an equitable salary structure. Professions built upon the ability to nurture and serve others must be given the recognition and status they deserve. A society that does not reward relatedness, compassion and empathy will inevitably leave women as victims and the society itself weakened.

Second, we must recognize the multitude of women who have no choice because of poverty and understand that we have a moral imperative to work to change their social realities. If we believe a woman's wellbeing is linked to her ability to make choices, then we have a responsibility to make choice a reality for all women. We have a responsibility to express our outrage at a cultural and economic system that continues to work against and oppress women. Economically, women as a group are poorer today than before the advent of the women's movement. The opportunity to choose satisfying labor outside the home remains a distant prospect for most women. In this sense real liberation for most women, allowing true choice and freedom from psychological and economic constraints, has not yet come into existence.

A Woman's Role
by Vivi Leavy

What should a woman be and do? The women who founded the Social Science Club wanted to expand the existing vision of a woman's role in life. They invited speakers to consider the questions, read books providing the answers, discussed the issues and presented their own papers. Through the years, as Mary Tucker noted in her verse for the Club's tenth anniversary: "...perhaps the favorite topic of this tireless S.S.C., was Woman, past and present, and what she was to be." Long-lived founding member Charlotte Calkins recalled those words at the Club's annual lunch in 1924 and even today's Club members periodically present papers on women and their roles. There have been changes though. In the Club's first decades a woman's duties as mother and homemaker, and the difficulties involved, were an important part of the conversation. In later decades the discussion shifted to how women should advance their capabilities in society and finally in the workforce.

In the winter of 1890 Club meetings were decimated by illness so instead of the usual presentations, the women read Frances Power Cobbe's series of lectures collected in an 1881 book, *The Duties of Women*.[2] Cobbe was an Irish reformer, journalist and suffragist whose arguments for the emancipation of women were based in her religious and ethical views. As a child of God, woman was the equal of man and her legal status should reflect that. Cobbe explained that few men realize that women have "brains to be cultivated and wills seeking also, like their own, for the free use of whatever powers we may inherit." She went on to say, "It is our task to make society more pure, more free from vice, either masculine or feminine, than it has ever been before." The way to accomplish that was through "the one only safe, true way of progress — the way of Duty." She defined duty as conscientiousness, unselfishness, temperance and chastity, and went on through the rest of her lectures to expand on why and how women should exemplify those qualities. This way of framing the issues must have been deeply reassuring to early Club members who were surely churchgoers: half the founding members were wives or daughters of ministers. Echoes of Cobbe's eloquent words appear in the Club's discussions.

In March 1892 future Club president Adelaide Blodgett gave her views on "The Age of Woman." This was the first of a series of presentations on the role of women but hers was the only one by a member of the Club. Her main point was that women are principally useful to society as an inspiration for great men. As usual in such essays Blodgett traced the roles of women in history starting in ancient Greece. She spoke of "mechanical improvements and educational progress, and of the improvements of great men's ideals as emancipation advances." Would Frances Cobbe have blanched? The discussion which followed included the "mythological symbolism" of women and Goethe's "eternal feminine," the idea at the end of *Faust Part II* that men strive because women inspire them. Alice Buswell, a young Smith College graduate, was taking notes for the record that day, and from her flat tone it is obvious that she considered that nothing new or interesting had been said.

A few years later in April 1899 Club member Mabel Hall, the first head of the Nonantum Industrial School and future principal of the Newton Private School, a co-ed college preparatory school, presented an "End of the Century Outlook for Women." Hall noted that women had made so many advances in the previous 50 years that it was "well to pause in the rush of progress and consider what women really want." For her, what women wanted was a women's club. The club movement was probably "the greatest form of development. Their influence being of great import in all the phases of human life." She went on to pose and then answer a number of questions about clubs: "Is the club life a helpful state of society? Does it threaten home life? Are the differences between the masculine and feminine mind lessening by the broad education now open to women, or are these fundamental and ineradicable?" It is too bad we aren't told how she answered these queries. Hall also "touched on women's outlook in politics, in society and in business, showing her opportunities but thinking it better for her not to enter the political or business field generally. She thought women and men should work side by side each in his or her special way, with no struggle for supremacy." She also emphasized her belief in education, "thorough training and practical use of all powers," as long as women remained in their proper sphere.

Club member Anne B. Wheeler gave the next full consideration of the state of women in November 1905. She called her talk, "The Evolution of the New Woman and Some of Her Problems." She set her remarks in a Christian context which would have been completely familiar to Cobbe and then reviewed the history of women from Sappho through Aspasia, to renaissance women who "filled chairs of philosophy and law," to famous English and French women of the recent past. She noted that in America "gradually schools of higher learning have opened their doors to [woman's] gentle touch, until today she stands not above or below but beside her brother and co-worker." Although she mentioned the need of an increasing number of women to work outside the home, her focus remained on a woman's domestic life. "Woman should aim to make her home a center of rest and comfort. The failure to realize the larger meaning of life, the diversity of interests of husband and wife, the clubs and secret societies that in so many cases make of home merely a lodging place, are largely responsible for domestic discord." Women must prevent discord.

In 1912 Club members embarked on a series of papers over the month of January with the theme, "Women in the Progress of Civilization." They covered the state of women in non-Christian Europe (condescendingly); women in Christian Europe (admiring only England); women immigrants (quoting Jane Addams); women as seen by novelists ("firm, sympathetic guidance is necessary for readers"); and women as seen by foreigners (Matthew Arnold disliked the "American voice of women.") The last presentation in the series was by Rosa Fuller on "The American Woman As Seen by Her Family." She compared the women of the Club to "a paper of assorted needles, straight and fine, bright and as true as steel, with clear vision, capable of coming to the point; of good temper and easy to guide, but when pressed too hard or driven rudely, apt to go to pieces." What a domestic image, fitting for women whose horizons were wider than their mothers' but who still felt most comfortable within the home and perhaps afraid of falling apart if they took on too much.

The tone of Club member Mary Speare's presentation on "Women's Achievements" in January 1929 is refreshing. Women had successfully joined the workforce in the First World War, and their perspectives had changed. While she started her review of women in the time of Plato, she proceeded to "the great victories since the first convention of women's rights in 1848, showing in each phase the century-old struggle of feminism culminating in the welcome of women today in the professional world." Women had made it out of the house. The reason for their success was not very different from Cobbe's or Blodgett's conception, however. "Underlying all leadership, Speare emphasized woman's greatest achievement, her womanliness, her mother-heartedness, her inspirational power." Mary Speare went on to describe in some detail the work of the social reformers Lady Astor (Nancy Langhorne before marriage) and Albion Fellows Bacon and the war relief work of physicist Marie Curie, all role models for the women of the SSC in the mold of the revered Jane Addams.

There is a big gap following Mary Speare before the topic of women was taken up again. By April 1962 when Ruth Simpson presented "The Emancipated Woman Re-examined," women had once more joined the workforce for the duration of the Second World War and then found themselves back home afterward, more unwillingly than before. "This may be called the era of the feminist revolution," she began. Simpson contrasted the emancipated women of the Club's early days with those of her own day. Then, "It was felt that women were not fitted physically or mentally for the rigors of the intellectual life and were jeopardizing their chances for matrimony. . . . Today one-third of the students in colleges and universities are women. Over 80% marry, and those who do not, find life

211

more satisfying and stimulating than ever before. The limit of a woman's professional education is that of her own individual drive for learning. More and more women are going into the professions." Ruth Simpson's focus was clearly on women moving into the world of paid work. She said, "The one type of woman who is new in this century is the one who is part of the world she lives in, who desires and expects to integrate within herself the functions of wife and mother, mistress and housewife, citizen and individual, wage earner and lady. She has not yet completely adjusted to her new role; it is still in a period of transition. The majority of women seem to settle for a compromise less strenuous, with part-time employment the answer for some, or volunteer, church and cultural work. Middle-aged women are re-entering the labor market in an increasing number and also going back to studying."

A decade later in February 1972 Patricia Bell put the events she saw going on around her into the context of the women's movement through the years in her paper, "Modern Woman Emerges." The women she chose as exemplars were political not social reformers: Lucy Stone, Eleanor Roosevelt and Betty Friedan. Patricia Bell was a Smith College classmate of Betty Friedan and took part in a survey she circulated at their 15th reunion in 1957, the answers to which contributed to Friedan's groundbreaking 1963 book, *The Feminine Mystique*. Bell related how Friedan, a free-lance writer "sensed as she traveled the country a malaise and a feeling that there was a growing belief that education was making women masculine and frustrated. This feeling was preventing many women from developing their full potential. The answers [Friedan] received convinced her it was not the education that was causing the frustration but the fact that these women did not fit into the 'feminine mystique' which was abroad in the land. She set about to pinpoint this mystique in her book." Although Cobbe might not have understood all the terms of this argument, the goal, that woman should attain her full potential, is essentially the same as Cobbe's aim that a woman should regard herself as equally and fully a child of God.

Interestingly, since Betty Everett's 1979 paper, "Changing Roles for Women," Club members have not addressed the topic again. The general question, 'What should a woman be?' has evolved into the much more individual one: 'Given all the choices now before me, what should I do?' Perhaps more important, the typical Clubwoman is no longer an energetic 40-year-old mother whose household obligations have lifted enough to enable her to take on some outside projects and who is struggling with issues of what and how much. Today's members of the Social Science Club are apt to have completed or be well settled in their careers, often ones much like those of the husbands of earlier members.

Women at Work, Then and Now

by Anne McKinnon Larner

When it comes to the issue of women's work — at home or in the workforce — the women of the Social Science Club of Newton in 1890 and 2010 share more in common than one might think. From a 21st century perspective, the world for women professionals at the beginning of the 20th century was fairly limited. But limitation is relative. Club members from both eras expressed optimism about the broad opportunities that had opened up in their own lifetimes for women like themselves. Also, many noted continuing discrimination against women in certain jobs and professions; they struggled with support systems that were and still can be problematic (household help, au pairs, after-school care); and they bemoaned no-win choices forced upon them by societies that had and still have an ambivalence about women's roles as both manager of a household (and children) and competitive professional worker.

Dream and Reality at the Beginning of the 20th Century

In a presentation to the membership in 1890, Ethie M. Bigelow stressed the need for education, and specialized training, stating that such preparation would serve young women well in business and in life. Her paper revealed the possibilities members saw for their daughters and some of the barriers they themselves hoped to dismantle. While a handful of the Club's younger members at the time were fortunate to have had a college

213

education, most members in the early years had not. Insufficient training and education and a culture that saw business and the professions as a male domain limited the options for women like the members of the Club.

> In training boys for their life work it is taken for granted that they shall conduct all branches of business and consequently they are taught details with thoroughness. With girls this training is omitted in general, as she is expected to engage in active business simply to bridge over the time between school and marriage when someone will give her the support which has been the main object of her struggling. Once in a while an independent self-reliant woman manages a business, a farm, an orange grove, edits a paper or invents successfully — but as a rule women are inclined to shrink from responsibility or publicity and naturally defer to men in business matters.
>
> *But of late years a gradual change has come about and nowadays girls are not considered bold or lacking in domestic virtues because they follow out their tastes and become teachers, doctors, or lawyers, or even aldermen and mayors.*[3] [emphasis added]

While Bigelow emphasized the positive, some members of the Club at that time encountered stumbling blocks. Mary Whiton Calkins became a member of the Club after receiving a B.A. degree from Smith College in the late 1880s. Soon thereafter Calkins took a position at Wellesley College teaching Greek. A year or two later Wellesley offered her a position teaching psychology (her primary interest) if she was able to complete a year's focused study in the subject. Following her father's intervention with President Eliot, Calkins was allowed to unofficially study psychology under William James at Harvard. Subsequently she received permission also to work unofficially with Hugo Münsterberg who James brought from Germany to head the psychology laboratory at Harvard. At the end of her studies, Calkins requested to be examined, and a committee put her through the paces of a traditional exam for a Ph.D. which she passed with high praise. Harvard refused to confer a degree despite support for her from James and Münsterberg because she was a woman and had not been a registered student.[4] Several years later Radcliffe offered Calkins a doctorate but she refused the offer on principle. Despite the lack of the advanced degree, Calkins enjoyed a long-distinguished career holding various positions at Wellesley College for over 30 years. She also became the first female president of the American Psychological Association in 1905.[5] Her experience exemplified both the possibilities and the obstacles facing women with dreams and ambitions.

According to the U.S. Census of 1900, 28% of Massachusetts women of working age (then set at 10 years) were employed. Over 40% of those working labored in factories and a third worked as domestics. In general young women from well-to-do families (including Social Science Club members) did not work. By social convention and in certain instances by law married women were barred from gainful employment.[6] Even for single women who had finished schooling, the norm in the social circles the Club membership came from was not to work. On occasion, driven by ambition or finances, single women taught school or worked in a library, but more often they devoted their time to charitable work or church matters and were supported by parents or siblings. Club experience reflected this pattern. Of the 22 Club members who were single and residents of Newton between the years 1900 and 1910, only five can be found in any U.S. Census or *Newton City Directory* with an occupation listed either during those years or the several decades before or after. The five with work listed included two physicians, a teacher, a secretary and a librarian. The evidence suggests the other 17 never were employed even though 12 of them were in the prime employment ages of 22 to 45 between 1900 and 1910. The census data is consistent with the March 1894 Annual Report in the Club's records:

> The members are mostly women occupied with home affairs, and for this reason the Club presents what is a most significant feature of this age. At no other period of history have [such] home-abiding women occupied themselves

with studies in politics and social economy. To these women, this is a relaxation from household routine.

Many of the members gained their training as teachers in their youth and others have served upon the Board of Foreign Missions. The Club welcomes young members and has always had in its membership college graduates. One of these young members, Miss Mary Whiton Calkins, a graduate of Smith College, is now instructor in psychology at Wellesley College. She is the author of a valuable work upon profit sharing. Miss Alice H. Bassett is vice president of the Massachusetts Association of Working Girls' Clubs and a member of the board of directors. Miss Alice Buswell, also a graduate of Smith College, is president of the Newton board of the Massachusetts Association of Working Girls' Clubs and is a member of the Committee of Instruction in the state association. Both Miss Bassett and Miss Buswell are members of [our Club's] Vacation House Committee.

The Club was rightly proud of its members' accomplishments, whether it be their training, employment or community charitable work. Cornelia Jackson,[7] a Club member from 1893 to 1902, was a librarian on the first staff of the Newton Free Library when it opened its doors in June 1870. By the time she joined the Club she was 57 and focusing on charitable work. Jackson lived in the

Cornelia Jackson, librarian and Club member. old family homestead with two unmarried sisters who were not Club members. Her sister Ellen gave 'drawing lessons' — the only one of the three consistently noted in census records as working. Florence Butterfield, on the other hand, was just 34 when she joined the Club in 1905 and managed for two years to juggle work as a secretary with Club duties before resigning from the SSC. Mabel Hall joined in 1886 at age 20 and resigned in 1902 when her increasing responsibilities as an educator made it difficult to continue.[8]

By 1899 Club membership included a physician, Dr. Clara D. W. Reed, with a second joining the group in 1904, Dr. Deborah Fawcett.[9] Clara Reed joined the Club near the end of a long career. Dr. Reed was born in 1840 in Alstead, New Hampshire. At 17 she married William Whitman who was killed in the Civil War, leaving her with an infant daughter Viola. In 1869 the young widow married George F. Reed. After her second husband died in 1874, Clara Reed turned to the study of medicine, graduating from the Boston University School of Medicine in 1878.[10] She spent a number of years practicing medicine in Bellows Falls, Vermont, before moving to Newton where she practiced for more than 25 years before her death in 1911.

Deborah Fawcett also graduated from the B.U. School of Medicine, but joined the Club in 1904 at the beginning of her career when she was fresh out of medical school and just 33 years old. Dr. Fawcett lived to be 81 and practiced medicine in Newton for more than 40 years. She also did further medical studies in London and Heidelberg.

Dr. Fawcett was a native of Northern Ireland who came to the United States as a young girl. She moved to Newton in the late 1890s. In her first full year in the Club Fawcett caused quite a sensation by running for the Newton School Committee, challenging an incumbent. The Club supported her with enthusiasm and helped finance her campaign. The following bolded, boxed notice on the front page of *The Newton Graphic* above the fold no doubt carried the fingerprints of her Club supporters who knew how to 'arrange' front page announcements:[11] They aggressively pushed her credentials as a physician.

Why vote for Dr. Fawcett

1st Because she is a **PROPERLY QUALIFIED WOMAN** and we feel it a duty to secure a fair representation of such women on our school board.

2nd Because today we have only **ONE** woman on the

board and **FOURTEEN** men.

3rd Because there is no physician on the board and in view of the fact that she has made a special study of nervous and contagious disease, also of sanitation, we feel that her service would be of **GREAT** value, **ESPECIALLY** as touching ventilation, fumigation and in dealing with some of the most [word obliterated] problems that confront educators today. Namely: physical training as well as mental, and over work which causes us so many nervous breakdowns among our young students.

4th Because as a **QUALIFIED** woman she is entitled to the support of every citizen who believes in women on the board.

5th Because this is not a question of **PARTY AFFILIATION**, but it is your opportunity to elect the **RIGHT WOMAN**.

Though she was not successful in her bid for the seat against an entrenched incumbent Herbert Stebbins, Dr. Fawcett made a strong showing and excited many women to action.[12]

The women of the Club were familiar with a number of female doctors besides their fellow Club members Reed and Fawcett. As early as 1892 the Club invited Dr. Julia Dutton who lived and practiced in Newton to speak to the membership about the prevention of nervous disorders. Her main point to the members was the importance of women educating themselves about physiology and the causes of diseases with the purpose of preventing suffering and the loss of life. Another physician, Dr. Julia Plummer of Boston, spoke to the Club in 1894 about the need for help for young women who had become pregnant out of wedlock. She was looking for financial assistance for Talitha Cumi, a home for unwed mothers in Jamaica Plain that she was associated with for more than 20 years, but also cautioned the women about the importance of educating their own daughters about sex and the challenges of dealing with sexual attraction.

Members were so impressed with Dr. Plummer that they arranged for her to speak to their own young daughters about sexuality and social mores at a special gathering the following month.

The 1905 business section of the *Newton City Directory* listed 85 physicians either working in or residing in Newton. Of the 85 at least 16 were females. Use of initials instead of given names masks the sex of five of the listed doctors. So it is fair to state that at least 20% of the listed doctors were women. The 1900 U. S. Census tagged the percentage of female doctors nationally to be 6% at the time. Boston registered 18% of physicians as female in that same census. With Boston as the site of the first co-ed medical school (Boston University Medical School) and one of the first female-founded and female-run hospitals focused on the health of women and children (New England Hospital), the city and surrounding communities were natural magnets for women physicians.

A 1910 report from the Carnegie Foundation on the state of medical education in the United States and Canada stated, "Medical education is now in the United States and Canada, open to women upon practically the same terms as men. If all institutions do not receive women, so many do, that no woman desiring an education in medicine is under any disability in finding a school to which she may gain admittance. Her choice is free and varied. She will find schools of every grade accessible." The report did note that women at that time lacked the same opportunities as men for intern privileges and that situation needed to be addressed. All in all the opportunities for women to become physicians in the Boston area were quite promising as the 20th century began.[13]

While females often comprise 50% or more of medical school classes today — B.U. Medical School's most recently available statistics show the entering class 55% female — progress has not been a straight line. Iolanda Low a current member of the Club and a physician with a Harvard M.D. degree was one of seven female students in a class of 140 that began studies in 1949 — the fifth year that Harvard Medical admitted women. Gains made for women in the late 19th and early 20th century in medicine disappeared in the 1920s and 1930s and aspiring doctors like Low often found tougher restrictions in the 1940s and 1950s than women like Clara Reed and Deborah Fawcett had found 50 to 60 years earlier.[14]

Other Women at Work: Helping the Help

The women of the Social Science Club at the beginning of the 20th century were concerned about other women besides themselves. While they struggled with issues about their own lives and the possibilities for their daughters, they pushed for reforms for women of more modest means who had no choice but to work to support themselves or their families. Club members advocated for decent working conditions in factories and equitable pay for female teachers. They also gave considerable time and thought to the issues and challenges of domestic service. This was an issue they knew intimately both from study and personal experience.

The 1900 U.S. Census indicates that just under one-third of working women in Massachusetts were employed in domestic service at the turn of the century — the second largest employment sector after manufacturing. At that time to be a servant to a middle or upper class family generally meant to live in. Data collected by Club member Dorothy McClure Wilson in the mid-1930s showed domestic service as the top occupation for Newton women in that decade. Between 1900 and 1930 much changed in domestic service. Clubwomen around the country along with other social reformers played key roles in effecting some of those changes.

Although census data at the city level (as opposed to the state or federal level) is difficult to access for the late 19th and early 20th centuries, a perusal of street-level data for the Newton corner area (e.g., Waverley Avenue, Franklin, Park, Church, and Sargent Streets and Billings Park) reveals a significant majority of homes listing live-in servants in 1900 — most commonly one or two servants but sometimes three or four. Large homes, many children, care of aging relatives or unmarried female siblings and the absence of technical advances[15] we take for granted today all contributed to the need for household help. Studies of that period also indicate that live-in help had become a status symbol for many families as well as a key to allowing middle-class and wealthy women the support that freed them to participate actively in community affairs, including club work.[16]

Of the 27 Social Science Club members listed in the 1900–01 yearbook as officers or key committee members, 21 listed live-in servants on the federal census that year, collectively employing 28 domestic helpers.[17] Sixteen employed just one servant, four families employed two and one family employed four. No detail was available on day help, but anecdotal evidence suggests some families used additional day help at least periodically. The Club members' live-in servants listed in the census were overwhelmingly female, white, single and between 20 and 30 years old. Typically they had recently emigrated either from Ireland or English-speaking Canada. (Seventeen of the 28 listed servants fit this description.) Among the Club members' employees there were also four black servants — three females and one male, all from the south — as well as several men from Armenia and individuals from Norway, Bohemia and Scotland. Census data from 1900 to 1920 coupled with comments by Club members suggests turnover was constant, with long-term service to one family a rarity.

In December 1902 Laura Drake spoke to her fellow Club members about her solutions for addressing the "servant problem." At the time Drake was 32, did not yet have children, but was responsible for a home that included, in addition to her husband, her mother-in-law, a boarder and one servant. Drake's thought was to put the relationship between a domestic servant and her employer on a more business-like basis, including a signed contract with protections for both parties. Drake had discovered research by Mary Trueblood, a graduate of Mount Holyoke, who was commissioned by the Massachusetts Bureau of Labor to do a report on domestic service in Massachusetts. Trueblood conducted a large series of confidential interviews with women in Lowell, Haverhill, Lynn, Brockton and Fall River about their work as domestics. She analyzed their concerns and prioritized their needs.

Drake reported three priorities that women articulated in their interviews with Trueblood: personal time off for relaxation and vacation, bathroom privileges and physical space within the home for receiving callers. Though still relatively new at running a household, Drake understood that only by meeting the needs of the servants as well as those of the mistresses could the "problem" be addressed. Her desire to form a "club of a half dozen ladies and a number of girls from shops and factories who were willing to do housework under the right conditions" and get them to draft a contract of mutual benefit seemed a step in the right direction. While she utilized someone else's research to develop her thinking, she understood that developing an effective contract would take hands-on work by a group of employees and employers working together.[18]

Eight years later in February 1910 Sarah Ivy, as part of a Club series on household help, suggested forming working girls' clubs for household employees in part as a vehicle for training employees and in part to provide support and socialization for the domestics. She spoke of the challenge of living in close quarters (servant and mistress), often without friendliness. "The personal relations are not frank and open and the result is envy and jealousy on the one side and a spirit of criticism on the other." She suggested the need for a strong dose of the golden rule. Ivy and Drake were but two of a handful of Club members who focused presentations on issues of household help in the first decade of the new century.

Domestic service was a frequent topic of interest for many women, not just members of the Club. Popular magazines of the period such as *Cosmopolitan, Ladies Home Journal, Harpers' Bazaar* and *Outlook* often carried articles about servants and servant-employer relationships.[19] Such articles together with solid research published around the same time by Professor Lucy Maynard Salmon of Vassar College provide a detailed picture of the 'problem' both Drake and Ivy tried to address. From the employer's perspective the chief issue was difficulty in finding and retaining good help. The typical domestic employee stayed less than one-and-a-half years according to Salmon's survey work. Available help was seldom experienced, usually had no exposure to a middle-class American environment and was often restless and discontent with the limited excitement available working in a household. Issues from the employee's perspective fell into two categories — issues with working conditions and issues with the social consequences of employment as a servant. Long hours with unpredictable time off headed the list of difficult working conditions.[20]

> [Unlike the shop girl, the live-in servant is as] bound to the house as an old serf to the land. She cannot go sailing down the road for an hour in the middle of the day. She is not free for the evening, with its excitements of the streets, the cinemas, and the soldiers in the park. She has to live other people's lives from the moment she gets up till the moment she goes back to bed. She is at best a well kept prisoner.[21]

The low social position that domestic service entailed was the key social complaint that limited the pool of women willing to accept such work or to stay in such work for any length of time. Unwillingness to be called a 'servant' topped the list of complaints in Salmon's survey of employees. The sense of disrespect in always being addressed by one's given name when other women are addressed respectfully as Miss or Mrs.; having no social space to entertain or even offer a friend a cup of tea; the social isolation — "I belong to the same church as my employer, yet have no share in the social life of the church," reported one employee respondent to Professor Salmon — all underscored the low status society placed on the job.

Traditional household maids and cooks were not the only domestic employees that raised concerns with Club members. The seamstress or dressmaker was also an issue. In 1910 at the same February meeting at which Sarah Ivy spoke of relations with traditional domestic workers, Helen Howes Gleason made a presentation on the issues with dressmakers visiting the home. In the early 20th century dressmakers were often itinerant live-in employees who worked a circuit of customers, staying for several weeks with a family to meet their seasonal clothing and household sewing needs. The greater Boston area had a limited number of custom dress shops where one could make arrangements for additions to one's wardrobe, forcing many families to settle for the traveling seamstress. Gleason compared the upset caused a household by having a seamstress in the house with the other alternative of ready-made garments which often "are ill-fitting and shoddily made." Ready-made also created the problem of meeting one's 'twin' at a social gathering or walking down the street. "Yet if having the sewing done at home unfits one for one's other duties, that is not right,"Gleason said, quoting a ladies magazine of the era.[22] Club minutes do not elaborate on exactly what Gleason saw as the problem between seamstress and mistress but it is reasonable to assume that, on top of any cultural issues, the presence of the seamstress disrupted household routine. Unlike the situation with traditional live-in servants, the employee in this case rather than the mistress was in charge of the time. The seamstress was there for a set number of days and the family had to conform to her schedule, attending fittings as she needed. Competent seamstresses were in limited supply so an unhappy mistress was in a tough position with limited acceptable alternatives.

The work of reformers like Lucy Salmon, staff at the Women's Educational and Industrial Union and researchers at the very active Massachusetts Bureau of Labor seeded community discussions such as those at the Social Science Club with their studies and survey work. They were all part of a force that slowly but surely together changed the face of domestic service.

> Gradually the life of the servant began to change through a combination of servants' struggles for more personal freedom and, ironically, the rise of the middle-class women's social reform groups concerned with questions of child and female labor, among other issues. Together, maids and social reformers began to call for a restructuring of domestic service. [S]ervants' hours were gradually shortened, domestic responsibilities were made more manageable and living conditions began to be re-negotiated.[23]

The exodus of women from domestic service into factory work (with its shorter working hours) as well as the advocacy of reformers and Clubwomen forced changes in working conditions for domestic help and also started a shift from live-in to live-out relationships between servants and employer families. And an improving quality of ready-made garments provided mistresses with acceptable alternatives should a dressmaker's visits become too disruptive for the household. Also contracts became more common just as Laura Drake had urged.[24]

While the street-level data for the 1930 U.S. Census documents a good number of live-in servants remained on Franklin, Park and Church Streets as well as Waverley Avenue and Billings Park, research supports that by 1930 the trend was clearly moving toward live-out help for those able to employ household assistance. The Great Depression and World War II completed what the reformers began.

Today the percentage of families that employs live-in help is very small. The occasional *au pair* or nanny is the most common live-in. With easy access to quality prepared foods, professional cleaning services, day-care and after-school programs and a host of work-saving appliances, even households in which all adults are employed full-time seldom require the services of live-in help.

Women's Suffrage

by Vivi Leavy

Obtaining the right to vote for women, the key aspiration of the first wave of feminism, was only one of the many subjects which engaged the women of the Social Science Club in the Club's first two decades, even though it was a particular project of Lucy Sawyer, their president during six formative years (1888–1894). While Club members were divided on their support for general women's suffrage and even municipal suffrage, when it came to school committees, where Massachusetts women had been given the right to vote in 1879, they encouraged each other to use that right and supported women candidates, sometimes with Club funds, from very early on.

The first mention of suffrage in the Club records is typical. In November 1887 when the Club was in its first year, Sawyer read a letter telling members about recent elections in Kansas, the only state in the union affording women full municipal suffrage at the time. Lucy Sawyer was most likely a member of the Newton Equal Suffrage League and well placed to keep SSC members informed. Municipal suffrage was a topic of particular interest having been voted down once in the Massachusetts House in 1881 but heading toward another vote.

In November of 1889, Sawyer, now Club president, told members that the Suffrage League had asked her to have the Club devote a morning's discussion to the topic of suffrage. This may not have been well received since no further mention of it occurred, and the diplomatic Mrs. Sawyer would never insist.

Finally, in early 1891, the question of whether women in Newton should have the right to vote in city elections came to the fore. Club member Adelaide Gilman was the second wife of Gorham Gilman, a state senator active in suffrage issues. He seems to have regarded the SSC as a useful place to exchange views. On February 25 the notice of State House hearings on women's suffrage was read out at the start of a Club meeting followed by Senator Gilman's "remarks on the duty of women to vote for members of the school board." That was followed up a month later on March 25 by a straw vote at Senator Gilman's request: How many would refuse the right of suffrage if granted? — Nobody! How many thought women's suffrage would be an advantage to the city? — 14 of those present. How many thought it would be a disadvantage to the city? — six members. How many would accept the right of suffrage if granted? — 20! Can we assume only twenty women were present? Normal meeting attendance in those days was more than 50. Suffrage was obviously not a straightforward issue for these Clubwomen.

That wasn't the end of the suffrage discussion for that year though. On April 22 Russell Ballou, husband of member Augusta Ballou and editor of the Universalist newspaper, *The Christian Banner*, spoke to members gathered in their home on "Women and Natural Law." As reported, he gave a straightforward analysis of how natural law worked and then added a few personal observations, that there was a failure on the part of mankind to notice the force of these laws and that women had a natural tendency to rely too much on faith. "The progress of women as a result of the working out of natural law was discussed next and an inimical treatment of the suffrage question given. . . . From the standpoint of natural law we must agree women's best work is done in the domestic sphere," he said. His listeners did not let these conclusions go unchallenged. Mary Stetson "gave some incidents from her experience in temperance work showing where in her opinion the votes of women are most needed. . . . Mrs. Wilson spoke of the duty of women to study political science. . . ." At the end of the discussion Orinda Hornbrooke, ever the traditionalist, spoke out against suffrage "pointing out the local and transient nature of this privilege, even for men, and speaking of the power already possessed by women without this right."

A year later opinions on suffrage among the women were still divided. An appeal from the School Suffrage Association was read out at a February 1892 meeting urging the women of Massachusetts to use their right to vote to improve the schools. "Mrs. Wellington made some very eloquent remarks in support." About half the women present voted that they were ready to join a movement "for awakening interest among Newton women." Their mixed enthusiasm was not unusual. Throughout Massachusetts only a small proportion of eligible women actually voted in school committee elections. The women of the SSC discussed the topic in December 1893 pointing to the difficulties in registering before voting.

During the early 1890s Lucy Sawyer, aided by Lydia Wellington, offered tickets to the Annual Suffrage Supper and reported on it to members afterwards, handed out suffrage circulars and, when urged, spoke on the topic. At the special annual luncheon in April 1893, to which representatives of many Boston-area women's clubs were invited, Sawyer "touched on the subject of suffrage." Her remarks were followed up by Elizabeth Peabody, Mrs. Gregory and Miss Orcutt,[25] all saying "many women are negligent of duty in not availing themselves of the privilege of voting upon so

227

important a matter as the choice of those having our public schools in charge." Peabody was the eminent educator Elizabeth Palmer Peabody, then in her final year of life and the keynote speaker of the event.

The suffrage question was most thoroughly debated by Club members in January 1894, the year before the matter of municipal suffrage for women was put to state voters, including women, in a non-binding referendum. Mary Stetson alerted her colleagues to a petition on municipal suffrage to be presented to both houses in the State House. Members were asked to consider the subject and be prepared to vote on the question themselves at the next meeting. Should the Club, as a club, sign the petition? The recording secretary, Elizabeth Whittier, described what happened:

> Then followed a conscientious discussion of that subject in all its bearings on the public weal and woe. Mrs. Wellington and Mrs. Stetson eloquently advocated the advantages of assuming the duties and privileges of municipal suffrage while Mrs. Hornbrooke, from her point of view, thought that women lack the business training to satisfactorily perform the duties pertaining to the government of a city, and that in its broader sense, suffrage would prove an inconvenience and not a benefit. Mrs. Tucker voiced the opinion of many present in declaring a belief in suffrage for women, but not in universal suffrage for either men or women.

The question was put to a vote and tabled. There was not enough agreement to send the petition forward. Considering that Lydia Wellington and Lucy Sawyer were founders of the Club, that Mary Stetson was a director and that Mary Lathrop Tucker was a future president, and all spoke for the measure, it is clear that Orinda Hornbrooke, though one voice, represented the opinions of many silent members.

In March 1894 the Newton Equal Suffrage Association offered to supply a speaker on suffrage. The Club voted to accept this offer and on March 21 Alice Stone Blackwell, the daughter of the suffragist Lucy Stone and a well known advocate of women's suffrage in her own right, "in a quiet logical manner presented the Equal Rights Doctrine." She quoted from a Massachusetts statute saying that a married mother has no legal right to her child — the father is the legal owner. Inequality of property rights keeps a 'help-meet' from sharing in her husband's rights. The advancing status and influence of women was considered. She quoted [Mary A.] Livermore, "We have two eyes to see, similarly we need two views of a subject." This is especially applicable to suffrage. It should be "a common bond of interest to talk it over." The subjects are not so abstruse as they seem. "It is useless to say women should not touch politics since politics touches them in so many ways." Blackwell's talk was interspersed with pertinent reminiscences, incidents and anecdotes and she ended with a touching appeal to thoughtful women, says note-taker Whittier.

The president, the politic Lucy Sawyer, "thanked her for furnishing so much food for reflection demanding intelligent thought even if contrary to traditional prejudices." The discussion touched on the likely fate of suffrage in manufacturing districts. Catholic clergy opposed it and their influence was greater on women than on men. "We have a solid foreign vote against it." "The president, while not opposing the subject, spoke of the added care and responsibility which would come to already over-taxed mothers who would feel their moral obligations in political affairs." To which Miss Blackwell replied that "a change of interests is restful in the long run."

As she did so often, Wellington, the Club's first president, had the last word, "We should be willing to work for the future and look upon this as a great step in civilization for which from our recent study, we are well-prepared." She went on to say that "we should not be 'nervously feminine' but consider carefully and use the power we have."

Lydia Wellington's encouraging words really were the last recorded in the Club's records on the subject beyond a very short note from a business meeting in May 1906, "Endorsement of equal suffrage urged." The municipal suffrage referendum went before Massachusetts voters, very few of them women, in 1895 and was overwhelmingly defeated. Municipal suffrage for women arrived along with general women's suffrage with the

Nineteenth Amendment in 1920, but the news didn't make the pages of the Club's record books.

By then the women were making their mark on city and state politics through petitions and direct action, through establishing the first vocational education in the city, setting up programs for immigrant mothers and children, speaking on conservation issues to other clubwomen and civic groups, running a branch of the National Consumers League and personally urging the governor to close a nearby bar. In 1894 members voted to reimburse Lucy Sawyer for $9 she had spent to promote the candidacy of Mrs. Martin on the school committee. Ten years later they supported one of their own, Dr. Deborah Fawcett, as she ran unsuccessfully for school committee. That strand of political activity continued throughout the Club's life. Club member Adelaide Ball was elected the first woman member of the Newton Board of Aldermen in 1953. In 2011 as many as 10% of the Club's members have held elected municipal office at some point in their careers.

What about the second wave of feminism in the 1960s, when there was a renewed push to pass the Equal Rights Amendment? Equal rights had at least two important aspects. One was legislative, to solve on a national level some of the problems of women's rights and ownership that Alice Blackwell had alluded to in 1894; the another was equal opportunity in the work force. Women were seeking employment in increasing numbers, former members of the Social Science Club among them. It seems that many women who wanted to take part in the social movements of the time did so through other organizations. Club records have almost nothing to say about active interest in the Equal Rights Amendment or the war in Vietnam but a lot to say about the diminishing numbers of Clubwomen. Members researched and analyzed social movements and wrote papers about them instead of joining them as their foremothers in the club had once done.

Social Science Women in the New Millennium

by Anne McKinnon Larner

In the Club of 2010 every current member has held a professional job and most have 20 or more years of work experience under their belts. Some members have worked continually since finishing college or professional training; others took time off to raise children before returning to previous work or re-inventing themselves; while still others continue to seek new directions and challenging opportunities though close to or past conventional retirement age. This is a very different reality than that experienced by members 100 years earlier when job opportunities for women were limited and social convention too often barred married women from the professions.

In today's Club all members have completed post-secondary education or training (college or nursing school) and a majority have earned at least one graduate degree. A number have two master's degrees, two members have Ph.D.s and one has a M.D.[26] Today's Club member is well educated by any standard, not just for women. Not only has educational opportunity expanded, work options have also increased many-fold. The work experience of current members varies widely. As in 1900 at least ten have spent some time as teachers, either K-12 or at the university level. In addition several have worked as librarians. Nursing or nursing education has attracted at least three members while five have been involved in the arts either as artists, teachers or part of the support system of gallery/museum workers. Five current members have worked in the science and math fields — from chemist to computer software developer to the biotechnology industry. The remainder includes linguists, editor/writers, social workers, financial managers and accountants, musicians and a lawyer. Current active and inactive members also include four who have held elected office: two as Newton aldermen, one as a Newton school committee member and one as state representative. Of the four women, two have held leadership positions (president of the Board of Aldermen and chairperson of the School Committee) and one ran a strong though unsuccessful campaign to become the first female mayor of Newton.[27]

231

It's almost as if the Club of 2011 is an in-the-flesh manifestation of the promise Ethie Bigelow spoke of more than 120 years earlier.[28]

Women of today's Social Science Club lead busy lives but that does not preclude volunteer work. Here five members of the Club join WGBH president David Ives for a Channel 2 public television auction. They are (from l. to r.) Jean Husher, Thelma Fleishman, Brooke Lipsitt, Marian Mandell and Gretchen Friend.

Giving Voice to the Club in the 21st Century
by Kate Stout

To bring the current Club and its members alive in the pages of this book a questionnaire was sent out to all members in the fall of 2010. Of our current membership of 50 — 38 active, 12 inactive — 25 members responded. They were asked to reflect on how the Club has changed over the years, how opportunities for women have changed since they were young, what challenges they encountered balancing family with working, how women's issues have impacted their lives and, finally, if they were groundbreakers. This last, in many ways, proved the most interesting — and inspiring — as the stories, while charting careers, are often stories of endurance, courage, camaraderie and are told here with a clear sense of the inanity of much of what they went through. Some answered openly and others asked to be anonymous. Virginia Woolf said it simply, and said it all, when she opined: "For most of history, Anonymous was a woman."

Let's start, then, with some of our groundbreakers.

When I started an MBA program at the University of Pittsburgh in 1967, I was the only woman in the program.

— anon

[I was the] first one in my family to graduate from college. Also to take the challenge of stepping away from being practical to become an artist.

— Cynthia Maurice, Social Science Club member since 2008

I wasn't really a groundbreaker but I got into a ground-breaking field. After college I worked at the Boston Lying-in Hospital where I did a little bench chemistry but mainly washed test tubes. [Then] a friend working at MIT said that since I had helped her with her math in high school, I would probably make a good programmer. So, armed with a B.A. in biology and a recommendation from my friend that I had been good at high school math, I applied for the job with Lincoln Laboratory. After a month of head-scratching, the group offered me a job. I was intimidated by M.I.T. and I was turned off by the idea of becoming a nerd at 23. Largely because of the encouragement from a woman doctor friend at the B.L.I., I decided to try it out. My first tasks at Lincoln Lab were to write massive amounts of code for a human factors application. After that I went on to writing code for an early time-sharing system and then worked on starting to develop the Arpanet, which eventually became the Internet.

— Liza Martin, Social Science Club member since 2004

I was the first woman elected and re-elected president of the Newton Board of Aldermen.

— Brooke Lipsitt, Social Science Club member since 1993

Being one of seven women in the fifth class to 'allow' women to enter medical school along with 140 males [made me a groundbreaker]. There has been a nearly 100% change in attitudes: I now teach medical school classes that are over 50% female. Salaries for women unfortunately still are below those earned by the opposite sex; also promotions tend to be unequal.

— *Iolanda Low, Social Science Club member since 2006*

I was the first woman to practice law at the firm of Sugarman and Sugarman, the first woman on the finance committee in the city of Newton and the first woman to chair the public facilities committee in the city of Newton.

— *Sondra Shick, Social Science Club member since 1998*

I won a rare opportunity to spend six months helping to set up care and hospital training for the five Native American tribes — Choctaw, Chickasaw, Cherokee, Seminole and Creek Indians — in Talihana, Oklahoma.

— *Emily Hubbs Scott, Social Science Club member since 1959*

As production manager at Little, Brown & Co., I was invited to a party given by the company head of manufacturing at his club — the Union Club on Park Street [in Boston]. I don't remember how the message was conveyed but I was informed that the Union Club had a women's entrance in the rear of the building. The more I thought about this the more I didn't like it. My counterpart, Cliff, smelled trouble. He said to me, "Carole, please don't make a fuss. I'll go in the women's door with you — you won't have to do it all by yourself." I couldn't bring myself to accept his offer. When the big day came, I sailed right in through the front door along with everyone else. And — nothing happened. Nothing at all. The sky didn't fall. No one said a word and everyone had a nice time at the party. I don't know if a new precedent was established that night [or not].

— *Carole Simon, Social Science Club member since 1999*

Carole Simon was also a member of the second class at the Harvard

234

Business School to accept women and is still a career woman to this day. Since 1985 she has had her own accounting practice. "By accident I became a CPA. When I say 'by accident' what I mean is that when growing up I had never even heard of accounting. I learned about it while I was at the B School."

Truth be told, however, most of the members of the Social Science Club, 2010, were, if not individual groundbreakers, part of a wave — a tsunami — of seismic change, not only in how society views and values women but also in how they feel about themselves. In the last half of the 20th century, anything — virtually anything — became possible for women to achieve. They could dream, they could be, they could do. So many of the members of the Club today are what they could not have dreamt of being when they were children. Witness Carole Simon. To women coming of age now when all is possible, the struggles, inequities and burdens of low expectations seem the stuff of exaggeration. But they are not.

For most of the current members of the Club, childhood aspirations were often curtailed by propriety. Says Duscha Weisskopf, Social Science Club member since 1987, "Since I was born in 1924 I 'assumed' that wives were supposed to stay home with their children. Thus I worked before I had children and started to work again after my two youngest were in high school."

Marie Baroni Allen, Social Science Club member since 1997 recalls her delayed awakening:

> I did little career planning while in high school since everyone knew I would become a teacher — other options were secretary, nurse or nun. So I went along my merry way preparing to be a teacher and then teaching at the secondary level. It wasn't until I was in my early 30s and was a department chairperson that I gave serious thought to 'what I wanted to be when I grew up'.

And this from a woman who entered college in 1961 with a triple major in mathematics, chemistry and physics! In 1980 Marie left teaching, shocking all who knew her, to work in the private sector, eventually making her way into fields commensurate with her interests and academic training — pharmaceuticals and biotechnology, the latter as a technical operations executive.

For other women the aspirations of childhood bumped up unequivocally against the 'Do Not Enter' sign of all-male professions. Gender-limited career options are fewer and harder to find, but not yet impossible. Speaking personally, I wanted to grow up to be the first female Whitey Ford — that is, the first left-handed woman pitcher in major league baseball. Alas, had I been born today the chances of that would still be bleak, talent notwithstanding. Vivi Leavy, on the other hand, "wanted to be a cowboy. My gender got in the way. I really couldn't figure out any other role I wanted to play in the woman's world." Today, gender would not hold her back although a dying profession might. Gretchen Friend, Social Science Club member since 1991 and a past president, recalls a more telling, in its very familiarity, experience:

> I always wanted to be a detective/FBI agent but was told
> it wasn't an option by my high school guidance counselor
> in the 1950s. A friend of my parents' who was a real FBI
> agent (he helped crack the Brinks robbery case) told me
> that women could not be agents, and that if I wanted to
> join the FBI it could only be as a secretary. Since it was
> apparent to my guidance counselor that I wasn't destined
> to be a brain surgeon, my choices were either nurse or
> teacher. I had two years of college where I changed my
> major every semester trying to find something that would
> interest me as much as being a sleuth.

The majority of current members worked outside the home at one point or another, sometimes deferring careers until their children were well into school, some forced into it by divorce. Many give credit to supportive husbands. Most had serious careers in diverse and often male-dominated professions — science, medicine, newspaper publishing, technology, law, business, etc. Those with children, to a woman, remarked on the difficulty of balancing the demands of family with the demands of the workplace.

Arlene Bernstein, Social Science Club member since 2009, sums up this conflict:

> When I found a position in the Wellesley Public Schools and was working full-time, I often felt that I had to dash home when the school day ended. I also never felt that I had enough time to prepare as much as I wanted to for the classes that I taught. When I was home, there were endless home-making/parenting responsibilities — I enjoyed them but they did not afford me enough time to pursue all the job-related interests that I had.

A few determined women did it all. Even though 'having it all' had its penalties as artist Cynthia Maurice relates:

> I pushed two baby girls in the carriage [while] marching for women's rights and having consciousness raising groups in the early 70s. Now my daughters, grown, take it for granted that husbands will share housework and income; that their femininity is not challenged if they choose a profession that formerly was associated with males. They had immense opportunity and freedom without the hesitation, self-doubt or conflict of homemaker versus career. It has taken me a lifetime to allow myself to be in the studio versus being at home caretaking everyone.

Anne Larner's experience was similar:

> While my mother was very supportive of my doing whatever I wanted re: a career, society's 'acceptable options' affected me. I was very conscious of what fell within the acceptable range and struggled with what price one might pay for going against the grain. My two daughters have not been limited by that kind of social pressure.

Of course there are war stories cherished by many, the sort that will be used to dazzle grandchildren with how feudal life in these United States could be for working women even into the late 20th century. Here are the choicest experiences to come from the questionnaire:

Although by the 1960s teachers were predominantly women, female teachers were discriminated against. Even at that time there were school systems that would not allow married women to teach. Pregnant teachers could teach only as long as it was not apparent they were pregnant. In those days there was no maternity leave so you were forced to resign your position. Essentially each time you became pregnant you lost your job, benefits and seniority.

— Marie Baroni Allen

In 1970 when looking for my first job after receiving a master's degree in biology, I went to an employment agency. They literally had a pink door and a blue door with the jobs category listed beside each. I couldn't make them understand that positions for my background were listed on the blue side. There was also the indignity of having to take a typing test, you know, just in case! Eventually I found a job at Brandeis University working for a world famous biochemist. It was me and one female graduate student in a lab of 16 people. Flash forward 37 years. My job required I attend seminars on how to interview possible hires. No blue and pink doors. In fact just about everything from my first interview is now illegal.

— Sue Fish, Social Science Club member since 2008

I came across a study in the Wellesley Library many years after failing the Foreign Service oral exam pointing out that there were only two women among the 200 or so men that made it the year I applied, a strong indication of discrimination against women candidates. I was not shocked at all. They had asked me one of those now forbidden questions: Do you plan to marry? When I answered that I did, they spent quite a while pointing out how difficult that would be: Do you expect your husband to follow you from one posting to another?! Well, I had also forgotten the significance of the Gadsden Purchase and had not read enough Harold Nicolson. The Foreign Service convinced me I was not made of the right stuff.

— Vivi Leavy

Not all current Club members are ardent feminists. Almost certainly, many of the members who did not answer the questionnaire fall into this category, some because they were wives and mothers first and foremost; others because they feel they missed out and don't wish to 'go public'; and some simply saw the challenges presented them as the norm:

Betty Freidan's book *The Feminine Mystique* was published in 1963 during my senior year in college. I was already on my way to living the 50s single- girl's life in the Big Apple and paid it no attention. So I went to New York City and discovered the only job I was offered was as a secretary. When I asked for a better job, I was offered a position as secretary to a more important person. It took substantial effort to land a 'professional' position. I saw it as my fight, not a communal one. By the time I focused on women's issues, many years later — probably not until after I was married — I considered myself a post-feminist, i.e., I never supported women because they were women. Rather, I looked for individuals of either sex who treated women as equals. I still do.

— *Brooke Lipsitt*

And this: "There was an expectation, even among college graduates, that marriage was something that was supposed to happen within a couple of years after graduation. I played by the 'rules' and was divorced in a few years. After the divorce and the switch from teaching to business, I don't think I was seriously impacted by women's issues."

—*anon*

And of course there were moments of true grace: Libby Gerlach, Social Science Club member since 1999 and long-time keeper of the Club's budget, recalls a rare occurrence given the times and her age: "My professional life developed after I got divorced. After teaching math for 12 years, I took a computer programming class to retrain teachers. I was 57 or so and wound up working for a small computer consulting firm started by some ex-IBMers. It was a wild ride, my first business experience, and we were all making it up as we went along." Later, fed up with her boss whom she describes as a bully, she quit "without thinking how hard it might be to get another job at the age of 63 or 64! I applied for a banking job and was lucky enough to find a perfect fit — and I worked at it for another eight years."

This is my own experience: After my mother died, I learned she was writing two different newspaper columns when I — her fourth and unexpected child — was born. She felt with a new baby at home she had to give up her newspaper work. In this crucial way I lived one of my mother's dreams, to be a journalist and professional writer, spurred on by DNA, I guess, because if she lived at all vicariously through me, she did so silently.

But for all the travails experienced by Club members as they negotiated tricky and changing times, whether they stayed home with the children or left the home to fight, wittingly or not, for parity in the workplace — as Dr. Iolanda Low puts it so succinctly, for "acceptance as both a 'Mrs.' and an 'MD' by my peers" — virtually all have benefited directly or indirectly from strides made during the second half of the 20th century. Club member since 1997 Jean Kennedy sums them up best: "Independence in travel, business opportunities, leadership in volunteer organizations, ministers/priests in churches, retaining one's maiden name upon marriage. Educating women to be equal to men . . . still improving on that one. The invention of the pill to control when to have children, if at all. To have opportunities to travel and study in foreign countries, unchaperoned!"

Perhaps the biggest difference in opportunity between our mothers' era and ours is that of education — not just higher education but the social education of Americans and, more specifically, of the male segment of the population. As women have learned — and been given society's permission — to exercise our competency in professions across the board as well as in the home, a real bridge to new and equal opportunity for women has been forged. Now our horizons are limitless.

Endnotes

1   Phyllis Schlafly is a conservative pundit known for her opposition to feminism. She founded the pro-family interest group, The Eagle Forum, in 1972.

2   Available on line from the University of Toronto. http://www. archive. org/details/dutiesofwomencou00cobbuoft

3   Social Science Club, Record Book, Vol. 2, Mar. 19, 1890.

4   Harvard would not accept her as a regular student because she was a woman.

5   Boyer, Paul. *Notable American Women: 1607-1950: a Biographical Dictionary, P-Z*, Volume 3; see Appendix III for Mary Whiton Calkins.

6   Most public school districts barred married women from teaching at this time. That began to change in the 1940s and 1950s.

7   Cornelia and her sisters were three of the 12 children of William Jackson, the entrepreneur and abolitionist, who built the Jackson Homestead on Washington Street and his second wife Mary Bennett.

8   Hall was the first head of the Summer Industrial School and later the principal of the Newton Private School, a co-ed, college preparatory school.

9   Reed was active in the Club for about 10 years and Fawcett for approximately 13.

10 At this time a high school diploma was sufficient for admission to many medical schools including Boston University.

11 The announcement was not signed and not identified as an advertisement. During the early 1900s the front page of the *Newton Graphic* carried commercial advertisements and lists of social announcements. The social announcements (including Club meeting announcements) ran in traditional newspaper columns with none standing out because of format. This announcement for Dr. Fawcett was most unusual.

12 In 1905 the only ballot women in Massachusetts could exercise was to vote for school committee members. At this time, school

committee candidates ran by party. Fawcett ran as an Independent, but won many write-in votes in both the Republican and Democratic primaries, including votes for alderman.

13 Flexner, Abraham, *Medical Education in the United States and Canada Bulletin,* Number Four (The Flexner Report), Carnegie Foundation, 1910.

14 Walsh, Mary Roth, *Doctors Wanted — No Women Need Apply: Sexual Barriers In the Medical Profession 1835–1975,* New Haven, Yale University Press, 1977.

15 Clothes washers and dryers, vacuum cleaners, automatic furnaces, and easy access to quality service providers and prepared foods were unavailable in 1900.

16 Deane M. Hotten-Somers, "Relinquishing and Reclaiming Independence: Irish Domestic Servants, American Middle-class Mistresses, and Assimilation, 1850–1920," *Eerie-Ireland: a Journal of Irish Studies,* Spring-Summer, 2001, pp. 185–197.

17 U.S. Census, 1900.

18 It's unclear what became of Drake's effort to form such a group.

19 "Suppose Our Servants Didn't Live with Us," "Why I Never Have Trouble with My Servants" and "Domestic Service from the Standpoint of the Employee" are just a sampling of typical titles.

20 Salmon, Lucy Maynard, *Domestic Service,* New York, The MacMillan Company, 1897, Chapters VI, VIII, IX.

21 "On Being a Servant," *Living Age,* Sept. 9, 1916, p. 821.

22 Ibid.

23 Hotten-Somers, p. 191.

24 Ibid.

25 The given names of women who were not Club members (Mrs. Gregory, Miss Orcutt, Mrs. Martin) were omitted in the records and also, necessarily, here.

26 Analysis of biographical information from all Club members including existing records and responses to queries, December 4, 2010.

27 As of the end of 2010 Newton has yet to elect a female mayor, although three women have officially run for the post.

28 More detailed biographical material on current Club members is being added to Club archives at the Newton Free Library during 2011.

Jean Kennedy enriched her 2010 paper, entitled "Uganda: Change Through Education, One Child at a Time," with photo boards she brought to share with the members. The 2010–2011 study topic was "Africa: Further Consideration."

APPENDICES

Appendix I

Social Science Club Timeline

January 22, 1886	First meeting. Lydia Wellington is elected president, Charlotte Calkins vice president and Lucy Sawyer secretary.
February 9, 1887	Mary Frances Linder's Club constitution is accepted.
Spring 1888	Club takes on teaching sewing to 12 girls in Thompsonville, the first step towards the Vacation Industrial School.
March 1889	Booklet listing members' names is printed.
February 1890	Club accepts invitation to join Massachusetts branch of the General Federation of Women's Clubs.
March 5, 1890	Club dues set at $2.
Summer 1890	Vacation Industrial School opens to boys; carpentry class offered.
January 20, 1892	First scholarship to Hampton Institute student, $70.
January 25, 1893	Club president Sawyer prepares a Club history for exhibit at World's Columbian Exposition in Chicago,.
May 3, 1893	Club votes to join the newly formed Massachusetts State Federation of Women's Clubs.
March–May 1895	Club leads the effort to form the Newton Federation of Women's Clubs.
March 4, 1896	First motto proposed: "Suit the action to the word; the word to the action."
May 6, 1896	Celebration of 10th anniversary at the home of Mary Billings.
February 1898	The motto "Privilege is Obligation" and the Club colors (green and white) are adopted.
April 1898	Club moves from members' homes to Hunnewell Club;

	membership limited to 100.
November 1898	Club Bureau of Information established to provide a pool of screened local workers available for members to hire.
1899	Social Science joins the Consumer League; it is concerned with fair labor practices, particularly for women and children.
1900	Membership is 100.
1901	Doing needlework during guest speakers' talks is banned.
May 1, 1901	Celebration of 15th anniversary with a luncheon at the Hunnewell Club.
May 1902	Request made to city to take over Vacation Industrial School; Club has contributed $6500 to date.
1903	City denies request to take over Vacation Industrial School, cites need to build support in Board of Aldermen.
1904	Consumer League becomes international. Club passes resolution to have a woman on the School Committee.
Autumn 1904	City matches Club's $400 for support of Industrial Vacation School expenses; school now under management of superintendent of Newton Public Schools.
1905	Club underwrites campaign of member Dr. Deborah Fawcett for School Committee. Lucy Sawyer, the guiding spirit of the Club and the force behind the Vacation Industrial School, resigns.
1906	First suggestion of summer picnic.
February 7, 1906	Evening reception at the Hunnewell Club with live music and song to celebrate Club's 20th anniversary.
1908	Club makes final contribution of $400 for Vacation Industrial School as the city of Newton takes over.
January 18,	25th anniversary celebrated at the Hunnewell Club;

1911	three original members present: Harriet Stone, Orinda Hornbrooke and Charlotte Calkins.
1915	Introduction of a unified study topic for each year's program.
1917	Club votes to contribute to the salary of a nature study teacher at the high school; $200 voted for war relief ($100 to Syrian and Armenian Relief, $50 each to French and Belgian).
1918	Patriotic song is sung at each meeting.
1920	Club dues raised to $4.
December 19, 1923	First musicale. Fiedler Trio performs.
January 2, 1924	First mention of a college scholarship; $200 raised and awarded.
November 10, 1926	40th anniversary celebration; with Negro spirituals as entertainment.
1933	Active members number 60.
1934	Institution of the penny collection to raise money for milk for underprivileged children at the Stearns School Center.
January 22, 1936	50th anniversary of the Club.
April 29, 1936	"Letitia's Triumph," written by Lenice Ingram Bacon in honor of the Club's 50th anniversary has first performance.
1939	Penny collection switches to Rebecca Pomroy House, but still for milk.
November 20, 1940	War Relief Committee established with Sarah Buchan Jewell as chair.
January 8, 1941	Four cases of clothing sent to British relief.
November 12, 1941	Club votes to dispense with first meeting of every month as a 'temporary [war] emergency.'

January 14, 1942	Mary C. Merritt appointed as information agent to keep the Club informed of what can be done for soldiers stationed locally.
March 11, 1942	590 books collected for army camps, 16 pairs of minesweeper gloves made.
November 9, 1943	Club's War Relief Committee collects Christmas bags for veterans of the last war.
February 1946	As war measures, number of meetings is reduced to 15, penny collection switched from milk to cod liver oil, members' annual luncheon fees donated to the Club for distribution to charities.
April 24, 1946	60th anniversary celebrated with hats and music appropriate for each decade.
December 3, 1947	Fifty cents per member special assessment is voted to build up the general fund.
February 4, 1948	Club votes to return to pre-war practice of having the annual luncheon at a public place.
March 15, 1949	Hope Mudge's bequest used to purchase silver tray.
January 25, 1961	"Letitia's Triumph" re-enacted to honor the Club's 75th anniversary.
April 1971	A tribute to Irene Hamilton Young includes a reading of her poem Die-Hards in celebration of the Club's 85th anniversary.
1976	Major revision of the bylaws is carried out, dropping, merging and renaming committees to streamline Club leadership.
1978	Club moves to home of Emily Hubbs Scott for meetings.
1979	January/February meetings are omitted for the first time.
1984	After 92 years Hampton Institute Scholarship is discontinued in favor of the college scholarship fund.
April 30, 1986	100th Anniversary celebration at Brae Burn Country Club; joint meeting between the Social Science Club and the Eight O'Clock Club; Club president Andy Marshall

	presents a paper on Club history.
1991	Bylaws, constitution, history and duties are published as a separate booklet.
1994	Custom of wearing hats and gloves ats and gloves at the annual meeting is instituted at luncheon; welcome potluck at Emily Hubbs Scott's house becomes welcome tea with sitting president hosting. Bylaws are revised.
Winter 1995	Institution of January and February brown bag lunches, informal gatherings at a member's home.
1997	Poetry and philosophy are added to the meeting program.
1998	Meetings move from Emily Hubbs Scott's home back to Grace Church.
2002	Club pin is designed by Gretchen Friend and presented to scholarship recipient; also sold to members for the first time.
Summer 2005	Summer picnics shift from Lisa Beeuwkes's Jamestown, Rhode Island, summer home to the home of Kate Stout on the Sudbury River in Concord.
2006	Bylaws are revised to include a dissolution clause and reflect the current Club practices.
2007	Active members total 40, a high point in recent decades.
2008	Membership files are computerized by Susan Kaplan and Gretchen Friend.
April 2009	Annotated Bibliography compiled by Kate Stout contains readers' notes of the first 122 years of the Club's archives which are housed atNewton Free Library.
May 6, 2009	Emily Hubbs Scott honored at the annual meeting luncheon for 50 years of membership.
April 2010	New membership procedure adopted eliminating secret-ballot vote.
April 29, 2011	125th anniversary celebration at the Jackson Homestead. Publication of *From Hearth to Horizons: 125 Years of the Social Science Club of Newton*.

Appendix II

Social Science Study Topics Since 1886

1886–88	Prison Reform
1888–93	General Topics
1893–94	Rise and Decline of the Moral Thought of Nations
1894–1900	General Topics
1900–01	The Elements of Sociology
1901–02	Education
1902–09	Varied Topics
1909–10	The Domestic Plant
1910–11	General Topics
1911–12	The State: The Commonwealth of Massachusetts
1912–13	Modern Philanthropy, Women in the Progress of Civilization
1913–14	Varied Topics
1914–15	Constitutional Development
1915–17	Varied Topics
1917–18	Pan-Americanism
1918–19	General and Varied Topics
1919–20	Americanization
1920–21	Education, Negro Problems
1921–22	Russia, English Novelists
1922–23	History, Poetry, English Novelists
1923–24	Development of Life, Geologic Periods, Vocational Training
1924–25	Man and the Movements of Our Early History
1925–26	Development of Our Country
1926–27	China
1927–28	Pioneers of Thought

1928-29	The New Age
1929–30	Contribution of the Races to American Civilization
1930–31	Rivers of the World: Highways of History
1931–32	Ten Notable American Women
1932–33	The Challenge of the Old Order in Present-Day Europe
1933–34	Broadcasts from Fields of Research, *Literati* of the Post-war Period
1934–35	Our Southern Neighbors
1935–36	Japanese Neighbors
1936–37	Experiments in the Solution of Social Problems
1937–38	The Drama of the Mediterranean
1938–39	Contemporary Leaders
1939–40	Modern Housing
1940–41	India
1941–42	Some Aspects of the English Novel
1942–43	Russia
1943–44	China of Today in the Making
1944–45	Boston
1945–46	Territorial Expansion of the Changing World
1946–47	Education of the Changing World
1947–48	Peace within Our Boundaries
1948–49	Defense Outposts of America
1949–50	Contemporary Art and Science
1950–51	Great Highways
1951–52	Personalities Behind the Evolution of American Foreign Policy
1952–53	Spiritual Forces in the World Today
1953–54	We Who Built America: A Nation of Many
1954–55	Arabia and Its Impact on the Western World
1955–56	American Women Emerge
1956–57	Africa South of the Sahara
1957–58	The United Nations
1958–59	Man Among the Stars

1959–60	Nobel Prize Winners in Literature
1960–61	From These Roots: Forerunners of Today's Civilization
1961–62	Contemporary Trends
1962–63	South America
1963–64	Benefactors to Culture
1964–65	Personal Preference
1965–66	Human Rights and Famous Trials
1966–67	Sweep of Nationalism in the Far East
1967–68	Pre-Bulfinch to Logue: Architectural Boston
1968–69	The Comic Spirit of America
1969–70	The Dynamics of Change: 20th Century Revolutionary Concepts
1970–71	The American Indian
1971–72	Personal Preference
1972–73	Oceanography
1973–74	How New is the Commune?
1974–75	Two Hundred Years of Taxes and Troubles
1975–76	From Newtown to Newton
1976–77	The Signers of the Declaration of Independence
1977–78	Contemporary Women of Influence
1978–79	Environmental Concerns
1979–80	Age of Transition
1980–81	Focus on the East
1981–82	Stars and Space
1982–83	The Near East
1983–84	Personalities of the 20th Century
1984–85	Nature on the Rampage
1985–86	Study the Past and Shape the Future
1986–87	The World's Continuous 'Hot Spots'
1987–88	Famous Explorers
1988–89	The North American Indian in the 20th Century
1989–90	United States: A Nation of Immigrants
1990–91	Critical Issues for Women Today

1991–92	Personal Choice
1992–93	Great Builders and Building Projects in History
1993–94	Nobel Peace Prize Winners
1994–95	Women in the Arts
1995–96	On The Road To...
1996–97	Out on a Limb
1997–98	Monkey Business: Issues in Ethics
1998–99	Unfinished Business: Reform for the 21st Century
1999–2000	The American Century in Review
2000–01	Globalization and the Environment: Where are We Going?
2001–02	Discoveries, Inventions, Inventors, and Their Impact on Our Lives
2002–03	How the World Celebrates: Pageants, Parades, Fêtes and Festivals
2003–04	Roles of Women in Shaping the Modern World
2004–05	Masterpieces and Masterminds
2005–06	Literary Lights
2006–07	The Hub of the Universe
2007–08	Shifting Sands
2008–09	Famous Feuds
2009–10	Africa
2010–11	Africa — Further Consideration

Appendix III

Some Early Members of the
Social Science Club of Newton

Of the women who were movers and shakers in the first 15 years of the Social Science Club, only Anna Bailey has her own listing in Who's Who in New England. Information about others is scant, although often husbands can be identified. The following listing is very partial and includes the most active women about whom some information could be found. The founding members were: Mary Calkins, Charlotte Calkins, Orinda Hornbrooke, Lucy Sawyer, Harriet Stone and Lydia Wellington. Only some addresses could be identified.

Bailey, Anna Leland (joined 1895) m. Alvin Richards Bailey, February 14, 1884, d. 1916. Anna grew up in Somerville, one of two girls to take the full classical course at Somerville High School. She studied music at the New England Conservatory and was a successful teacher before marriage. She organized classes for study in various areas before women's clubs were generally recognized. A Unitarian, Anna Bailey was a member of the Newton Suffrage League, Newton Hospital and Day Nursery Associations. She was a member and the historian of the Daughters of the American Revolution and wrote its history 1891-1906. She was an officer of the Social Science Club and Newton Federation of Women's Clubs. For 20 years, she was a member of the West Newton Women's Educational. Mrs. Bailey held many other memberships including the Appalachian Mountain Club, New England Women's Club. Alvin Bailey was a member of the Eight O'clock Club.
550 Centre Street.

Baker, Susan J. (joined 1888) m. William M. Baker. Susan Baker was the first non-founder to become president of the Club from 1895 to 1897. Her daughter Annie was a member for a short time as well.
602 Centre Street.

Ballou, Augusta W. (joined 1891) m. Russell Arnold Ballou (b. 1827, d.

255

1895). Russell Ballou was a Universalist minister and editor of The Banner (a Universalist newspaper) in Augusta, Maine. He came to Boston to edit the Christian Leader. In 1863, he entered real estate where he had a 30-year career.
140 Church Street.

Bates, Emma Barstow (joined 1887) b. 1867, m. William Carver Bates (b. 1838, d. 1910). William Bates was in the insurance business. He was also an author and editor and a member of the New England Genealogical Society and the Boston Mycological Society. He claimed descent from early settlers of the region.
13 Belmont Street.

Billings, Mary M. (joined 1887, changed to honorary 1901) m. Charles E. Billings (d. October 19, 1893). Mary Billings was a Trustee of the Newton Hospital. She hosted the Social Science Club's 10th anniversary luncheon at her large home. Charles Billings was senior member of Billings, Clapp and Co., manufacturing chemists, Boston. He was also director and president of 'one of the New England' railroads, a member of the Eliot Church and a staunch contributor to its building. King's Handbook calls him "the millionaire importer of drugs."
85 Franklin Street.

Blodgett, Adelaide (joined 1887) m. William H. Blodgett. Adelaide Blodgett was Club president 1897–1900, after which she became president of the Newton Federation of Women's Clubs. William Blodgett was a carpet merchant in Boston.
645 Centre Street.

Buswell, Alice Maude (joined 1890, left 1899) m. Dr. Harvey Parker Towle, December 1898. She gave a paper on vacation homes for working girls at the Convention of Working Girls' Clubs in Boston, May 11, 1894, and gave the welcome for her graduating class at Smith Female College Class Day in 1889. A year after her marriage, she and her husband moved to Marlborough Street, Boston, where they raised three surviving daughters. Harvey Towle was the son of a Boston fur dealer and attended Harvard College, Class of 1888. He was a dermatologist with a widely known study of the therapeutic use of x-rays. He practiced at Massachusetts General Hospital and taught at Dartmouth and Harvard.
92 Franklin Street.

Buswell, Susan (joined 1889) m. Charles H. Buswell. Susan Buswell was an active member of the Newton Hospital Aid Society. Charles Buswell was "a Boston merchant" according to King's Handbook.
92 Franklin Street.

Byington, Louisa J. Workman (joined 1892) m. Ezra Hoyt Byington, D.D. (b. 1828, d. 1901). Louisa Workman grew up in Worcester. Ezra Byington was a Congregational clergyman and author of a study of John Eliot and other works.
100 Franklin Street.

Calkins, Charlotte Grosvenor Whiton (joined 1886), b. 1840, m. Wolcott Calkins (b. 1831), d. 1937. Charlotte Calkins served two terms as president of the Social Science Club. She also headed the local branch of the Consumer League (1904). Wolcott Calkins became a Presbyterian minister and came to Newton in 1880 as pastor of Eliot Church, a position he held until 1895. He was the author of several books.
22 Bellevue Street.

Calkins, Mary Whiton (joined 1886) b. 1863, d. 1930. Mary Calkins received a B.A. degree from Smith College in 1885, an M.A. in 1888. She held various positions at Wellesley College from 1887 to 1930, starting as instructor in Greek and ending as research professor of psychology. Her only sister, Maud, died in 1883; she had three brothers. Calkins studied at Harvard through the intervention of her father with President Eliot. Her doctoral committee unanimously recommended her degree but Harvard would not award it. Hers was the first psychological lab in the United States and she published steadily. She was the first woman president of the American Psychological Association, in 1905, and also became the first woman president of the American Philosophical Association, in 1918 (academically, psychology developed out of philosophy).
22 Bellevue Street.

Creegan, Melissa W. (joined 1887?) m. Rev. Dr. Charles Cole Creegan, d. 1897. After she and her husband moved from Newton to New York City in the 1890s, Melissa Creegan served as Vice President of the Women's Board of Missions. Her full-page obituary in the church monthly omitted her Christian name. Charles Creegan was a Congregational minister. He was secretary of the American Board of Commissioners of Foreign

Missions and wrote several books about the lives of missionaries. In 1880 as superintendent of Congregational Churches in Wyoming, Utah, New Mexico and Colorado he founded 18 churches in those states.

Drake, Laura Bell (joined ?) b. Nov 14, 1870, m. Louis Stoughton Drake, January 15, 1894, d. January 1, 1936. Laura Drake was a proponent of swimming for health and worked to bring a public 'bath' to Newton. Louis Drake was a genealogist who in 1896 self-published a long thorough history of the Drake family in England and America. He later was an importer/exporter of East Indian and Chinese goods, as indicated in surviving advertisements from 1917 and 1918. His company Louis S. Drake, Inc., was owned by his brother-in-law, the lawyer Stoughton Bell. Louis and Laura were probably cousins.
Auburndale.

Ellison, Mary Elizabeth Richardson (joined 1890) m. William Peleg Ellison. Mary Ellison was an active member of the Newton Hospital Aid Society. William Ellison was a financial manager of trust estates, a trustee of the Newton Savings Bank and Mayor of the city, 1882-83.
15 Vernon Street.

Ensign, Angeline Faxon Barber (joined 1893) m. Charles Sidney Ensign (b. 1842). Charles Ensign was a lawyer and historian. He was a member of the New England Historical Genealogical Association and served as a member of the Massachusetts House, and as a Newton alderman. He ran unsuccessfully for mayor. He was a member of the Eight O'clock Club.
113 Galen Street.

Farquhar, Alice (joined 1890, left 1892, re-joined 1899) m. David W. Farquhar. David Farquhar was active in politics and served as an alderman. He was a delegate to Benjamin Harrison's nominating convention according to King's Handbook, which includes a photo of his house.
Corner of Durant and Pembroke Streets.

Gay, Mrs. Levi (joined 1887?). Levi B. Gay was the publisher of Banker & Tradesman. He was probably the son of Newton resident Charles M. Gay, publisher of Littell's Living Age.
303 Franklin Street.

Gilman, Adelaide S. Sears (joined 1888) m. Gorham Dummer Gilman (b. 1822, d. 1909). 'Senator' Gorham Gilman went to sea in 1840 at the age of 18. An entrepreneur, he started several export/import businesses before settling in Newton. Adelaide Gilman was his second wife. Mr. Gilman established Gilman Brothers, a wholesale pharmaceutical business. In his *Bulletin of Pharmacy* obituary he was noted as "a conspicuous figure, not only in the drug trade but in civic, Masonic and religious affairs." He served as a representative and a senator in the state legislature, as a Newton alderman, and also as consul general for Hawaii in Boston. In 1887 he entertained Queen Kapiolani of Hawaii at his residence.
9 Baldwin Street.

Hall, Mabel T. (joined 1886). Mabel Hall was the first head of the Summer Industrial School. By 1914, she became principal of the Newton Private School, a co-ed, college preparatory school.
60 Elmwood Street.

Hardon, Anna Wallace Wilson (joined 1886) m. Henry C. Hardon, 1859. Henry Hardon was a principal in the Boston public schools.
28 Copley Street.

Hayward, Sarah Jane Hale (joined ?) b. Westbrook, Maine, December 30, 1845, m. Albert Francis Hayward, June 11, 1879, d. July 28, 1920. Sarah Hayward was a member of both the Social Science Club and the Newton Highlands Woman's Club. Albert Hayward was a confectioner and later president of the New England Confectionary Company. The Haywards had no children.
Newton Highlands.

Hornbrooke, Orinda Althea Dudley (joined 1886) m. Francis Bickford Hornbrooke, D.D. (b. 1849, d. 1903), d. 1920. Originally from Cambridge, Orinda Hornbrooke was a descendent of Thomas Dudley, an early governor of Massachusetts Bay Colony. She joined the American Ornithologist's Union as an associate member in 1897. Francis Hornbrooke was pastor of Channing Unitarian Church, Newton (1879–1900). He was a member of the Boston Browning Society and wrote an appreciation of Browning's poem, *The Ring and the Book: An Interpretation* (Little Brown & Co.), which was published after his death. Mrs. Hornbrooke also wrote a biographical sketch of her husband for the Channing Church. Rev.

Hornbrooke's statue by Cyrus E. Dallin is in the Newton Free Library. He was a member of the Tuesday Club.
68 Lombard Street.

Jackson, Cornelia T. (joined 1893), d. 1903. Cornelia Jackson was librarian at the Newton Public Library and founder of the Santa Claus Club which operated out of the Jackson Homestead.
527 Washington Street.

Linder, Mary Frances Farlow (joined 1886) b. December 1, 1844, m. George Linder, Jr., June 26, 1867. Mary Frances Linder was one of two members who joined in January 1886 and is sometimes listed as a founding member. She drew up the first draft of the Club's Constitution in February 1887 but resigned when it was sent for revision to a committee that did not include her. Her older daughter, Mary Blanchard Linder, also belonged to the Club for a very short time. Both women were members of the Museum of Fine Arts and donated items of historic interest to it. George Linder, Jr., was the son of George and Matilda Smallwood Linder of Newton. Mary Frances and George Jr. had five children: George, John Farlow, Mary Blanchard, Alfred Horner and Ethel Bigelow. George was a merchant with Linder & Meyer, 118 Milk St. Boston.

Pearce, Miriam Badlam (joined 1894) m. William Houghton Sprague Pearce. William Pearce was a cellist and a composer. He wrote the Constitution (Old Ironsides) March, Summer Days (a ballad) and other popular songs. He was the grandson of Charles Sprague, the 'Banker Poet' and had an insurance office at 87 Milk Street, Boston.
185 Newtonville Avenue.

Ripley, Estimate Ruth E. Baldwin (joined 1888) m. Nathaniel L. Ripley. Nathaniel Ripley was a jeweler at 383 Washington Street, Boston. Their son William Zebina Ripley (b. 1867, d. 1941) the anthropologist, political economist and professor at MIT and Harvard, was a frequent speaker at the Social Science Club in the early 1890s. He gained fame for his racial theories and as a railroad economist.
618 Centre Street.

Sawyer, Lucy Newhall (joined 1886, changed to honorary in 1905), m. J. Herbert Sawyer, d. 1908). Lucy Sawyer was vice president of the

Newton Non-Partisan Woman Suffrage League as well as president of the Social Science Club. She was acknowledged as the force behind the Nonantum Insdustrial School. J. Herbert Sawyer was treasurer of "a great manufacturing corporation in Boston" according to King's Handbook. He was a director of the New England National Bank in 1908 and a member of the National Association of Cotton Manufacturers.
Hammond Street, near Beacon Street, Chestnut Hill

Springer, Annie Maria Smiley (joined 1893) m. Elestus Martin Springer. Elestus Springer was the founder of Springer Brothers, Boston, manufacturers and dealers in ladies' cloaks. A Republican, he was on the vestry of Grace Church, Newton. Their home described as a "charming, vine-covered stone cottage," is pictured in King's Handbook.
187 Kenrick Park.

Stanley, Augusta M. Walker (joined 1884) m. Francis Edgar Stanley (b. 1849). Francis 'F.E.' Stanley taught school, became a photographer and artist, and with his brother Freelan invented the Stanley Dry Plate and became president of the Stanley Dry Plate Company in Newton. It was sold to George Eastman in 1903. By then he and his brother had developed the Stanley Steamer auto (1897) which held the world auto speed record in 1906. He was killed in an auto accident in 1918.
638 Centre Street.

Stanley, Flora J. R. (joined 1886) m. Freelan Oscar Stanley. Freelan 'F.O.' Stanley worked with his brother Frank to invent the dry plate photographic process and then the Stanley Steamer. F.O. Stanley also built the Hunnewell Club which opened in 1887 and where the Social Science Club held its meetings.
337 Waverley Avenue.

Stearns, Emily Williston Clark (joined ?) m. Frank Waterman Stearns, 1880) Frank Stearns was a member of the family dry goods company, R. H. Stearns, Boston. He was also a Republican, a bank director, an Amherst College trustee, and a Congregationalist, probably at the Eliot Church.
269 Park Avenue.

Stetson, Mary E. (joined 1888) m. John Stetson and later widowed, d.

1909. Mary Stetson served as Club vice president, director and delegate to the City Federation. She was known for prodding the members to actually carry out their decisions.
133 Park Avenue.

Stone, Harriet Hodges (joined 1886) m. Lincoln Ripley Stone M.D. (b. 1832), 1864. Originally from Salem, Harriet Stone was elected recording secretary of the Club in March 1890 but resigned during that summer. She apparently rejoined later although she does not appear as a speaker. Lincoln Stone trained at Harvard and served as a medical officer with the Massachusetts troops in the Civil War. He was taken prisoner. After the war he practiced medicine in Newton.
178 Bellevue Street.

Tucker, Mary Lathrop (joined 1886, changed to honorary 1901) b. June 27, 1848, m. Fred H. Tucker, October 21,1880, d. 1919. Mary Tucker was particularly interested in conservation. In 1899 she addressed the Massachusetts Horticultural Society on the subject of roadside treatment. Her Handbook of Conservation was published in 1911. Mrs. Tucker wrote a good history of the involvement of the Social Science Club with the Nonantum Industrial School for Mirror of Newton, Past and Present, published by the Newton Federation of Women's Clubs in 1907. Fred Tucker was a Ward 1 school committeeman, a trustee of the Eliot Memorial and a member of the Eight O'clock Club.
206 Church Street.

Wellington, Lydia Davenport Colburn (joined 1886) b. 1836, m. Henry Wakefield Wellington (b. 1814, d.1899), 1872. Originally from Dedham, Lydia Wellington was the first president of the Club. She resigned in the mid-1890s due to ill health although she lived for a long time thereafter. Originally from Lexington, Henry Wellington was an entrepreneur who founded a Boston dry goods firm, Wellington Bros. & Co., and built the Wellington Building at the corner of Bedford and Chauncy Streets, Boston, of red Maine granite from a quarry he had once owned. Lydia Wellington was his second wife. In 1869 he became a director and later treasurer of the Silver Lake Manufacturing Company, a cordage mill in Newtonville. In 1882 he built a home on Fairmont Avenue near the mill. He was an early abolitionist and a friend of William Lloyd Garrison, Theodore Parker and Ralph Waldo Emerson.
42 Fairmont Avenue.

Whittier, Elizabeth W. (joined 1890) m. Justin Whittier. Elizabeth Whittier, who had a clear hand and a lively voice, served many terms as recording secretary of the Club. Justin Whittier was in the leather business in Boston. They lived at the Hunnewell Hotel and then "The Hollis" in Newton Corner.

Sources:
Marquis, Albert Nelson, Ed., Who's Who in New England, Chicago: A.N. Marquis & Co., 1909.
New England Historical and Genealogical Register,
http://www.americanancestors.com/the-register.
Newton City Directory, 1887.
Newton Federation of Women's Clubs, Mirror of Newton, Past and Present, 1907.
Social Science Club of Newton Yearbook 1900-01.
Sweetser, M.F.S., King's Handbook of Newton, 1889.
Twenty Thousand Rich New Englanders, Luce & Bridge, Boston, 1888, Google Online Book Archive.

Acknowledgments

Special thanks go to the following people for their able assistance in making this project a success. Georgina J. Flannery, M.S., reference librarian for the Newton Collection at the Newton Free Library, was a source of knowledge and cheerful assistance to all the readers and writers engaged in exploring Club archives held in the library's Special Collections room. Susan Abele, former curator of manuscripts and photographs for Historic Newton, located information and photos for us in the Jackson Homestead archives and was steadfastly encouraging and enthusiastic about this book. Also much gratitude goes to Brooke Lipsitt for assiduously proofreading this manuscript. Finally, Michelle Roach and Vicki Johnson lent technical expertise and a much-appreciated booster section to the layout and design of From Hearth to Horizons *which kept the designer both sane and on-course.*